Another Kind of Public Education

Another Kind of Public Education

Race, Schools, the Media,
and Democratic Possibilities

Patricia Hill Collins

A Simmons College/Beacon Press
Race, Education, and Democracy Series Book

BEACON PRESS
BOSTON

Beacon Press
25 Beacon Street
Boston, Massachusetts 02108-2892
www.beacon.org

Beacon Press books
are published under the auspices of
the Unitarian Universalist Association of Congregations.

This book is published as part of the Simmons College/Beacon Press
Race, Education, and Democracy Lecture and Book Series and
is based on lectures delivered at Simmons College in 2008.

Text design and composition by Wilsted & Taylor Publishing Services

Library of Congress Cataloging-in-Publication Data

Hill Collins, Patricia.
   Another kind of public education : race, schools, the media, and democratic
possibilities / Patricia Hill Collins.
      p. cm. — (A Simmons College/Beacon Press race, education, and democracy
series book)
   "Based on lectures delivered at Simmons College in 2008"—T.p. verso.
   Includes bibliographical references.
   ISBN-13: 978-0-8070-0018-2 (hardcover : alk. paper)
   ISBN-10: 0-8070-0018-3 (hardcover : alk. paper) 1. Racism in education—
United States. 2. Public schools—United States. 3. Education in mass media—
United States. 4. Democracy and education—United States. I. Simmons College
(Boston, Mass.) II. Title.

LC212.2.H55 2009
371.82900973—dc22   2008046809

Contents

Preface
Another Kind of Public Education

On August 28, 1963, Martin Luther King Jr. stood on the steps of the Lincoln Memorial in Washington, D.C., and delivered his famous "I Have a Dream" speech to an estimated 200,000 to 300,000 people gathered at the March on Washington for Jobs and Freedom. One line stands out: "I have a dream that my four little children will one day live in a nation where they will not be judged by the color of their skin but by the content of their character."[1] Some would say that the outcome of the 2008 presidential election has been either the realization of King's dream or evidence of its failure. We can speculate endlessly about how and why Barack Obama won and John McCain lost, but this may not be the best use of our time. For the United States and the globe, too much is at stake to concentrate too closely on winners and losers.

Quite frankly, no one wins and everyone loses if the social issues that face growing numbers of the world's population are not given serious thought. We know the list—environmental degradation, illiteracy, poverty, HIV/AIDS, a global fiscal crisis, hopelessness, and

violence in all its forms—these issues all require critical analysis coupled with new action strategies. No one wins and everyone loses if
we continue to think of the world's population itself as divided into
winners and loses. Who wins, for example, if the children and youth
of the world lose?

This framework of winners and losers is unlikely to shed light on
the complex issues of our times. In this context, political parties or
any other group that claims to have quick and easy solutions may itself be part of the problem. When times are tough, people look to
leaders to give them hope and tell them what to do. It is seductive
to see our most cherished leaders as responsible for solving problems—
vesting them with authority enables us to praise or blame them for
the answers they propose and the results they do or do not produce.
Yet the more sobering realization is that they can only lead us where
we are willing to go. We each must learn to think for ourselves as
individuals, but we also must learn to act collectively. We are each
unique, yet we are also part of something bigger than each of us.

I think that the United States is at a turning point in its history,
and it should look to the lessons of world history for guidance. Blind
faith in strong leaders has gotten many groups of people into trouble.
In countries where a small group seizes power and imposes its will on
an unwilling populace, we recognize that shift of power as an illegiti-
mate coup. But we are less skilled at seeing how individuals and groups
manipulate structures of power for their own ends, often within legitimate structures of government. For example, the National Socialist
German Worker's Party (better known as the Nazi Party) was elected
to office in Germany in 1933. There was no palace coup—the Nazis
did not seize power by force. Instead, a legitimate democratic election
brought them to power and, once in office, they so quickly changed
the rules of the game that they eviscerated the meaning of democracy.[2] There are numerous cautionary tales like this about democratic
power being wrested from an unwilling public, or worse yet, willingly
relinquished by a public that confused its own interests with those of

its elected officials. In democratic societies, people who passively follow the rules and uncritically obey their leaders open up their countries to undemocratic outcomes. Unquestioned obedience may be the best way to run an army, but it can be the death knell for democracy if a citizenry chooses this path.

The United States prides itself on being one of the greatest democracies of all time and calls upon each individual citizen to defend democracy from its enemies. These enemies, however, do not include the historically imagined enemy of brown or black youth, more often depicted as America's problem than its promise. These enemies do not include the nameless, faceless, yet ethnically imagined terrorists that we have been encouraged to fear in the post-9/11 environment. Rather, the greatest internal enemy of American democracy is more likely to be an uninformed and uncritical American public that can be manipulated by soothing political slogans, feel-good photo ops, and endless rounds of shopping.

What the United States needs is another kind of public education—one that encourages us to become an involved, informed public. What this country needs is a recommitment to schools and other social institutions whose mandate lies in delivering the kind of public education that will equip us for this task. We miseducate the public and students when we dumb down big ideas and shy away from politics. We do not need a public that stands on the sidelines, cheering political candidates like they were heavyweight contestants in boxing matches; or a public that passively listens to political commentary with an ear attuned for the latest putdown. Voting, for example, is more serious than calling in one's opinion to *American Idol*, or text-messaging one's fan favorite to *America's Next Top Model*.

In *Another Kind of Public Education: Race, Schools, the Media, and Democratic Possibilities*, I argue for another kind of education, one that better prepares the American public for democratic action in our contemporary social and political context. Two core questions shape this entire project. First, what kind of critical education might the

American public need to picture new democratic possibilities? Second, what changes can we envision in schools and in other important social institutions that might provide this critical education? Because these questions can never be answered in any one book, I focus my discussion in this book on four important themes.

First, I emphasize the persistent effects of race in a seemingly color-blind society. Because of its history, race has been tightly bundled with the social issues of education and equity in the U.S. context. Moreover, in the current, seemingly color-blind context where the next generation of Americans is increasingly of color, the United States must find a way to build a democratic national community with an increasingly heterogeneous population. Rather than equating excellence with elitism—the posture that encourages keeping people out—we might define excellence as being compatible with diversity. Only by involving a range of points of view in the democratic process will the United States get the kind of innovation that it needs. I posit that grappling with this deeply entrenched challenge to U.S. democracy should yield provocative ideas and new directions for dismantling similar social inequalities.

Second, I focus on schools as one important site where these challenges are negotiated. Because public schools in America are vested with the responsibility of preparing each generation of new citizens, schools are inherently political. I also focus on pedagogy as a crucial component of democratic practice. Teachers perform vitally important duties that go beyond simply delivering job skills or acting as simple conduits for information. Rather, teachers are frontline actors negotiating the social issues of our time. Teachers are the ones whom black and brown youth turn to for guidance for upward social mobility. Teachers can be facilitators or gatekeepers of fundamental democratic ideals.

Third, I focus on the media. If you define public education as public institutions teaching us about our place in the world, schools are by no means the only institution educating young people and the broader public. In this book, I would like you to watch out for how kids get another kind of public education, beyond school-based learning, from the media. Whether we like it or not, for youth, the media provides an education that often contradicts and supplants school-based learning. New technologies are the currency of youth, and a critical education requires a media literacy that prepares youth to be critical consumers of media as well as cultural creators.

Fourth, I speak to and about youth. When I think about the American public, I visualize a heterogeneous population of youth, characterized by vast differences in wealth, religion, appearance, sexual orientation, gender, linguistic competency, immigrant status, ability level, ethnicity, and race. Some are in schools, others are not, and all are trying to figure out their place within American democratic institutions. I see the talent and potential in this heterogeneous population as crucial for American democracy. Yet I also see tremendous differences in opportunities that are offered to youth. In this context, just as school is inherently political, so is this youth population.

As young adults in early-twenty-first-century America, youth see the challenges that face them—a deep-seated worry about the uncertain future that awaits them in such volatile times; a growing disenchantment with the seeming inability of the United States to provide equal opportunities to a sizable proportion of its youth of color; their impatience with parents, teachers, clergy, and others who struggle with the rapid technological shifts that brought the wonders of the Internet and cell phones. But mostly, the politically savvy among them see the significance of themselves as the next generation of leaders.

Youth will not be following us. Rather, we will be following them. I want them to be prepared to lead me in directions that eschew complacency and put some genuinely new ideas on the table. I do not want to follow them down a path of hopelessness; rather, I want to look to them to envision and take action for new possibilities that I could not consider in my life. Therein lies the critical significance of delivering another kind of public education to youth. They will inherit not only social issues, but also the responsibility for addressing them. To meet these challenges, youth will need another kind of public education that equips them with tools to take informed action.

As you read, I'd like you to keep in mind several factors that shaped this book. First, *Another Kind of Public Education* grew out of my activities as a public intellectual and sociologist of race. The issues that I investigate come not primarily from academic settings but also from the ordinary conversations of everyday life. I talk with different kinds of people on a regular basis about a wide range of topics. I don't seek out issues—rather, they come to me through my talks on college and university campuses, conversations with friends and neighbors, chats with people standing in line in supermarkets and airports, and commiseration with people after my exercise classes. Because I have been working on the ideas in this volume for some time, the arguments presented here have been honed through dialogue with a variety of people.

My career as an educator constitutes a second factor that influenced this book. I have spent over twenty-six years teaching in public state systems of higher education. Before that, I spent four years as a university administrator and six years teaching elementary and middle school in the community schools movement of Boston, Massachusetts. As a lifelong educator, I understand how important teachers are at all levels of education. I also see how education is vitally important to solving the crucial social issues that confront democratic societies such as ours. Thus, I write not only as a scholar of education, but also as a practitioner. In this book, I draw upon many examples from my own teaching, not as examples of best practices to emulate, but rather as examples to carry the main ideas of my argument.

Third, this book had a specific catalyst, a factor that influenced how I wrote it. *Another Kind of Public Education* was developed from a series of lectures that were originally given in spring 2008. When I received the invitation to speak to the public as part of the *Race, Education, and Democracy* lecture series at Simmons College, I had been thinking about these ideas for some time and had this title in mind for the actual book. The invitation to participate in the lecture series could not have come at a better time. The chapters presented here reflect a choice of language and tone commensurate with the lectures. Unlike much of my other writing here, I occasionally use a more personal, informal style. Whenever possible, I have also incorporated some of the many rich ideas that characterized each lecture's question-and-answer period. The fact that these were lectures helps explain my ambition for the book—to bring to a general audience a line of thinking and ideas that are usually talked about in scholarly conversations. I remind readers that public dialogue and debate is the cornerstone of democracy, and I was fortunate enough to develop this book in that context.

Fourth, I should point out that this approach to using conversations with a wide range of people and, in this case, the more focused dialogues of the *Race, Education, and Democracy* series constitutes a contemporary expression of a long-standing thread within American democratic social thought. In writing this book, I consulted not just current debates about education but also a broader conception of public education that draws inspiration from traditions of American pragmatism. John Dewey's work on democracy and education, as does that of W. E. B. Du Bois, Jane Addams, and Alain Locke among others, has a special place here. In the early twentieth century, thinkers such as these emphasized the significance of educating the American public for democracy in a rapidly changing society. We face similar challenges today. I draw inspiration from and amplify their historic calls for linking democracy and education. I place myself (modestly, but ambitiously) in a tradition of public intellectuals speaking to these issues.

Finally, the intertwining themes of race, schools, the media, and youth are woven throughout the entire book. The volume focuses on racism and its effects on American youth, yet I suggest that if we can diagnose racism, we can envision new democratic possibilities. In what ways do schools perpetuate racism and other forms of social inequality, and what can parents, schools, teachers, and students do about it? How might youth in a consumer society speak the truth to a powerful media that now holds sway? What will it take to prepare youth from heterogeneous backgrounds for the challenges they will face in sustaining democratic institutions?

Each of the four chapters explores some aspect of these questions. In chapter 1, "What Does the Flag Mean to You? Education and Democratic Possibilities," I sketch out the big questions about race, education, democracy, and possible paths for the future. In chapter 2, "Social Blackness, Honorary Whiteness, and All Points in Between: Color-Blind Racism as a System of Power," I introduce a domains-of-power framework to analyze racism in a seemingly color-blind society. In chapter 3, "Would You Know It If You Saw It? Practicing Resistance in a Seemingly Color-Blind Society," I explore how the domains-of-power framework might help us think through anti-racist practices in educational settings. In chapter 4, "Somebody's Watching You: To Be Young, Sexy, and Black," I take a closer look at African American youth, one important population that is most heavily affected by these changes, as well as the media as one important site where these themes are played out.

Writing the bulk of this book without knowing the outcome of the November 2008 elections was a real nail-biter for me. With hindsight, I am glad that I did not know. Not knowing required that I thought more broadly about the core ideas of my argument, the ideas that are larger than any political party, any media figure, and the specific expression of broader issues concerning democracy as they are expressed at this historic moment. At the same time, two major events of fall 2008 that may define this historical moment have direct implications for my arguments. The election of Barack Obama as the first African American president of the United States constituted a historic moment for American democracy. This was a time for celebration and a reminder of the promise of American democracy. The global fiscal crisis that grew in importance in fall 2008 also has significant implications for the arguments presented here. The job loss, credit crunch, and mortgage foreclosures suggest that economic issues will rise in significance in the near future. I make reference to these events when possible in this book. But because I do not engage either of these events in depth, I encourage readers to think about how current events that have unfolded since fall 2008 shape the main ideas presented here.

Today we confront our particular variation of the struggle to craft an American democracy that builds upon new opportunities (such as the 2008 election) and that simultaneously is adequate to the challenges of our times (namely, the global fiscal crisis). We can learn from the achievements and unsolved problems of prior generations who grappled with the same overarching questions, but we must craft our own answers to the problems of our times. There are no easy solutions. Instead, there is the need for another kind of public education so that we, as a public, are up to the challenge.

I

What Does the Flag Mean to You?

Education and Democratic Possibilities

By the time I began my senior year at the Philadelphia High School for Girls, my public school education had almost silenced me. The days of playing the lead in my preschool's pageant or chattering away with my elementary school friends were distant memories, all but erased by my school district's tracking policies that left me marooned in overwhelmingly white settings. I rarely spoke in any of my classes. As a working-class African American girl, I knew my place in a school that catered to middle-class white girls. I could stay if I didn't make waves. So I sat and I listened.

Given my chronic silence, I was surprised when my twelfth-grade English teacher asked me whether I would be willing to deliver the Flag Day speech at Independence Hall. What an honor—to sit on the dais erected at the site of the Liberty Bell and the Declaration of Independence, and to participate in a ceremony held at this birthplace of American democracy. I had no doubt about my ability to write a speech or to deliver it. All I had to do was answer one simple question: "What did the flag mean to me?"

I thought writing the speech would be easy, yet when I got home, crafting it turned out to be far more difficult than I'd expected. When it came to issues of the American flag and its Black American citizens, growing up in my African American neighborhood had apparently raised more issues than I anticipated. What did the flag mean to my father, I wondered? Despite serving in a racially segregated army, his service in World War II left him a proud veteran with a strong commitment to the flag. Risking his life to defend the flag did not shield him from racial discrimination at home. Despite his status as a veteran, banks refused to grant him the low-interest loans that were routinely offered to white veterans, which would have enabled my family to buy a house in the burgeoning suburbs of Philadelphia.

What did the flag mean to my mother? She rarely mentioned anything to do with politics. By the time I was in high school, she had given up her dream of attending college and becoming an English teacher. Her secretarial job at the Department of Defense helped pay the bills, yet she was never recommended for promotion. Instead, as I discovered years later, she spent years training her bosses, all of them white men who routinely started out as her subordinates. Year after year, she got up and simply went to her job, reading a book on the subway as respite from and reminder of her unceasing work and her dream deferred.

What could the flag mean to me in this context? I was doing all that I could to be ready if and when the doors of opportunity that had been closed to my parents opened for me. I got good grades, was a church organist, a Sunday school teacher, played the trumpet in my high school band and orchestra, and I even made all my clothes. I was on the path to success. Yet I was also plagued by the growing recognition that the American ideal of a meritocracy was a myth. How was it, I asked, that the flag could signify the lofty ideals of democracy suggested by my public school education, yet my parents and others like them struggled so hard to improve their lives, with many, like my mother, never achieving their dreams? Why was I having such difficulty writing this simple flag talk? I wondered.

Despite my misgivings, I wrote what I thought was a muted, respectful speech that expressed my true feelings. My speech was no
knee-jerk tribute to Old Glory. Instead, it aimed to breathe life into
the principles that the flag seemingly represented. My speech stated
my commitment to the democratic ideals that the flag engendered—
in particular, fairness, equal opportunity, and justice for all. Yet it also
tentatively questioned the contradictions that surrounded the flag.
Unlike now, when I speak of racism so openly, I said nothing about
race in that talk, but I remember that race was on my mind.

I took my speech to my English teacher and waited anxiously
while she read it. After a few minutes, she calmly remarked, "Patricia, we need to make a few changes." Out came the red pen. When
she was done, she said, "I've made a few minor changes. Please look
them over and, once you make them, your speech will be fine." When
I got home, I reviewed her comments. I had expected her to correct
my grammar, yet I was stunned to see that, with the strokes of her
red pen, my teacher had completely changed the meaning of my entire speech! Gone was my ambivalence about the meaning of the flag
and, by implication, the meaning of democracy. The speech that she
expected me to give was an uncritical celebration of American patriotism.

When she invited me, I sensed that I was selected to give the
speech because I was African American. By that time in my educational career, I also understood that you had to be careful what
you said in school because none of my teachers really cared what I
thought. If I said what I really thought, it could be dangerous for me.
I had strong opinions about race, school, and democracy, but there
was no place for my opinions in school. This speech incident stands
out for me as one of the first times that I took a stab at saying what
I thought, albeit in a muted, tentative fashion. But this speech was
also the first time that I became painfully aware that I was selected

because I was perceived as being a certain kind of black person.[1] I was expected to deliver a specific message about race and democracy; namely, that because race doesn't matter in America, democracy has been achieved.

Looking back on that experience, and before telling you later in the chapter what I decided to do, I want to share some lessons that I took from it. For one, this incident points to the significance of schools as gatekeepers for what can be said and done. It was no accident that this gatekeeping experience happened in a school. From the perspective of a sociologist like myself, schools do many things in a society other than teach academic facts and skills. Schools are places that mold ideas, that, through a variety of ways, in a so-called hidden curriculum, reward us for seemingly appropriate ideas and behaviors and punish others. Schools do more than teach. They control access to jobs, sort people into groups, attempt to control what we think and say, attach privilege to some and not to others, and, via these activities, perpetuate social inequalities or, on the other hand, foster fairness.

For another, all of this was unspoken. Ironically, as is the case with many contemporary forms of communication about race in America, meanings are exchanged without the word *race* ever being mentioned. My teacher never ordered me to say certain things and avoid saying others—that would have been a case of censorship, a frowned-upon practice in a society committed to free speech. Instead, my teacher wanted me to deliver a racial message with my body, through my visibility in a media setting, and through editing my words, she made it clear what message I was expected to convey.

This incident also speaks to the ways in which African Americans, Latinos, indigenous peoples, poor and working-class people, and new immigrant populations can be silenced within mainstream institutions. It is no longer the case that historically marginalized groups are simply *excluded* from good schools, jobs, neighborhoods, and the like. Rather, the terms of their *inclusion*—the rules that regulate their participation—have grown in importance. One such rule is that Western civilization is better than all others and that all are welcome within it if we uphold this belief. Back in that high school classroom, my teacher tried to teach me to support this idea by telling me that I was not a credible witness for my own experiences. According to her, my standpoint on the flag and American democracy lacked value if it contradicted her own.

Seeing how my version of truth and that of my teacher differed dramatically led me to question the very criteria that are used to determine truth itself. Why do we always believe certain people and routinely disregard others? How did we come to think this way? More importantly, who gets to decide which rules we will follow in determining what counts?

This all leads back to questions of ideas, democracy, and the centrality of education to power. Democracy speaks to issues of political power. Here in this book I emphasize that ideas matter in the exercise of political power, and that democracy is not a finished product but rather is constantly in the making.[2] In the United States, what counts as legitimate knowledge about the meaning of democracy? When it comes to the democratic process, do the ideas of some people count more than others?

Because my teacher disagreed with me and made it clear that she would decide which speeches would be heard at the Flag Day podium and which would remain unspoken, she has become, in my mind, the symbol of what I have come to see as an army of gatekeepers whose purpose is to silence alternative points of view such as mine. From where I stand today, it is clear that many individuals as well as many different groups are still denied access to the power of the podium. Their ideas are ignored, dismissed, and/or co-opted, all in the name of fostering both a false homogeneity and a feel-good multiculturalism that obscure our understanding of important issues that confront the American public. Including pictures of individuals from marginalized groups on the covers of college catalogs or hiring friendly women of color as receptionists for major corporations does not mean that universities or businesses take seriously the ideas of women or people of color.

Experiences such as these raise several broad questions. In what ways do schools perpetuate racism and other forms of social inequality? What will it take to prepare youth from heterogeneous backgrounds for the challenges they will face in sustaining democratic institutions? What kind of critical education might youth and the American public need to envision new democratic possibilities? What can parents, schools, teachers, and students do in response to these concerns? These questions ask us to think about schools as key sites for educating the public about democracy, not simply as institutions that teach people how to fit into social inequality.

EDUCATING THE PUBLIC

Numerous thinkers and activists in the United States have claimed that American democracy requires an educated public that understands the benefits and obligations of citizenship. Philosopher John Dewey is credited as being the major proponent of this point of view, but many thinkers have advocated for a broad-based, inclusionary public education that prepares each individual for democratic citizenship. Anna Julia Cooper, W. E. B. Du Bois, and Jane Addams, among others, saw a certain kind of education as fundamental for democracy. They also believed that without a sustained commitment to social justice, democracy would remain an empty promise.[3]

Schooling mattered in Dewey's schema, but he had something far more radical in mind than school reform. John Dewey argued that a successful American democracy required an educated public and that public schools should be central to citizenship education.[4] Within this robust understanding of public education, teachers, scholars, educators, and everyday citizens each might bring distinctive points of view (or experienced truths) to the common endeavor of strengthening American democracy.

Moving toward this vision of democracy is no small task because it requires negotiating a basic contradiction that lies at the heart of American society. On the one hand, democracy is the law of the land. Despite deeply entrenched social issues that have confronted each generation, American society has demonstrated a resiliency that has enabled it to weather a bloody civil war, absorb successive waves of immigration, and change its ways in response to protracted social movements. The United States has managed to survive massive reorganization of its capitalist economy, as evidenced by major shifts in its labor market. People have moved from jobs in agriculture, to manufacturing, and then to the contemporary service economy. Workers in the high-tech sector today do jobs that could not even have been imagined a generation ago.[5]

On the other hand, deeply entrenched hierarchies of class, race, gender, and ethnicity that persist from one generation to the next have compromised this very same democracy. Catalyzed by the conquest and colonization of native peoples, slavery, the subordination of women, and an unfettered capitalist class system, opportunities and treatment of individuals reflect their placement in persistent hierarchies.[6] Collectively, these social inequalities mean far fewer opportunities for upward social mobility for large numbers of people than those provided to the few individuals, like myself, who do manage to maneuver the institutional barriers of class, race, and gender inequality. In essence, depending on where you stand, American democracy constitutes a reality, a promise, a possibility, or a problem.

Within this broader project of negotiating a national, democratic community, some groups have more at stake than others in changing things, whereas other groups have more of a vested interest in maintaining the status quo. In the United States, African Americans, Latinos, native peoples, new immigrant populations, and similar subordinated populations have consistently pointed out how elite groups manipulate education to convince the American public to view social inequalities of race, class, gender, ethnicity, and sexuality as natural, normal, and inevitable. "If you can control a man's thinking, you do not have to worry about his actions," claimed prominent African American educator Carter G. Woodson.[7] Woodson was one of a long line of educators who emphasized the necessity of challenging dominant understandings of social inequality by providing a critical education for African American youth. Woodson was not advocating an education that would allow African Americans to become more technically literate slaves who would be more useful to their masters. Instead, he pushed for another kind of education; namely, one that linked knowledge to practices of social responsibility as citizens and collective struggle in defense of democratic principles.

Black Americans do not have a monopoly on this vision. In a global context, many thinkers and activists from diverse traditions have also recognized the crucial link between gaining a critical education and empowering a disenfranchised public. For example, educator and theorist Paulo Freire's important book *Pedagogy of the Oppressed* presents a powerful model for using literacy campaigns to educate Brazilian peasants not simply about reading skills, but also about political awareness.[8] Both Woodson and Freire advocate for an expanded kind of literacy that would enable disadvantaged groups to improve their own lives and, in the process, better society.

Beliefs and worldviews produced by elite groups stand in complex relationship to racism, sexism, and similar systems of domination. On the one hand, elite points of view are seen as being far more legitimate than others, thus explaining their visibility within institutions of public education as well as the organization of educational institutions themselves. People are encouraged to trumpet the benefits of elite beliefs even if it may not be in their own best interest to do so. My teacher, for example, may well have sincerely believed that the flag already had delivered on its promises to its African American citizens and all that remained was to celebrate it. Armed with these assumptions, she saw her job as teaching us to wave the flag at the public so quickly that few would question its meaning. Ironically, this very same teacher was most likely underpaid because she was a woman and denied opportunities much as my mother was.

Because elite ways of looking at the world are so pervasive, they are often taken for granted. At the same time, many people reject dominant beliefs. People of color; poor people; women; lesbian, gay, bisexual, and transgendered (LGBT) people; students; and other subordinated groups routinely produce alternative interpretations that challenge prevailing wisdom. These alternative interpretations reject uncritical habits of mind—such as my teacher's—and, by implication, dominant views of American democracy itself.

Disempowered people can develop, in the words of W. E. B. Du Bois, a "double consciousness" concerning their placement in power relations.[9] On the one hand, for reasons of survival, they must understand (but not necessarily believe) how the powerful see them, usually as less intelligent, less morally capable, less hardworking, less beautiful, or all of the above. Disempowered groups armed with this knowledge often mold their ideas and behavior to the expectations of more powerful groups. For example, in a society where men have such power over women that they view women as sexual objects, women learn to anticipate male behavior—they adjust their style of dress to repel or attract men; they refuse to go out unaccompanied at night; or they fall silent when men talk, all in response to knowing how men view and treat women.

On the other hand, disempowered people can develop a distinctive consciousness or "way of knowing" about their oppression that stems from having to adjust their behavior in response to the whims or the demands of more powerful groups.[10] Sometimes an individual develops an oppositional consciousness through wit and good luck. But often individuals draw upon ways of knowing that have developed within subordinated groups from one generation to the next. For example, African Americans have developed cultural messages that refute dominant ideas about African American inferiority and that create alternative perspectives not only on themselves but also on whites.[11]

Applying this notion of double consciousness to the realm of education identifies some challenges for students and educators, especially those who have been marginalized in U.S. society. Black American and Latino learners, for example, have to engage two dimensions of public education. On the one hand, they must learn to value sufficiently the ideals and traditions of schooling itself so that they can achieve within existing norms. On the other hand, they must challenge current practices that claim to represent those same norms. Charting this path requires living in this space of double consciousness where one draws both from school-based traditions as well as one's own experiences (cultural traditions). Managing this complexity takes a high degree of skill, dedication, and self-reflection. Stated differently, disempowered learners must find a way simultaneously to survive within institutions that were not set up with them in mind and to synthesize the best of what the school teaches and what they know from their life experiences. By doing this, such learners push public schools to fulfill their promise of preparing citizens for democratic participation.[12]

Those of us who believe that democracy grows stronger when more voices are heard realize that centering our education on issues that matter to us sharpens our critical-thinking skills. The better the public's ability to analyze social issues, the better equipped they become to act as first-class citizens. Elite groups rule, in part, by suppressing dissent and not simply by arresting dissenters (as is done in some countries). They repress the critical thinking of women, poor people, African Americans, Latinos, native peoples, immigrant groups, and sexual minorities, creating situations where people live with ignorance instead of engaged, critical analysis. As a result, disempowered groups far too often replace what might be original analyses on a variety of topics (in my case, the meaning of the flag) with formulas that uncritically celebrate the very things that oppress us.[13]

This is why education constitutes a crucially important social institution in American society. On the one hand, it is a premier institution through which dominant interpretations are passed on from generation to generation. We all know that textbooks express the point of view of those who write and publish the books.

On the other hand, educational institutions strive to cultivate the values and habits of democracy. Schools are frontline institutions for putting teeth into democratic possibilities in the U.S. context.

Schools are at the center of these debates, primarily because education remains the sole American institution that is vested with the responsibility of teaching kids about democracy and citizenship. Schools teach the history of U.S. democracy and simultaneously are institutions for contemporary patterns of democratic inclusion. What they teach about democracy in formal school curricula, as well as how schools are organized to promote or suppress democracy (the "hidden curriculum"), is central to helping the young envision new democratic possibilities.

Debates about education are often treated as technical concerns of professional educators. But we all have a stake in what happens with schools. Shortsighted squabbles about identifying best practices for teaching reading to poor kids or raising the achievement test scores of inner-city learners can obscure the centrality of schooling to the practice of democracy. Moreover, because teachers and school personnel are frontline actors in working with kids from diverse backgrounds, they see firsthand many of the issues that escape policy makers. To educators, many educational debates, such as those about school resegregation, are not abstractions; rather, they inform school practices from everything to what's in a given textbook, to how classrooms should be organized, to whether the racially homogeneous sports team should venture out of its neighborhood to play with kids who might hate them.

Instead of viewing educational debates as special-interest topics for teachers, we might instead look to these very same debates as ways to help us envision democratic possibilities. I see three current approaches to democracy, each of which might inform school practices and policies. Moreover, each might also suggest different democratic possibilities for building a democratic national community from the heterogeneous population now living in the United States.

ASSIMILATION, MULTICULTURALISM,
AND OTHER DEMOCRATIC POSSIBILITIES

Educating the public to decide which directions American democracy should take is now more important than ever. Education constitutes a crucial site in negotiating democratic possibilities. Certainly, prior generations have faced the challenge of crafting a democratic whole from a heterogeneous population, but never in the context of a shrinking globe with substantial environmental challenges, of threats of terrorism that point out how vulnerable interdependence makes us when those at the bottom no longer play by the rules, and where high-tech weaponry makes the annihilation of the world possible. At the beginning of the twenty-first century, we confront one of the most important issues of our times. We must find a way to make democracy work.

In the post-9/11 context, we have been encouraged to see democracy as a thing, a finished product manufactured in the West that advanced capitalist societies can give to the less fortunate. Yet in reality, democracy is a *process*, a way of building community and getting business done—it is typically something that is not bestowed upon us by people at the top, but rather something that bubbles up from below. Strong democratic societies meld the different talents, experiences, and skills of their citizenry to build effective neighborhoods, schools, workplaces, and communities—that is, strong public institutions grounded in local participation.

When it comes to the multiple ways that democracy can be imagined and organized, the United States has a unique history. The origins of the nation came from a revolutionary movement that sought to replace rule by a king with rule by the people. Yet from its inception, this democratic ideal of an empowered people or citizenry has been in tension with the actual people who originally lived in what is now the United States, or those who voluntarily or involuntarily came to live here. The people of America are far from homogeneous, and this heterogeneity has been central to the country's democratic possibilities. America's heterogeneous population has had vastly different experiences within American democratic social institutions, and as a result, it holds very different perspectives on the meaning of democracy. A growing, changing, heterogeneous population makes democracy in the United States context an ongoing process, not a finished product.

In the post-9/11 environment, the United States once again faces the question of how to conceptualize its democracy with a diverse national population and in a greatly changed global context. What are the possibilities for democracy for such a heterogeneous national community still plagued by substantial social inequalities? What might it mean for such a heterogeneous national community to continue to remake its democracy in times of domestic financial crisis and global political and economic reorganization? Clearly this task of envisioning democratic possibilities in the current context is not easy. How Americans conceptualize democracy itself shapes how we see ourselves in it, how we assess its current state of being, and what changes, if any, we think should ensue.

Here I sketch out three approaches to democratic possibilities. Each approach can be seen in how public schools are organized and in how they see their mission or overall purpose. Because these approaches are focal points, they also have tremendous implications for how we think about race and power in the current context.

Assimilation constitutes one model of democratic possibility. Under its tenets, crafting democracy involves sacrifice by its citizens. Individuals are encouraged to put aside their differences for the greater good of the group. Based on traditions of voluntary immigration, the guiding metaphor for assimilation is the melting pot whereby new immigrants exchange individual and cultural differences for full American citizenship.[14]

Assimilation models have their strengths. For example, citizens can place the needs of the country before their own individual aspirations in ways that ensure the safety and future of everyone. Assimilation models stress sacrifice for the greater good, or voluntary submission to norms that are bigger than personal self-interest. When U.S. citizens support democratic institutions, the government builds solid bridges and roads, quality schools, and public libraries. Assimilation models ensure that democratic institutions watch out for the public good and citizens pay taxes and fulfill civic obligations, not simply because they expect to get a return on their investment, but rather because by doing so, they invest in the future of democracy itself.

Assimilation models also have their drawbacks. For one, assimilation can force people to shed worthwhile cultural traditions. This has certainly been the case with white immigrant groups who shed their distinctive ethnic cultures to assimilate into a new white American identity.[15] In this way, assimilation models counsel that to get their rights, individuals must suppress or ignore differences of race, gender, class, sexuality, age—in essence, everything about them that is distinctive. For another, assimilation models withdraw protection from all those who refuse to assimilate. In this way, assimilation is often forced upon individuals and can be used to suppress dissent. For example, for many decades, U.S. policies upheld taking Native American children from their families, putting them in boarding schools, forbidding them to wear native dress, and speaking their native languages. For another, assimilation raises the question of which norms and values will become standards to which individuals should assimilate and which should be avoided. If standards are not decided in some sort of democratic fashion, then assimilation can set up permanent winners and losers. Historically in the United States, becoming American meant becoming white.[16]

Multiculturalism constitutes another possible model for envisioning democracy. This is the model that many educators have struggled to achieve, in part because the multicultural model emerged as a reaction to forced assimilation. Here the guiding metaphor is the salad bowl, the notion that democracy might contain within it many groups with different histories and agendas. Diversity would make democracy stronger by mixing a wealth of ideas in the bowl brought by the various ingredients (races) in it.[17]

Multiculturalism does have its advantages. For one, multiculturalism respects group-based cultural distinctiveness. This can be a real asset to African Americans and similar groups whose cultural practices are routinely derogated. For another, multiculturalism recognizes the significance of group-based histories to the issues of today. Ronald Takaki's book *A Different Mirror: A History of Multicultural America* surveys the histories of many groups who contributed differently to U.S. democratic institutions. Takaki offers an important corrective to approaches to U.S. democracy that elevates the achievements of white men above those of other groups.[18] Multicultural approaches also help avoid the problem of seeing social problems as originating only in the domain of personal experiences. Via its attention to group-based histories, multiculturalism fosters discussion of systems of power that produce social groups and differences in their group-based experiences.

Multiculturalism also has its disadvantages, though. For one, some multicultural initiatives have evolved into benign celebrations of cultural differences, such as differences in food and clothing. Because these approaches detach social groups from social inequalities of class, race, and gender, for example, they tend to erase the workings of social power. For another, by fostering competition among groups for increasingly scarce resources, multiculturalism can aggravate balkanization. Groups competing for resources are tempted to define themselves as different from one another, as African American or Latino, for example, instead of viewing areas of overlap and convergence. Another drawback of multiculturalism is that multiculturalism can suppress differences within a group. For example, the ways in which the needs of women and men within the Latino population might differ, or the specific political needs of LGBT people in African

American populations, become suppressed to the seeming greater good of the overall group. In this sense, within the confines of multicultural group politics, the mechanisms used to foster group solidarity resemble the policies of forced assimilation. Individual members of the group may be required to subordinate their distinctiveness and assimilate into the group's political agenda.

When it comes to envisioning democracy, *mestizaje*, a third and emerging democratic possibility, draws from and yet potentially moves beyond both assimilation and multiculturalism. I use the term *mestizaje* guardedly because I do not think that we yet have adequate language to describe this third approach.[19] Instead, a diverse collection of makeshift terms describes various elements of this emerging social world. The guiding metaphor that comes closest to describing this new democratic possibility is the mixing bowl. The mixing-bowl metaphor describes an in-between place, much like the desegregated space between past practices of racial segregation and imagined futures of racial integration. The ingredients within the bowl are no longer distinct from one another. Moreover, unlike the fixed bowls of assimilation and multiculturalism, the mixing bowl is permeable and dynamic, reflecting in part the changes that occur within it.

This type of mixing and remixing draws inspiration from two major social developments of our time. The first consists of mass migrations of people so that people are no longer associated with a homeland where everyone looks alike. Take, for example, the players who represent France in the Olympics or the World Cup. The French team is so multicultural that it challenges notions of France as a place of homogeneity and assimilation. The second major social development flows from the speed with which new technologies have granted people access to cultures outside their everyday life experiences. Some argue that these two developments—migration and new technologies—have spurred a new global mass culture housed in an inside-out mixing bowl, a globe that contains entirely new social relations and forms of cultural contact.

A diffuse terminology has been used to describe changes in mass culture brought on by dramatic shifts in transportation (migration) and telecommunications (mass media and the Internet). The *hybrid*, originally used within biology to denote the mixing of species within nineteenth-century frameworks of scientific racism, now is so accepted that this historical meaning has been replaced by the notion of a fusion of two different technologies, for example, gas and electric energy to power a car.[20] *Syncretism* constitutes another term that is used to describe these new relations of mixing, primarily in the realm of culture.[21] *Creolization* constitutes another term to describe these new social relations, with ideas drawn from linguistics. The idea here is the creation of a new language so that people who speak different languages can communicate with one another. Neither speaker needs to relinquish his or her native tongue. Rather, Creole languages are border languages that reflect the desire or need for divergent people to communicate ("Spanglish," for example, is a Creole language).[22] *Fusion* combines structures and practices that typically would have been seen as specific to cultural groups.[23]

We no longer think of music, dance, and art from different places in the world as being pristine. Images of cultural purity mapped onto unique spaces where people naturally belong—for example, the image of Heidi with the yellow pigtails in a pinafore yodeling in Swiss mountains—are passé. Instead, we live in a world where music, dance, and art influence one another in multiple directions. Originals may still exist, but they may not. Take, for example, the case of rap and hip hop and how they have traveled around the world and all the separate, distinctive expressions of what may get created in one place. Rap is not simply copied and replicated in other places, but is, in fact, created yet again. The idea of sampling in music, the act of taking fragments of lyrics or sounds from everyday life and using new technologies to mix them together, gets at these relations. Rap and hip hop illustrate these trends. New technologies have enabled this cultural fusion to happen.

These myriad terms all provide clues to *mestizaje* mixing and re-mixing. Yet all focus on aspects of culture that emphasize belief structures and identities, not relationships of power. Not all cultural mixing has been friendly and consensual. Much of the cultural mixing that has shaped contemporary global geopolitics is the result of war, colonialism, imperialism, and empire.[24] These types of relationships were far more likely to be the catalyst for mixing and to produce contemporary heterogeneous global populations than negotiated trade. The term *mestizaje*, used to describe populations in the Spanish-speaking world formed from forced and consensual mixing of heterogeneous peoples, reflects these relations.

What are the implications of these three approaches to envisioning democratic possibilities? The best I can do is sketch out possibilities, not make predictions. First, these three democratic possibilities do not stem from logic but rather from historical trajectories of where the United States has been and might be going. They describe trends, anchors to use in thinking about public policy generally and educational policy in particular. One might ask: do public policies seem to be supporting assimilation, or are they more open to *mestizaje* social relations?

Second, each model has specific strengths and drawbacks that should be taken seriously. The U.S. legal system is based in ideas of individualism, and not taking assimilation seriously in a system that does can have serious consequences. Multicultural models that embrace difference and protect heterogeneity have served as an important corrective to the excesses of forced assimilation, yet they can replicate the pitfalls of either/or thinking in terms of winners and losers. *Mestizaje*, the dynamic fusion of differences, constitutes a provocative way forward, but because patterns of mixing are often not chosen but forced, it cannot be uncritically celebrated.

Finally, these possibilities may not be in competition with one another but may develop a synergistic relationship. Thanks to imperfectly desegregated schools, new communications technologies (cell phones and the Internet), and a powerful mass media (movies, cable television, iPods, YouTube, and so on) that has exposed global youth to an array of new ideas, a sizable segment of the U.S. youth population may already be mixing these three democratic possibilities.

The term *mestizaje* may come closest to the task of envisioning democracy, namely, conceptualizing communities in ways that might incorporate the best of assimilation and multicultural models, yet do so in ways that describe actual communities of how people actually live their lives. Moreover, there may be other emerging options that we have not yet conceptualized, that we have not yet recognized. But the issue is not so much to close off possibilities prematurely but to open up this issue of democratic possibilities to imagination. What do we have in mind when we envision democratic possibilities, assimilation, multiculturalism, *mestizaje*, or something else?

PRIVATIZATION AND THE CHANGING
MEANING OF *PUBLIC*

Given the current state of U.S. public institutions, these questions have taken on a new urgency. We must become concerned about the continual erosion of the public sphere in America and a variety of factors that discourage us from being engaged citizens. In the United States, who gets to speak and who is silenced, who gets to lead and who must follow, depend primarily on socially constructed categories such as race, gender, nationality, religion, social class, or sexual orientation. We may see *individuals* from these categories as freely expressing their individual beliefs—this is the power and purpose of mass-media spectacles—but the interests of *social groups* who are formed by and subordinated within these systems of inequality typically occupy second-class status in public policy.

I suggest that we replace this inordinate focus on individualism and the erasure of the bona fide interests of subordinated social groups with public debate about questions that can best be addressed by public policy debates. For example, we need a more vigorous debate in the public sphere about child poverty in America. The large number of Americans who lack health insurance, access to health care, or both is now on the national agenda, but public policy still lacks a nuanced analysis of group-based patterns of the uninsured, without which one-size-fits-all policies may be rendered less effective. Where is the public outrage about the effects of predatory lending on Latinos, U.S. Blacks, and immigrant populations that seems to be just as harmful as the old-fashioned redlining? Blaming first-time homeowners for signing up for subprime mortgages shifts attention away from fundamental flaws that exist in unregulated capitalist markets. Poverty, lack of health care, housing difficulties, military service as the job of last resort, underfunded schools—these social problems disproportionately affect rural whites, blue-collar workers, African Americans, Latinos, children, women, and similar groups whose race, ethnicity, gender, age, class, and citizenship status disempowers them.

Moreover, dissent from those who are most affected by social problems such as these, when it surfaces, is often ignored, if not dismissed. U.S. Blacks, for example, long have protested public policies of de jure and de facto discrimination, yet their dissent about prevailing racial norms was ignored, dismissed, and suppressed by government officials.[25] Current dissent about racial inequality meets a different form of suppression. Instead of responding to dissent by examining potentially discriminatory policies of social institutions and governments, we are offered examples of *individuals* who achieved against the odds. For example, the social problems facing poor and working-class African American women as a group, a status that reflects the convergence of class exploitation, racism, and sexism, is routinely ignored as a matter of public policy. Instead, we hear about the successes of individual, high-achieving African American women such as Secretary of State Condoleezza Rice or Oprah Winfrey. We forget that these women achieved against the very odds that persist today. Yet their success is used to mask persisting problems. How do the achievements of talented *individuals* such as these address chronic problems facing poor and working-class African American women as a *group*?

Despite the historical significance to democracy of both public institutions and an educated citizenry that is dedicated to upholding them, public institutions of all sorts in the United States are now under attack. From the 1980s to the present, concerted efforts by Republican administrations and their Democratic allies dramatically reconfigured the valuation of the meaning of the term *public* generally, as well as the social welfare state as the quintessential public institution. Elite groups launched sustained and often vicious attacks on public institutions during the 1960s and 1970s, the period when African Americans, women, and other historically oppressed groups gained jobs and became eligible for governmental benefits long enjoyed by others. This strategy was brilliant. Rather than directly attacking the groups themselves—behavior that would open them to charges of racism or sexism—they attacked the public institutions that had offered the most support for these groups.

When it came to race, for example, the attacks were seemingly color-blind. Yet the outcome of dismantling public-sector institutions was hardly racially neutral. For example, racial politics have framed social welfare policies such as Social Security, unemployment compensation, and services to poor children and families since their inception in the 1930s. African Americans often have borne the brunt of these racial politics. Two categories of workers originally were excluded from Social Security benefits: agricultural workers and domestic workers. African Americans were disproportionately employed in these areas and thus were excluded. Much political advocacy by African Americans has focused on gaining equal services from state institutions.[26]

By the 1960s, poor African American women were able to gain welfare benefits that had long been offered to white women, thanks to sustained political advocacy. Yet this success at gaining equal access to government services opened up the welfare state to criticisms of fraud and inefficiency. One subtext of these attacks was the implication that social welfare programs helped too many seemingly unworthy African Americans. The 1980s ushered in a series of initiatives whose goal was to deny services to the poor. Major initiatives focused on weeding people from the welfare rolls. Other initiatives went after the nuts and bolts of program administration—for example, an early proposal by the administration of President Ronald Reagan that ketchup be classified as a vegetable for school lunch programs.

Efforts to shrink the social welfare state also affected middle-class African Americans, but in a different fashion. Historical patterns of racial discrimination had largely excluded African Americans from good jobs in the private, corporate sector. For example, many educated African American men worked for the U.S. Postal Service because private-sector employers would not hire them. When post–World War II social movements successfully challenged racial discrimination in hiring, government employment opened up to African Americans before private-sector employment did. Many African Americans went to work for local, state, and federal government agencies, such that government employment became the backbone of the growth of the African American middle class. As a result, middle-class African Americans depended on public-sector employment more than other groups. Thus, while appearing to be a racially neutral policy, the Reagan cuts in government had a disproportionate effect on middle-class African Americans, not simply poor African Americans.[27]

Privatization, the ostensible antidote to the problems of public-sector institutions, now seems ubiquitous in the United States. Current efforts to privatize hospitals, sanitation services, schools, and other public services, and attempts to develop a more private-sector, entrepreneurial spirit in others (such as public radio and public television) by underfunding them or subcontracting specific services via seemingly competitive bidding, illustrate this abandonment and derogation of anything public. Ironically, at the same time, via subcontracting, private interests that favor the wealthy or that make certain people wealthy have hijacked public institutions. Various levels of government subcontract their traditional functions. From the prevalence of subcontracting in the war in Iraq to the growth of charter schools run by educational subcontractors with public money, privatization is increasingly widespread.[28]

This pressure to privatize American social institutions on the surface can seem to provide more choices for individual citizens. Solve the problem of failing urban schools by creating the choice of charter schools; eliminate the financial problems of Social Security by diverting part of the money into individual retirement accounts, political pundits proclaim. Who wouldn't want more choice about where to send children to school or how to spend his or her money? Privatization seems logical, yet does it really solve social problems? Many more people now have the right to choose to work wherever they want, yet one wonders whether communities where Wal-Mart, McDonald's, and the Army constitute the *best* choices have improved the quality of their residents' lives. Individual choice may come with the hefty price tag of an impoverished collective experience, namely, the erosion of democratic public institutions and a public that can support democracy itself.

This shift toward privatization has never been race-neutral. As critical race theorist Patricia Williams points out, this shift toward privatization and market-based solutions to social policy could not have been accomplished so smoothly without invoking American understandings of race:

> No longer are state troops used to block entry to schools and other public institutions—segregation's strong arm, states' rights, has found a new home in an economic gestalt that has simply privatized everything. Whites have moved to the suburbs and politicians have withdrawn funds from black to white areas in unsubtle redistricting plans. No longer is the law

expressly discriminatory . . . yet the phenomenon of laissez-faire exclusion has resulted in as complete a pattern of economic and residential segregation as has ever existed in this country.[29]

As Williams suggests, much of this push toward privatization has covert yet powerful racial undertones. Post–World War II suburbanization, once described by African American R & B artists George Clinton and Parliament in their 1975 song "Chocolate City" as "chocolate cities surrounded by vanilla suburbs," has sparked a third ring of even more vanilla, racially homogeneous exurbs. Through zoning practices that limit land-use practices, and social policies that block mass transit, many suburbs and exurbs support local governments that operate like private corporations.

Schools, for example, may be ostensibly open to the public, but the question of which members of the public qualify for quality educational services is strictly rationed. Within this "chocolate" and "vanilla" segregation, gated neighborhoods have sprung up, where residents tax themselves to support private police forces trained to protect them from obvious strangers. The resegregation of U.S. public education occurs in this context.[30]

So-called neutral public space open to all has not been immune from this growing race and class polarization that reflects a more general impetus toward privatization. As public spaces of shops and malls become increasingly hostile to Black Americans, Latinos, and/or poor people, especially young men, possessing the *formal* right of citizenship to be in public space may not translate into *substantive* rights of equal treatment in public places. For example, in 1995, when store security guards in an Eddie Bauer warehouse outlet outside Washington, D.C., suspected an African American male shopper of stealing, they evicted him from the store shirtless. Amazingly, he was forced to return to the store the next day with a receipt to prove that the shirt that had been on his back was in fact his.[31]

The outcome of all this is that ideas about the benefits of privatization encourage the American public to assume that anything public is of lesser quality. The deteriorating schools, health care services, roads, bridges, and public transportation that result from the American public's unwillingness to fund public institutions speak to the erosion and accompanying devaluation of anything deemed public. In this context, public becomes reconfigured as anything of poor quality, marked by a lack of control and privacy—all characteristics associated with poverty. "The living space of poverty is best described in terms of confinement: cramped bedrooms sleeping several people. . . . Not only is private space restricted . . . by the constraints of poverty, so too is public, institutional space, and purposely so . . . overcrowded classrooms, emergency rooms, and prison facilities," observes philosopher David Goldberg.[32] These ideas of lack of privacy, poor quality, and poverty all affect the changing meaning of the word *public.*

American society now reflects a distinct reversal—public institutions in the United States become highly visible locations that increase the value of privacy itself. Public places become devalued spaces that contain poor people, racial/ethnic minorities, undocumented immigrants, and anyone else who cannot afford to escape.

If we persist in seeing public spaces as populated by dangerous Black American, Latino, and Middle Eastern criminals and terrorists who have made the public streets unsafe; by "public children" from racial/ethnic groups and new immigrant populations who consume educational and social welfare services far exceeding their perceived value to society; and by women of all races whose inability to "catch and keep" an employed man, refusal to work, or both leaves them "married" to the state, we fail to nurture democratic processes.

THE WAY FORWARD:
IS BUYING IN SELLING OUT?

When it comes to American understandings of democracy, this devaluation of public institutions and of the very meaning of the term *public* creates a real dilemma. On the one hand, public institutions face defenders of past practices who, when confronting demands for more democratic decision making, are all too quick to cry out, "But we've always done it this way." Embracing the past as the best route forward, these defenders of past practices suggest that reestablishing their own traditions of family and religion will solve social problems. But this group fails to realize that American public institutions of prior eras were far less democratic and inclusive than they now are. This perspective equates scarcity and elitism with excellence and quality. Thus, the American public is encouraged to perceive public institutions as second-best (less excellent and of poorer quality) *because* such institutions are required to be more inclusive and democratic. In this context, freedom represents not the move *into* the public sphere but the move *out* of it. Groups with the resources to remove themselves from public schools, public transportation, public housing, and public health often do so, leaving behind a wake of underfunded public institutions occupied by seemingly less worthy individuals. Rather than committing to democratic institutions, self-interest groups eschew coalitions and alliances in favor of narrow, self-interested politics where they only care about their own group members.

On the other hand, groups who quite rightly point out that they have been historically excluded from democratic decision making expect American public institutions to become increasingly inclusive and provide services to all its citizens. When public institutions fail to deliver, these groups are understandably disappointed, angry, and ready to give up on democracy itself. If the federal, state, and local governments cannot operate democratically and seem to be tools of special-interest groups, then why should poor whites, African Americans, Latinos, unemployed blue-collar workers, and other groups who have not yet achieved the substantive benefits of citizenship support these institutions? The charter schools movement in Washington, D.C., Philadelphia, Los Angeles, and other urban centers may be an indication of this deep-seated disappointment with public schooling. If urban public schools cannot seem to educate African American and Latino youth, many parents and community activists feel they can do better. If public institutions do not care about African American and Latino children, why shouldn't parents and leaders create private alternatives to public schools? This default position illustrated by disenchanted groups who withdraw from the public sphere and create private initiatives (but often with public monies) presents real challenges for U.S. public institutions. The conflict that currently accompanies these competitive group politics threatens to shatter American public institutions, if not balkanize American society itself.

When it comes to ideas about making democracy work, people are encouraged to neglect supporting democratic public institutions in favor of pursuing their own narrow self-interests. So long as the victims of government shrinkage can be portrayed as the youth of seemingly unworthy populations, it is easier to be convinced of the benefits of privatization. In this context, there are clear losers—namely, youth and other populations who depend on well-functioning public institutions. But who, exactly, are the winners? If the fall 2008 global economic crisis is any indication, there are no winners under this system. When banks fail, people lose their homes to foreclosure (and those owners who can afford to keep their homes may find the value of their property plummeting), food is no longer guaranteed to be safe to eat, and Christmas toys may be toxic. No one wins. We all lose if our government does not watch out for our interests as a collective society. The magnitude of the global crisis casts a harsh light on our interdependence. The general victim here is a shrinking public sphere where groups that might bring multiple points of view that are needed to solve important social problems find shrinking public space to do so.

In this changing context, I think that it is important for us not only to recognize the scope of unregulated privatization and the impasse of narrow self-interest groups but also to analyze critically the terms of our individual participation in upholding or challenging these practices. We each grapple with the contradictions of trying to find our way through the maze of crosscutting relationships that characterizes contemporary American democratic politics. Each of us faces, on a daily basis and in our neighborhoods, at our jobs and where we play and worship, a series of decisions large and small concerning our relationship to American democratic ideals. Rather than looking to all the reasons why democracy struggles during our current time, we might just as fruitfully ask about the terms of our own participation in public institutions. What would get us to buy into supporting democratic public institutions? Is buying into a system that currently seems so flawed an indicator of selling out?

Because schools are a microcosm for these concerns, and because I am a teacher and a scholar, I often approach these issues within the context of schooling. Working with youth lays bare many of the broader concerns that I identify here about democratic possibilities. Schools typically claim that they value critical analysis, but they also advocate conformity to established ways of thinking. Schools are typically unwelcoming places for students who insist on being outspoken or politically active. Instead, many students perceive school success solely in terms of absorbing what their teachers want them to repeat back to them. Sadly, many teachers and school personnel interpret their jobs in a similar fashion. Both groups become passive consumers of schooling, as opposed to active citizens of their school communities.

Teaching undergraduates at the University of Cincinnati, a large, public institution, laid bare for me these contradictions between passively consuming information and actively pursuing an education, of believing that quiet, docile citizens are the most patriotic and seeing active, dissenting citizens as equally patriotic. Questioning whether their undergraduate education was molding them to be uncritical flag wavers, my students asked, "How will I know when I've sold out?" Or, in its more generic form, they wondered, "Is buying in selling out?" To get an A in that rough course, to land that elusive job, or simply for reasons of protection, how often would they be pressured to wave the flag uncritically in their classrooms, jobs, churches, neighborhoods, or even within their own families? How many parents who send their sons and daughters off for a tour of duty in Iraq really believe that they are doing the right thing? In a post-9/11 landscape where everyone becomes a prospective terrorist or enemy of the state, dare any individual rock the boat? Yet can democracy flourish if no one does?

This question, is buying in selling out? is far from simple. While I remain angry with my twelfth-grade teacher, all I can do is speculate about a complex situation. Perhaps my teacher's motives went beyond "waving the flag, smiling, and celebrating the 'success' of American democracy," even if she knew it was a lie. Perhaps she felt her job might be at risk if she allowed a student like me to give such an ambiguous (and apparently threatening) speech. Perhaps my teacher tolerated my presence and was forced to issue the invitation by higher-ups. I will never know her intentions and how she experienced the contradictions that she faced. She clearly appeared to buy into the prevailing social norms. What I don't know is how much, or even if, she sold out by doing so.

We all face similar contradictions in our everyday lives. The very question, is buying in selling out? rarely occurs to people who confuse either mindless patriotism or knee-jerk criticism with thoughtful, civic engagement. Because such individuals never think to question the terms of their own participation in racism, sexism, heterosexism, and similar systems of social inequality (they are either for it or against it), they perceive the truths that American institutions teach them as being the Truth with a capital "T" and love or hate this Truth accordingly.

This uncritical buying in to the terms of public discourse by those on the far right or the far left fosters no space for a critical patriotism that tests the visionary ideals of American democracy via pragmatic actions. Instead of educating the public and seeing the educated public as the site of informed debate, we suffer from dogmatic truths of the far right and the far left, filtered through discourses of an anti-scientific God or a Godless science. Why should we be surprised by the overlapping tendencies of people on the far right and the far left to believe that they have all the right answers? *The Jerry Springer Show* and *Divorce Court* TV programs become templates for the way many Americans think about and debate public issues. Gone are the days of measured conversation, taking turns, and examining multiple points of view. Instead, shouting matches replace informed dialogue, with the person left standing at the end of the fracas anointed as the winner. Knee-jerk critics on both the left and the right aren't necessarily being critical thinkers.

This sustained pressure to balkanize the American public and provoke it to engage in the political equivalent of gang war (talk of blue and red states sounds a lot like Crips and Bloods to me—the colors are even the same) has pushed many of us to a place of exhaustion.[33] I am tired of the kind of either/or thinking that says, "If you are not with us, you are against us." What exactly does it mean to be "with" the conservative, radical, liberal, progressive, capitalist, or socialist academic team? Is this like signing an exclusive contract with a sports team where one is fined, or worse yet, cut from the team if caught fraternizing with team competitors? Surely, figuring out solutions to important social issues such as the global credit crisis, poverty, joblessness, illiteracy, homelessness, domestic violence, infant mortality, disaster relief, obesity, the exponential growth of the prison system, and the national debt requires more nuanced analysis than sound bites on talk shows or ideological formulas from the far right and the far left. More importantly, the contentious practices that are associated with early-twentieth-century U.S. politics as usual mute the kind of critical thinking that is necessary for democracy itself.

The outcome of the 2008 election, which has installed Barack Obama as the country's first African American president, suggests that these same forces pushed large numbers of Americans into newfound civic participation. The 2008 election reversed the trend of politics as a sphere that the public has increasingly abandoned (as evidenced by years of low voter turnout in the past). Not only was voter turnout high in this recent election, entirely new populations participated by working for various candidates, both national and local. Youth, African Americans, and Latinos all demonstrated a more visible presence in the political process. These macro-level trends are encouraging, and I hope they will last, but what are the prospects for repairing the balkanization of everyday life?

The coalition that the Democratic Party in particular put together to win the 2008 presidential election suggests that a sizable segment of the American population has come to reject the political version of gang warfare that has held sway. I suspect that growing numbers of people are searching for political institutions that are more nuanced and complex. Most of us understand why the question, is buying in selling out? may be important, yet we remain uncertain as to how to answer it from one situation to the next. The dilemmas faced by my undergraduates simply place in sharper relief the questions that face us all as teachers and learners in our everyday lives, in our quest to become part of an educated public. In particular, we know that getting an education should change us; why get an education if you learn absolutely nothing new? Yet we also remain ambivalent about and in some cases critical of the very changes that we undergo. My undergraduate students on both sides of relationships of privilege came to see the harm done to themselves and to others by the social inequalities that shaped their everyday lives. Beliefs about the natural superiority of maleness, whiteness, heterosexuality, wealth, Christianity, and the "American way of life" no longer rang true for them, if they ever even did. Their ambivalence and uncertainty were unsettling, conflict-ridden, and often painful for them, but I can see no other way to develop skills of critical thinking without being willing to learn things that you really would rather not know at all.

Despite the pain of doing so, opening ourselves to the humanity of others changes us. Small moments can have a major impact—this is why our interpersonal encounters in everyday life carry such importance. For example, my beliefs about poverty shifted dramatically the day that I took my daughter to a public park in Cincinnati and watched her play on the swings with a poor, white Appalachian child. As I watched them play together, I was ashamed because I realized how my beliefs about racism had impoverished my ideas about U.S. poverty. Did I really believe that white children suffered less under poverty than African American, Latino, indigenous, or new immigrant children? Until that day, the face of poverty for me was typically not white. On another occasion, walking to my fancy San Francisco hotel, I saw a homeless man on a downtown corner who was lovingly feeding his cat. I could not ignore him. If he loved his cat as much as I loved mine, what did that say about our shared humanity? On another occasion, I marveled at a photograph of the bruised face of a woman whose husband had three times tried to kill her, yet who continued to return to court to prosecute him. She looked quite ordinary; where did she get the courage? On still another occasion, I picked up the newspaper and saw a photograph of the sad faces of teddy-bear-clutching, Latino first graders. As the accompanying article explained, because these six-year-olds spoke only Spanish, they knew that they would fail a required high-stakes test that was given only in English. Recognizing this potential trauma, the local Shriners' chapter gave the children teddy bears to help them weather the ordeal.

Privatization, the devaluation of anything public, frames these moments. Poor children, such as the little white Appalachian girl, are more likely to be found in public parks, whereas middle-class children play in suburban soccer games or enjoy play sets in their own backyards. Only failed men, such as the homeless pet owner I observed in San Francisco, show love for people and pets in public—so-called real men save those kinds of emotions for the privacy of their family rooms and bedrooms. Latino children whose parents have money would not dream of letting them go through the ordeal of the repeated planned failures that awaited the teddy-bear-hugging first graders. Private school, where they can learn English and perhaps even a third language in a supportive environment, is the answer to that problem. As for the woman whose so-called private drama of domestic abuse became played out as public spectacle in Ohio courtrooms, neighbors who hear the screams and see the bruises still wonder whether they should intervene in seemingly private family matters. Across these situations, class, citizenship status, race, and gender operate as subtexts that underlie ideas about the public.

We all stumble across moments such as these, if we agree to put down our filters and frameworks of race, class, gender, and ethnicity to let them in. Such experiences challenge the objectified, sterile categories of poverty, homelessness, apathy toward domestic violence, and anti-immigrant sentiment that routinely languish in public debate on these issues. Everyday platitudes such as "Anyone who is poor deserves it"; "Everyone can make it in America if they just work hard enough"; "She must have done something to provoke him"; and "If they don't like America the way that it is, they can just leave it" sound hollow when confronted with the humanity of those who have been ignored and often demonized within U.S. public policy.

Far too many in the American public resist thinking critically about issues such as these, let alone the meaning of democracy and how vitally important each person is to the success of U.S. democratic institutions. Working two jobs, neither of which provides adequate health insurance or retirement benefits, and relying upon television as your sole source of news will do that to you. So will working eighty-hour weeks in professional positions that demand more loyalty to the firm than to family. Living in neighborhoods segregated by class and race also plays a part. Fear of the unknown people who live in the "other" neighborhood on the other side of town, or in the "other" country on the other side of the globe can be crippling. In this culture of fatigue and fear, dogmatic thinkers on the far right and on the far left lash out at one another, stigmatizing healthy debate as unpatriotic and demonizing challenges to prevailing social policy as un-American. The rest of us are encouraged to watch this David and Goliath match of gladiators from the sidelines. Occasionally we cheer on our protagonist, typically failing to question the spectacle that is designed to distract us from questions such as why we have to work so hard, why we can't find a good job, why we get to spend so little time with our families, or why we lose hope that things will ever get any better.

The magnitude of the problems facing contemporary U.S. society means that each of us, from wherever we are located (politically, geographically, intellectually, or demographically), needs to begin to craft imaginative and innovative responses to these challenges to democracy. At its core, democracy is an aspirational construct, one that requires an ethos of hope coupled with action strategies to move it forward. Despite the challenges to democracy that I detail in this book, I remain hopeful. I do not think that all segments of American society have given up on democratic possibilities, despite considerable pressures from many sides that they do so.

For example, take American youth and their apparent significance in the campaigns leading up to the 2008 general election. The post-9/11 period clearly ushered in new challenges for U.S. democracy, but it also revealed some emerging, provocative generational changes. For example, the Center for Information and Research on Civic Learning Engagement (CIRCLE), a think tank that tracks the youth vote, found an impressive increase in youth voter turnout in the 2008 primaries. Examining the state data from CIRCLE's Web site, in states where comparisons can be made, almost all states doubled, tripled, or quadrupled their youth turnout.[34] What does this mean?

A large part of this population was clearly inspired by and participated in Barack Obama's successful bid for the Democratic presidential nomination. But it would be a mistake to attribute increased voter interest solely to the charisma or other qualities of any one person. Despite the fact that youth voters primarily supported Obama, we may not be able to make the claim that the candidate is wholly responsible for inspiring the increased turnout. Barack Obama may have been a catalyst for a phenomenon that was waiting for the right spark.

Are we witnessing a generational shift that might alter our ideas about civic participation and democracy itself? Unlike previous generations, this post-9/11 generation seems to be buying into democratic politics in new ways.[35] Yet even within this very promising development, we carry the legacies of the past into the present. Despite the rapid growth in the youth vote, it remains deeply divided by social class. A total of eight in ten young voters went to college or currently go—this is the population that is inspired to participate. Even with this encouraging development of civic engagement, our process ends up favoring higher-income, white, academically successful youth.[36]

Thus far, I've focused on the significance for democracy of developing an educated public, as well as some of the current barriers for its realization. Examples of these barriers include the shift toward privatization that has eroded public institutions of all sorts and seemingly aggravated a global fiscal crisis; a polarized political discourse that may take time to heal; the continued differential patterns of democratic participation by American youth that leave a sizable portion of poor and working-class youth out of the loop; and an unwritten racial subtext that, in a context of color blindness, makes it difficult to navigate these issues. These are formidable challenges.

At the same time, I see several hopeful signs, even in the context of fiscal crisis, that accompany Barack Obama's successful presidential campaign. First, the dignified, largely positive tone of the Obama campaign, and its success, suggest that the polarization of the American electorate need not continue. This campaign managed to organize people from varying walks of life, indicating that coalitions are possible around issues that people care about. Yet because coalitions are dynamic, no political party can count on its constituencies and always must work hard to build new coalitions that can address new political realities. The Obama campaign did this by reaching out to people whom prior Democratic campaigns had simply written off to the other side—including people in the so-called red states. The campaign suggests that, when it comes to social issues that people care about, there may be only one side.

Second, the campaign's use of technology (cell phones, the Internet, YouTube, and so on) suggests that new communications technologies provide new opportunities to bring people together. The very notion of what constitutes a public and how we might participate in it is being dramatically altered by these new technologies. Gaining access to many ideas can only help democratic institutions because the synergy of many ideas may be needed to solve our most pressing social problems.

Third, the election of Obama has been called historic in that it signals a new phase of racial politics for the United States. Yet the significance of this election lies not in using it as evidence that we have achieved a color-blind society and do not need to think about it anymore. Rather, its importance is that it signals yet another milestone along the path for full democratic participation for all people. African American history provides some important lessons in this regard. The abolition movement's success granted African Americans formal freedom. The Civil Rights movement's success created a legal platform for equality. The election of Barack Obama provides a tangible, symbolic victory—when people tell their children that they can be anything that they want, this is not just talk or an idle dream. Regardless of Obama's achievements as president, that psychological barrier has been shattered. Yet we cannot confuse one historic victory with the achievement of all democratic ideals. The election ushers a new phase for envisioning democratic possibilities where social institutions work for all.

In this rapidly changing social context, the core questions that catalyzed this entire project remain. How might another kind of public education enable us to envision new democratic possibilities? How might another kind of public education equip us to take charge of our democratic institutions and make them stronger?

CODA—MY FLAG DAY SPEECH

Looking back at the dilemma of my Flag Day speech, I see how it constituted a turning point in my intellectual development. Clearly more was at work than a simple disagreement between a teacher and student about the meaning of the flag. The invitation to deliver the Flag Day speech constituted an important opportunity. After years of silencing that was the cost of my public school education, I thought that my speech constituted an opportunity for me to break this silence. When my English teacher said to me, "No, you can't say what you think," I faced a dilemma. At the time, I had no adequate framework for thinking through the issues in my situation, or possible solutions to my dilemma. Instead, I was left with a visceral reaction that something was profoundly wrong with the situation.

Years later, upon reading the great African American abolitionist Frederick Douglass's classic speech titled "What to the Slave Is the Fourth of July?" I discovered that I was not alone in my reactions. Douglass's 1852 speech began by saying:

> Fellow citizens, pardon me, allow me to ask, why am I called upon to speak here today? What have I, or those I represent, to do with your national independence? Are the great principles of political freedom and of natural justice, embodied in that Declaration of Independence, extended to us? And am I, therefore, called upon to bring our humble offering to the national altar, and to confess the benefits and express devout gratitude for the blessings resulting from your independence to us? . . . I say it with a sad sense of the disparity between us. Am not I included within the pale of this glorious anniversary! Your high independence only reveals the immeasurable distance between us. The blessings in which you, this day, rejoice are not enjoyed in common. The rich inheritance of justice, liberty, prosperity, and independence bequeathed by your fathers is shared by you, not by me. . . . You may rejoice, I must mourn. To drag a man in fetters into the grand illuminated temple of liberty, and call upon him to join you in joyous anthems, were inhuman mockery and sacrilegious irony. Do you mean, citizens, to mock me by asking me to speak today?[37]

Douglass could not bring himself to celebrate the Fourth of July when his people remained enslaved. Had I known about his Fourth of July speech, I might more easily have seen the contradictions of my situation. But I had no way of knowing about Douglass at the time. Such is the consequence when we remain alienated from our own experiences and what they might teach us about race and democracy. This is the outcome of schooling that trains us through forced assimilation, failing to recognize that embracing multiculturalism and *mestizaje* might catalyze new ideas about the meaning of the flag.

What advice would you have given me? Should I have delivered my English teacher's version of my speech? Should I have tried to convince her that my speech was in fact better than hers? Perhaps I should have been subversive—I could have pretended to make the corrections but actually given my own speech on Flag Day itself. Should I have complained to her superiors about censorship in the school? Were there other alternatives that I had not considered that would have enabled me to have my say in arenas where the people whom I wished to reach could hear me? Hindsight always provides more clarity than when we are experiencing these moments of indecision. If I knew then what I know now, the choices would be clearer, but the best choice in that particular context might still elude me.

What choice did I make? Despite the opportunity my English teacher provided for me, I just could not see myself giving *her* Flag Day speech. Because I could see no other options, I went back to her and said, "I'm really sorry. I can't give this talk." It pained me to turn down that opportunity, especially the public recognition I might have received. Since that day, I have learned other strategies for dealing with the contradictions that accompany the question, is buying in selling out? I can make myself heard, even when no one has invited me. I recognize that the many communities through which I travel contain many differences that require a toolkit of diverse responses. Yet despite my many accomplishments, that Flag Day experience haunts me.

On that day, I could not find a way to speak truth to power that was riddled with so many contradictions. Instead, power silenced my fledgling efforts to articulate my truth. My teacher nicely thanked me and promptly found someone else. A few days later, I read about the event in a big spread in the major Philadelphia newspaper. A photo-graph of the Flag Day dignitaries accompanied the article. There she sat among the local luminaries—the one African American girl on a dais who was surrounded by smiling white faces. She was identified by name as giving a talk on what the flag meant to her. Yet because the article did not report her ideas, I do not know what she actually said. All I know is that in that published picture, she was smiling.

2

Social Blackness, Honorary Whiteness, and All Points in Between

Color-Blind Racism as a System of Power

I have, occasionally, been whitened. These situations, where I thought of myself as being not-white yet treated as if I were white, typically take me by surprise. I was not trying to pass for white (the case of the tragic mulatto of past racial eras), and my brown skin should have signaled those who whitened me that I was not-white.[1] Instead, I was whitened in more subtle ways. For example, after an ordinary conversation, an academic colleague gushed, "It's so nice talking to you—you're so articulate!" Unless we assume that all academic conversations are boring and incomprehensible, this seeming compliment makes little sense. I cannot imagine one white person saying this to another, or a man to a woman. However much it was intended as a compliment, this unconsciously coded remark—"you are so articulate *for a black person*"—makes sense in the context of color-blind racism. Even public figures who are as accomplished as Barack Obama can have those accomplishments recast within a whitening framework. Early during the 2008 Democratic presidential primaries, Joe Biden, who was running for president at the time and eventually became Obama's running mate, was asked to describe his opponents. His description of Obama proved to be controversial. Biden stated, "I mean, you got the first mainstream African American who is articulate and bright and clean and a nice-looking guy. I mean, that's a storybook, man." Biden subsequently apologized and explained that his words were taken out of context.[2] However, this strategy makes sense only if one envisions the mass of black or brown people as inarticulate or unclean. Barack Obama is an exceptional individual— editor of the *Harvard Law Review*, a successful lawyer, a U.S. senator, and now president-elect of the United States. Yet many people may persist in seeing him as an "exceptional black": one standard pattern of being whitened.

In another situation, I was amazed to find that I could be rendered "honorary white." I was on a South African tour bus headed to Zululand, a tourist village designed to expose foreign visitors to a sanitized form of African culture. Surrounded by European and American tourists who, by U.S. racial standards, were clearly white, I was the sole black face on the bus. Our white guide launched into her introduction to the Zulu, giving her rendition of their cultural patterns and beliefs. She chattered away about Zulu men, primarily why they leave their wives and why they engage in violent behavior, identifying social problems and interpretations of them that sounded eerily like U.S. discussions of African Americans. At one point in her narrative, she dropped her voice and confided in us that she had inside information on these Zulu practices—she got her information from her trusted Zulu maid. Armed with this information from her native informant, she said, "Now you know the Zulus, they're not like *we* white people. *We* white people stay married and take care of our children. *They* can't seem to help it—their situation is so desperate." And suddenly I thought, "Who is this 'we'? Have I become white? Am I invisible? What's going on here?" With hindsight, I see this experience as another example of being whitened, but for a very different reason. For the guide to give the same speech that she routinely gave to buses of white tourists, she needed to reclassify me as "honorary white." She could not tell that same story had I, in fact, been Zulu.[3]

Depending on the social context, blackening is also possible. You would think that black is just black, but being rendered socially black can come in many forms. Because *black* is a social concept just as *white* is, any individual can be socially blackened, often using related concepts of age, religion, ethnicity, class, or other markers of subordinate status. Blackening typically means being pushed down a social scale of some kind. For example, when I was in my mid-twenties, I started a new job as a fairly high-level university administrator. During my first month on the job, I walked into the office of the Dean of Students for my first scheduled meeting with him. Instead of welcoming me, the receptionist brusquely demanded, "What do you want?" Before I could answer fully, she interrupted me with a condescending: "You know, you [black] students . . ." I was so taken aback by her rudeness that I was rendered speechless. Fortunately for her, the Dean of Students came out of his office, greeted me, and introduced me to her. I could see the shock on her face. Because she rarely encountered any high-level African American administrators, she thought I was a black student and treated me accordingly. Through differential treatment, she had the power to blacken me in that social context, and, by implication, to whiten others.

There are many gatekeepers in life like this receptionist, and black and brown people, among others in the U.S. context, quickly learn to perform a complex calculus as to how much whitening clothing and behavior may be needed from one situation to the next. Absent social contexts or social cues that help whiten them, they can be blackened. People who are Latino, or Middle-Eastern, or women, or dressed poorly, or who either are out of their whitening context or do not explicitly whiten themselves are routinely ignored by people in positions of power and authority and can even be rendered invisible.

For example, I was unnerved one day when a colleague whom I knew from several faculty functions not only walked right by me but also looked right through me. I understand the absent-minded professor phenomenon—I am one upon occasion. But this felt different. Surprisingly, this feeling of being seen yet rendered invisible happened again on campus, but with a different colleague. I began to notice a pattern. Social context and my demeanor mattered. Apparently, some of my white colleagues could only see me as an individual if I were in a context where the rules sufficiently whitened me (faculty meetings, for example), or when not in such contexts, when I sent out helpful whitening social cues (clothing that clearly distinguished me from random African Americans on the street). Appropriating both sets of whitening cues was the winning combination—wearing a suit at a faculty meeting. In those settings, my faculty friends flocked around me, with their behavior implying, "There's my friend. I'm such a liberal guy; I have a black colleague." Yet, when I was strolling in student space on campus in casual clothes, out of the setting where I was the honorary white person, or, in any case, whitened, many struggled to see me at all.

Lest we forget, it's not easy being white these days, especially for whites in racially/ethnically diverse settings. In a new, seemingly color-blind context, whiteness no longer seems beyond question. For one, the elastic category of honorary white may be changing the very definition of whiteness itself.[4] By mandate or by choice, when monied or high-achieving segments of Latino, Asian, biracial, or black populations claim the benefits of honorary whiteness, they challenge the definitions of whiteness itself.[5] For another, challenges to whiteness come not only from those traditionally considered to be nonwhite. Some whites voluntarily blacken themselves, becoming "honorary" blacks, with varying patterns of prestige and penalty attached to their embrace of blackness. For example, in *Everything but the Burden*, Greg Tate suggests that whites often adopt and even benefit from black cultural patterns when they can avoid the racial burdens that plague

African Americans.[6] This group of whites may sample blackness, knowing that they won't pay a penalty. In a different vein, whites who participate in interracial dating are also pushing against the boundaries of whiteness. Those who have children, however, especially through marriage, may suffer a penalty for their seeming choice of an African American partner and may become more sensitive to the burdens of blackness.[7]

These situations fascinate me because they illustrate how the power to define race lies in the context and not necessarily in the person. The contradictions that accompany racial dynamics of honorary whiteness, social blackness, and all points in between can be maddening to those who routinely do not fit comfortably into assigned categories (light-skinned Latinos, Middle-Easterners, and affluent African Americans, for example). These contradictions are also evident to those of us who are differentially classified when we travel from one situation to the next. Travel across racial borders (through going into racially different spaces), class borders (through upward or downward social class mobility), or national borders (new immigrant populations trying to understand America's racial politics) routinely bump into sets of expectations that reveal the hidden structures of race. Travel reveals how race is neither something that is hardwired into a person, nor something that one finds on the individual's skin. Racism is not simply a system of moral failure that produces prejudiced white individuals. Racism, instead, is a system of power.[8]

Understanding the dynamics of racism as a system of power in a theoretical way sets the stage for developing pragmatic strategies for practicing resistance and catalyzing change. In this chapter and in chapter 3, I want to map out how we might think about racism as a system of power that, during the post–Civil Rights period (that is, the 1980s to the present), produces slippery and dynamic categories such as honorary whiteness, social blackness, and all points in between. My goal is twofold. First, I present a critical analysis of racism as a system of power that serves as a template for thinking through other similar systems (for example, gender, sexuality, ethnicity, religion, class, age, and ability). Second, I aim to create space to envision possibilities for taking action if we shift our thinking about the nature of social problems—in this case, the persistence of racism. Together, these two chapters sketch out core issues linking race and democracy in the contemporary U.S. context.

U.S. POLITICS IN THE POST—WORLD WAR II ERA: FROM COLOR-CONSCIOUS TO COLOR-BLIND RACISM

Like many other societies in a global context, the United States is no longer in the phase of color-conscious racism. Before the 1950s, color mattered, not just in the United States, but also in many other societies that segregated segments of their populations for purposes of economic exploitation and political control. Jim Crow segregation in the United States, genocidal policies against indigenous peoples in British, French, Spanish, Portuguese, and American colonies, and racial apartheid in South Africa all relied upon diverse expressions of racial segregation, whether the kind of actual physical distance that characterized the creation of the ghetto or the kind of social distance of slavery—segregation within narrow spaces of proximity.[9] Practices of segregation may have taken diverse forms, but across societies, color mattered, albeit differently from one location to the next. In the United States, for example, a finely tuned taxonomy of color regulated opportunity structures in every facet of everyday life. A belief system that installed white purity as the pinnacle of human worth and of Enlightenment civilization rendered all people of color not just other, but inferior. Historically, white made right, and it did so in a way that installed, in barrios, ghettos, reservations, and native preserves, military might as the court of first and last resort.

The momentous 1954 *Brown v. Board of Education* Supreme Court decision was designed to stamp out these forms of racial apartheid in the United States. By declaring that "in the field of public education the doctrine of 'separate but equal' has no place," the U.S. Supreme Court decreed that racial segregation violated the Fourteenth Amendment to the U.S. Constitution, which guarantees all citizens equal protection under the law.[10] If U.S. Blacks have been excluded from the best schools, the best jobs, or the best neighborhoods, the solution seemed straightforward—outlaw exclusionary practices and let African Americans in. Stop seeing color; move on from the embarrassing practices of the past where "good colored folk" had to relinquish their bus seats to late-arriving white passengers, or where notices of upcoming lynchings were published in town newspapers so far in advance that attendees had time to pack a lunch and take a train to the event. All-white anything was out—*Brown* aimed to bring brown children into public policy to arrive at a color-blind future where ironically, there would be no need for the *Brown* decision, nor to create any category of people who would be treated differently because they were brown.

Now, more than fifty years after the *Brown* decision, we have a clearer view of the reconfigured racial politics of the imagined color-blind future. On the one hand, some victories seem obvious. Talk-show host Oprah Winfrey has replaced the minstrelsy of Amos 'n' Andy, with Winfrey finding a way to get Americans to read books, a feat only dreamed of by many American teachers. A visible African American middle class has emerged, in part as a product of the desegregated institutions catalyzed by the *Brown* decision.[11] While neither as affluent nor as stable as its white counterpart, this new African American middle class has managed to position its children to receive better schooling and jobs.[12] The political sphere shows some seemingly unbelievable strides. In 2008, Barack Obama, the son of a white mother and a Kenyan father, ran an unprecedented campaign for President of the United States. As Obama racked up state after state in a steady march toward the nomination, it became apparent that he changed the stakes for African American candidates overall and for the political participation of people of color beyond the local level.[13] In these spheres of media and American culture, economics, and politics, color blindness seems to be paying off for a sizable number of African Americans.

While it is important to stop and acknowledge these accomplishments, it is equally important to note that others have been left behind. In a series of important social indicators, substantial gaps remain among African Americans, whites, Latinos, Asians, and Native Americans. For example, rates of poverty for African Americans, Latinos, and Native Americans remain consistently higher than for whites.[14] Health disparities among racial groups persist; for example, racial/ethnic populations are at higher risk of HIV infection.[15] The 2008 financial crisis in the housing industry saw a much higher rate of foreclosure among racial/ethnic groups than whites, a factor explained in part by patterns of predatory lending.[16] One of the most significant racial gaps remains in rates of incarceration and involvement with the criminal justice system.[17] Differences among racial/ethnic groups are also far more apparent, with color no longer bearing the badge of stigma for some racial/ethnic groups that it once did.[18] Thus, it is important to avoid either prematurely claiming racial victory (the color-blind perspective) or doggedly refusing to acknowledge racial progress. Rather, we must make sense of changes that are far more complex than simple victory or defeat.

To be brown is far more acceptable than it once was, yet to many of us, it feels uncomfortably like we've gone from politics that protects racial privilege through maintaining all-white spaces to a multicultural, colorful politics that relies on allegedly color-blind mechanisms to reproduce the very same racial privilege. Whites may less frequently find themselves in all-white spaces these days, but the existence of seemingly racially integrated settings (especially in the media) does not mean that white privilege has been dismantled.[19]

Thurgood Marshall, Derrick Bell, and other civil rights activists had no way to anticipate the current realities of a new color-blind racism. For example, the early trickle away from public schools by middle-class white parents who founded private white academies so that their children need not attend racially integrated public schools opened the floodgates of so-called white flight from public institutions of all sorts. Public schools, public health, public transportation, and public libraries are all now devalued in the face of market-based policies that say, "Buy it for yourself if you can."[20] Why take light rail if you can safely ride in your Hummer on dangerous city streets? If there are too many African American children in your local mall, then move somewhere else—Nordstrom's, Borders, and the Cheesecake Factory will follow you. Why sit next to a Latino teenager at the Loews if you can have a private theater in the comfort of your own suburban McMansion family room? Few businesses protest these trends—they sell more cars, shoes, books, slices of cheesecake, and DVDs if consumers reject the collective ethos that underpins notions of "the public." And what about social problems? Well, privatization should work there, too.[21] This eroding support for public institutions is rarely labeled as racial—the rules of color-blind racism make us much too polite for that—yet the roots of privatization can be traced to white reactions to the *Brown* decision.[22]

Given these contradictions between visible societal changes that can be seen as success and less visible social realities that suggest that racial inequality is still with us, it may be time to pause and evaluate racial progress in the post-9/11 political context. Quite simply, how have the African American children that the *Brown* decision aimed to help fared under color-blind policies? Here the record is disheartening. More than fifty years after the momentous *Brown* decision, far too many poor and working-class African American and Latino youth remain relegated to racially segregated urban neighborhoods and underserviced rural communities where their level of isolation persists.[23] In cities, poor housing, no jobs, gang violence, drugs, alarming rates of HIV infection, and a host of other social issues not only shape their view of themselves in the world but also the value that we place on their lives. Native American youth in cities and reservations alike often fare no better.[24] African American, Latino, Native American, and new immigrant youth are defined more often as America's problem, not its promise. Moreover, in the context of an American racial history that colorizes poverty, this visible ghettoization of African American and Latino youth masks the increasingly invisible impoverishment of large numbers of white American children.[25] Public institutions fail poor and working-class white youth, too. Apparently, the *Brown* decision's universalistic language of inclusion that promised *all* children in the United States equal opportunities does not apply to poor white youth, either. African American youth may be the poster children for this comprehensive failure of public institutions to provide opportunities, but they are far from alone in being affected by these issues.[26]

Much has changed in some ways, and yet the essential facts of racial inequality have not. Clearly, we cannot continue thinking about the realities of contemporary racism using hand-me-down theories from the past. What gets in our way to think our way out of these problems?

Post-Vietnam-War-Era Politics: Race and Patriotism

From the perspective of today, we can forget what a wrenching time the 1950s through the 1970s were concerning an entire generation's relationship with their government. War can be a solidifying event or a polarizing one—but in either case, strong feelings are always at play. The war in Vietnam was no exception. The roots of today's political realities took hold then. We forget that the Vietnam War catalyzed a wound in American society that has yet to fully heal. The very meaning of patriotism shifted dramatically during this period.

The Civil Rights movement demanded redress from government and used the democratic ideals of the U.S. Constitution to extract more accountability from the nation's leaders. After centuries of oppression, African Americans had few illusions about the government.

They did not trust it, but they saw activities such as filing lawsuits and running for public office as essential to racial redress in the United States. At the same time, they did not see the government as being the same as American democracy itself. For example, my father fought in World War II in a racially segregated army. Yet he was able to see the contradictions of American democracy—he remained a proud veteran yet routinely pointed out how racial segregation impoverished the country itself. He believed that the U.S. government could be improved and pressured it to improve.

In contrast, the Vietnam War era ushered in a basic distrust of government by an entire segment of the U.S. population.[27] In their relationships to big government and to ideas about democracy itself, race and class fragmented youth. For example, African American, Latino, and poor white kids were overrepresented in the army that actually fought the unpopular war in Vietnam, and when they returned, their service seemed disrespected by the massive antiwar protests of college-educated youth. When confronted with the possibility of being drafted, more affluent youth encountered for the first time the punitive government policies that were familiar in barrios, ghettos, and company towns of Appalachia. These events laid the foundation for a generational ambivalence about the role of government and democratic institutions. These events also polarized the country, raising questions about the ability of democracy to keep going in the face of such widespread upheaval.[28]

Following this period, an entire group of social issues fell through the cracks. Sustained public debate about some of the most contentious and important issues of late-twentieth-century American politics—affirmative action, abortion, gay marriage, school prayer, and tax reform—failed to materialize. Instead, beginning in the 1970s and accelerating in the 1980s, an us-versus-them, winners-and-losers mentality emerged, with a resulting winner-take-all approach to American politics that carved up the electorate and suppressed bipartisanship. The so-called hip hop generation, angry and nihilis-

tic, came of age during this era of shrinking opportunities and disenchantment with government. For this generation, government could
only be the enemy (expressed in their hatred for the police, among
other emotions) and market relations became the solution.[29]

In the post-9/11 period, an entirely new group is coming to power,
whose members have the potential to learn from the accomplishments and blind spots of this post–Civil Rights, post–Vietnam War
generation, as well as the issues of the hip hop generation. This
generation has come of age under the polarized partisan politics of
the late twentieth century and has been privy to the biting social
commentary advanced within conscious hip hop. This 9/11 generation was also old enough to have experienced the events of 9/11 as
their own lived memories. Many in this generation have been quite
clear about distancing themselves from polarized politics of any kind,
whether the pre–Civil Rights official policies of racial segregation or
the deterioration of civility in the culture overall. This generation
lives with Jerry Springer and scripted reality TV, with Oprah Winfrey
and Don Imus. Many in this generation want change.[30]

It is important to remember that youth have been on the front
line of important questions of envisioning democratic possibilities in
a U.S. and a global context. For example, youth were central actors
in all forms of political resistance during the Civil Rights and Black
Power movements. In some cases, they followed existing leadership,
while in others they pushed those leaders aside and led their own
movements.[31] The 1963 protests in Birmingham, Alabama, that were
aimed at ending the city's segregated institutions did not garner attention until African American kids started going to jail. Officials
locked up waves of kids, some of whom were as young as seven and
eight years old. Similarly, in South Africa, apartheid was brought
down in part because so many kids refused to go to school. Protesting
the flawed education that was offered to them in Afrikaans, the language of their white oppressors, this "lost generation" missed years of
formal schooling. The protest expressed in rap and hip hop, a youth

cultural phenomenon, advanced political criticism that took on global significance. More recently, one need only look at the image of the lone student staring down tanks in 1989 at Tiananmen Square to appreciate the potential power of youth activism.[32] In the historical and cross-cultural context of youth movements, the U.S. post-9/11 generation has many potential strategies and many new challenges. Racism constitutes one of many such challenges that youth have confronted before.

UNPACKING COLOR-BLIND RACISM: THE DOMAINS-OF-POWER FRAMEWORK

This generation that is coming of age at the turn of the twenty-first century needs a new language for analyzing the new color-blind racism of contemporary American society that has stymied its efforts to live up to the promise of American democracy. Members of this generation also need new forms of engagement with American social institutions to bring it about.[33] To develop this new language for engagement, in this chapter and the next, I propose a framework for how we might think about racism as a system of power that will be useful to this generation that is coming of age. Because we all love our children and do not want to see them destroyed by the history that we leave them, such a framework might also be helpful to their allies.

I suggest that we begin to think about what the generation that is coming to power might do about social injustice generally and about racism in particular. Moreover, because a sizable segment of this generation does bring with it a new sensibility concerning equality (even as it remains unrealized, as I argue here), it is important to place the racial analysis that I present here within a broader context of social inequality. In addition to race, gender, ethnicity, class, religion, sexuality, ability, and age, all have distinctive structures of power with their own individual histories. At the same time, these systems of power draw strength from one another, both in structuring social inequalities and in fashioning strategies for change. By analyzing race, I do not characterize it as the most fundamental type of inequality nor as the most important form of inequality. Rather, I focus on racism, especially color-blind racism during the post–Civil Rights era, as a system of power because it constitutes an especially deeply entrenched version of America's struggle for democratic social equality. Although the contours will differ, the framework that I develop here, as well as the strategies for practicing resistance that it might catalyze, can be applied to any form of social inequality.

People often invoke institutional racism to explain racial inequality but often do not specify the exact forms that institutional racism routinely takes. Instead, they rely on either/or thinking that paints racial inequality as caused by either institutional or personal factors.[34] I take a different approach. I propose that we think of racism as a system of power with four domains.[35] They are:

(1) A **structural domain** of power that shows how racial practices are organized through social institutions such as banks, insurance companies, police departments, the real estate industry, schools, stores, restaurants, hospitals, and governmental agencies. This is the structure of how racism as a system of power is set up, and how it is organized without anybody doing anything. This is the structure into which we are all born and we will leave behind when we die.

(2) A **disciplinary domain** of power where people use the rules and regulations of everyday life to uphold the racial hierarchy or to challenge it. The disciplinary domain is often organized through bureaucracies that rely on practices of surveillance.

(3) A **cultural domain** of power that manufactures the ideas that justify racial hierarchy. The cultural domain—through the media in particular—is increasingly significant these days, in constructing representations, ideas, and stories about race and racism as a system of power. The cultural domain is where we see the color-blind story play out.[36]

(4) An **interpersonal domain** of power that shapes race relations among individuals in everyday life.[37] This would be the domain of one-on-one

encounters and the area of personal choice. This domain involves ordinary social interactions where people accept and/or resist racial inequality in their everyday lives.

Table 1. The Domains-of-Power Framework

STRUCTURAL DOMAIN Institutional structures	CULTURAL DOMAIN Ideas and ideologies
DISCIPLINARY DOMAIN Organizational practices	INTERPERSONAL DOMAIN Relationships and communities

When thinking about the domains-of-power framework, you should consider several features. First, it is vitally important to notice that in most people's minds, especially if they believe that a color-blind society is a reality, the first three domains—the structural, the cultural, and the disciplinary—often disappear. As a result, their understandings of race and racism get collapsed into the interpersonal domain. Motorist Rodney King's question, "Why can't we just get along?" is representative of this thinking. Let's just all change our minds individually, and then everything else will change. While this is an attractive idea, for those on the bottom, changing society one person at a time would be such a slow process that it might not feel like change at all. While some domains may be more visible than others, all four domains are equally necessary for racism as a system of power to function.

A second feature of the domains-of-power framework is that racism is simultaneously structured and resisted *within* each domain as well as *across* all four domains. Thus racism is neither a top-down phenomenon, whereby people simply go along with laws and policies of discrimination, nor a grassroots phenomenon, whereby individual men and women engage in racist name-calling or racially discriminatory behavior. Anti-racist resistance is neither solely social movement actions to boycott, picket, sue, and protest racially discriminatory practices and organizations, nor is it restricted to complaining about the racial stereotyping on television. Individually and collectively, racism is produced and resisted *within* each domain of power as well as *across* all four domains.

Third, because each domain is an analytically distinct entity, each has its own characteristic set of questions that help us think about how racism is structured and how it is routinely resisted *within* that domain. For example, for the structural domain, we might ask: How do public schools and the media help reproduce racism, and how does anti-racism manifest itself within these particular social institutions? Because the disciplinary domain examines the dynamics of how racism operates, we might concentrate on examining how the rules of racism work and how they might work differently, if at all. Questions here might include: "Do some teachers interpret policies such as the No Child Left Behind Act in ways that 'dumb down' their classrooms? Do other teachers use those same policies to improve their instructional offerings? How do implementation strategies reflect the racial and class composition of the classroom?" For the cultural domain, the space of ideas and ideology, we might analyze the content of songs and music videos that depict young women of color as "hos" and young men of color as "pimps," as well as how young people of color themselves use new technologies to contest these representations of themselves.[38] Questions such as how racism is justified, what kinds of arguments criticize it, and what kinds of anti-racist society we might imagine belong in this domain. Because people live with racism in their everyday lives, we might ask how individual men and women from social classes, ages, and sexualities embrace their racial identities in ways that foster domination or emancipation.

Finally, the domains-of-power framework fosters more complex analyses of important social issues. It helps us resist the temptation to argue only in one domain and to focus on either oppression or resistance. For example, public schooling is an important issue that illustrates the interdependence of all four domains as well as how public education is a vital concern within each distinct domain. In this book, I talk about public education in the specific sense of schooling, an approach that taps a tradition of research and practice that is structural and disciplinary. Certainly much attention to public schools has examined the content of the curriculum as well as relationships among teachers, students, and parents.

But the broader notion of public education can also be accommodated within the domains-of-power framework. What are the ways in which each domain shapes how well the public perceives U.S. democratic social institutions to be working? How effectively is the American public educated about its rights and obligations in a democracy? Here the domains-of-power framework can be helpful as well. In the structural domain, inadequate funding for adult education, voter education initiatives, and civic education in schools mean that many Americans remain woefully informed about the basic topic of the structure of U.S. government. In the disciplinary domain, practices in the media (such as Internet censorship and rules set by the Federal Communications Commission) make it easier for some groups to control the flow of information and restrict it from others. The state of educating the public in the cultural domain is exemplified by mass media content that routinely overreports some stories as newsworthy (for example, the actions of petty criminals) while underreporting other types of criminal behavior (for example, white collar crime or government corruption). In the cultural domain, people are routinely bombarded with advertisements for everything from toothpaste to political candidates. One sees the outcomes of these factors in the interpersonal domain of power, where it is difficult to tell whether people are being educated for either citizenship or consumerism.

As I go through each domain, I focus on these two meanings of public education. I do so with a specific focus on youth of color, especially African American and Latino youth, populations that have been central to debates about public education itself. In the following sections, I use examples to illustrate the workings of color-blind racism in each domain of power. In chapter 3, I take up the question of resistance within each domain of power.

"AREN'T THERE LAWS AGAINST THAT?" THE STRUCTURAL DOMAIN OF POWER

In her book *Volunteer Slavery: My Authentic Negro Experience*, African American journalist Jill Nelson describes how her struggles to break into journalism provided her with a novel perspective on race in America:

> From a distance, it's easy to start thinking that white folks run things because they're especially intelligent and hardworking. This, of course, is the image of themselves they like to project. Up close, most white folks, like most people, are mediocre. They've just rigged the system to privilege themselves and disadvantage everyone else.[39]

Nelson's view of a rigged system describes how color-blind racism operates within the structural domain of power; namely, how banks, insurance companies, police departments, the real estate industry, schools, stores, restaurants, hospitals, governmental agencies, and other social institutions are organized to produce a rigged system. A racially rigged system produces consistent winners and losers —some groups benefit from one generation to the next, whereas others perpetually lose. Prior to the *Brown* decision, everyone knew that the system was rigged, yet far more African Americans than whites were bothered by the lack of meritocracy. In the post-*Brown* context, whites are more aware of the possibility of rigged outcomes but seem most concerned when rigged systems might disadvantage them.[40]

The *Brown* decision constituted an important milestone in a much broader struggle to change American social institutions that produced ongoing rigged results, not just for African American children but also for people whose national origin, gender, age, ethnicity, ability, and sexuality caused them to encounter rigged social structures. Social movements by African Americans, Latinos, women, indigenous groups, and LGBT populations, among others, took on the task of challenging the numerous ways in which the social institutions of American society were organized to reproduce inequality from one generation to the next. Within the United States, the shifting legal structure and concomitant reorganization of American society that characterized the 1950s and 1960s suggested that a more democratic, multicultural America was at hand.

The changes in the legal climate following the *Brown* decision were stunning. In a span of less than twenty-five years, several other legal reforms set the stage to eliminate a wide array of exclusionary mechanisms for reproducing social inequality. In addition to the 1954 *Brown v. Board of Education* Supreme Court decision, in the decades that followed, the Civil Rights Act of 1964 prohibited discrimination on the basis of race, color, religion, sex, age, ethnicity, or national origin; the Fair Housing Law of 1968 prohibited discrimination against people seeking housing on the basis of race, color, religion, or national origin; and the Voting Rights Act of 1965 repealed local discriminatory practices against African American voters (the act was amended in 1975 and 1982 to include linguistic minorities and was renewed in July 2006). The Immigration Act of 1965 removed barriers to immigration for people from primarily non-White nations. The 1967 *Loving v. Virginia* Supreme Court decision removed all legal barriers to interracial marriage. Title IX, the portion of the Education Amendments of 1972 that prohibits sex discrimination in educational institutions that receive any federal funds, affected women's equality initiatives in the majority of schools in the country, from elementary schools through college. The Americans with Disabilities Act of 1990 prohibited private employers, state and local governments, employment agencies, and labor unions from discriminating against qualified individuals with disabilities in job application procedures, hiring, firing, advancement, compensation, job training, and other terms, conditions, and privileges of employment. In 2003, in *Lawrence and Garner v. Texas*, the Supreme Court struck down an anti-sodomy law that had made it illegal for same-sex partners to engage in sexual conduct that was allowed for opposite-sex partners. Collectively, this new legal infrastructure provided a greatly changed institutional context for challenging deep-seated customs across virtually all segments of American society.

Because race was a catalyst for these widespread changes, one would think that a changed legal climate that outlawed color-conscious social policies would solve the long-standing problem of differential and inferior treatment for people of color. Many people think that passing laws against racism did away with that discrimination. Unfortunately, just as highway drivers may know that the speed limit is 55 miles per hour yet continue to drive at 80 (unless they see a police officer), passing laws does not mean that people follow them. While perhaps well intentioned, posting a "no racism allowed here" sign leaves much more room for interpretation than any speed limit sign ever did. In this context, we might ask, "Is the system racially 'rigged' now? If so, how?"

What we now have is an imperfectly desegregated society where some parts are racially integrated (but not color-blind), whereas other parts remain as isolated and disadvantaged as ever (for example, schooling for low-income African American and Latino youth). Certainly the *visible* "whites only" signs that upheld Jim Crow racism are a thing of the past. Yet the *invisible* effects of past racial segregation, as well as the workings of new forms of racial segregation, continue to shape American social institutions. Take housing and neighborhood patterns, for example. In their landmark book *American Apartheid: Segregation and the Making of the Underclass*, sociologists Douglas Massey and Nancy Denton describe the entrenched effects of residential racial segregation:

> [R]esidential segregation lies beyond the ability of any individual to change; it constrains black life chances irrespective of personal traits, individual motivations, or private achievements. For the past twenty years this fundamental fact has been swept under the rug by policymakers, scholars, and theorists of the urban underclass.[41]

Past color-conscious policies produced racially segregated neighborhoods through policies of lending, insurance, and racially restrictive covenants. For example, when my family decided to purchase a house in a racially integrated neighborhood in Cincinnati in 1981, our deed contained a clause that we could not sell the house to Negroes (meaning, I suppose, that if we bought the house, we could not sell it to people like ourselves!). When we questioned this clause, we were told that because such clauses were illegal, we could effectively ignore it (as the seller was clearly doing). During the same house-hunting trip, our agent drove us past the elementary school during recess so that we could see the neighborhood children at play. Clearly embarrassed, our agent stated that "we're not supposed to do this, but it does give you a good sense of the [racially integrated] neighborhood." Racially restrictive covenants and informal practices such as these were once widespread. Laws forbidding race to be taken into account in real estate were an important first step. Yet because property is so central to the workings of racism, regulating everything in the past from marital laws (inheritance of property) to restricting the sale of residential property to African Americans and Latinos (ostensibly to protect property values), the disposition of property is a central feature in color-blind racism as well.

Social policies that produce racially disparate effects may be more difficult to spot in seemingly color-blind contexts than my past experiences with racially restricted covenants or the act of driving past the elementary school to assess the racial character of a neighborhood. In a color-blind context that eschews the use of racial terminology, other terms stand in for race in ways that make the use of racial language unnecessary. Take, for example, the growing significance of the use of ZIP codes. ZIP codes confer rights and status. For example, where kids live (their ZIP code) shapes the schools they attend as well as perceptions of people who live in that ZIP code. One study of hiring patterns in Chicago found that employers used ZIP codes to screen job applicants. Assuming that applicants from certain ZIP codes would be poor employees (largely because of the schools they attended), employers routinely did not call applicants in for interviews who were from these specific ZIP codes. Not surprisingly, the residents of the less desirable ZIP codes were overwhelmingly African American and low-income. Via this seemingly color-blind policy of using a ZIP code, employers could engage in racial screening without calling it such.[42]

Seemingly color-blind contexts are also characterized by policies that appear to be racially neutral yet have racially disparate effects. For example, high-stakes tests—such as the SATs, Graduate Record Examinations (GREs), and statewide standardized tests necessary for graduation—appear on the surface to be racially neutral. Under the tenets of color blindness, such tests are intended to measure achievement and thus are a tool in ensuring fairness (those with higher scores should receive more social rewards). Yet when African Americans routinely test more poorly than whites (even if they come from identical social class backgrounds), differential outcomes seem best explained by other factors that must lie within the student or his or her culture. Claude Steele's notion of the "stereotype threat" offers an alternative explanation other than fair tests that accurately measure bona fide differences among students or test bias that inaccurately measures student achievement. Steele suggests that these tests themselves may be racially neutral, yet African American youth may perform more poorly if they perceive that they are high-stakes tests and that race will be considered as a factor.[43] Beyond issues of test fairness, the broader question concerns the purpose of testing. These tests sort people for social benefits. If the testing process produces racially disparate effects, we must question the ways in which high-stakes tests contribute to racial inequality in seemingly color-blind contexts.

In the structural domain of power, social policies within one social institution can catalyze racial inequality in others. Because they are important social institutions for race relations, schools often receive the lion's share of attention. Yet schools constitute one social institution where what happens in other social institutions affect not only the schools but the kids who attend them. For example, property taxes directly affect patterns of school funding. The local tax base in urban areas is low because these are often disproportionately minority, high-poverty-concentrated areas. The effects of low school funding lead to large class sizes, high teacher turnover rates, lack of classroom resources, and uncertified teachers. These factors, in turn, foster high dropout rates (because students don't meet the graduation requirements or because they don't want to attend inferior schools). Lacking the credentials that are needed for today's job market, such students enter adulthood at a disadvantage. Without a high school diploma, they struggle to find a legal job that pays a decent living wage, so some youth turn to illegal activities. As a result, many of these young people go to jail, and because jails are routinely holding cells rather than rehabilitation centers, inmates who reenter communities are unable to find jobs (because they have a criminal record or because there are no jobs) and usually end up back in jail. The entire community suffers from the low earning power of many of their residents, a factor that aggravates the low tax base and high poverty rates. So who is at fault when a particular African American teenager ends up in jail? Not just the school system, certainly.

One social institution that, along with schools, has a greater impact on the lives of young adults than on either children or adults illustrates some key dimensions of the structural domain of power. A sizable segment of African American and Latino youth are locked up.[44] Beyond the fact that U.S. rates of incarceration are the highest in the world, prison serves as the template for other social institutions that youth encounter. One can see how social institutions interlock: ghettos, schools, and prisons begin to resemble one another in ways where people move smoothly among them.[45] Similarly, the policies and regulations from one institution help uphold those of others: for example, differential sentencing, high-stakes testing, and ZIP code screening in labor markets appear to be independent phenomena, yet each ultimately influences the other. The significant point here is that the incarceration of African American and Latino youth is structural—incarceration does not *originate* in how individual parents and teachers treat kids (the disciplinary domain), or in media images of African American kids and Latino kids as less capable, dangerous people (the cultural domain), or even in how kids who are living under prison-like conditions treat one another (the interpersonal domain). Rather, this particular group is on lockdown in a carceral society.[46]

"I'M WATCHING YOU": THE DISCIPLINARY DOMAIN OF POWER

The structural domain of power establishes the parameters of social organization as well as the rules and regulations that uphold them. In contrast, the disciplinary domain of power focuses on the dynamics of how individuals and organizations exercise power; in other words, how people enforce and resist rules and the techniques and practices of organizations that regulate populations. The disciplinary domain does regulate how one person treats another, yet the behaviors in the disciplinary domain typically stem from differences in power in the structural domain. Within schools, for example, teachers or professors, students, parents, administrators, and custodial staff all occupy different positions of power and authority that enable them to treat others in certain ways. The disciplinary domain references two sets of behaviors—how the rules of organizations regulate who can say and do what, and how people actually carry out these rules in their day-to-day behavior.

Common practices for disciplining children (for example, threats of spanking, time-outs for misbehavior, or rewards and prizes for co-operation) get at processes of disciplinary power. Moreover, the school experiences of poor and working-class African American and Latino kids make a compelling case that their schools aim to discipline them for their place in a racially stratified, class-based society. In *Bad Boys*, a study of a multiracial elementary school in a California community, Ann Arnett Ferguson studied how African American boys dispro-portionately ended up in what the school called "punishment rooms." School policies required that all kids who misbehaved were to be sent to the first punishment room. But what counted as misbehaving re-flected the race, gender, and class of the child. Ferguson documented that African American boys were more likely to end up in punish-ment for the same behavior that was overlooked or excused in other children. Moreover, this school had a second punishment room for especially recalcitrant children, and Ferguson found that African American boys were disproportionately sent to this room. Ferguson reported feeling uncomfortable sitting in this room—to her it felt much more like a prison than the first punishment room. The second room was hot and airless, and it seemed to say to the boys, this is your future if you don't behave.[47] This example gets at the interaction between the structural domain of power (namely, the policies that make ghettos, schools, and prisons interlock to form a carceral soci-ety for many poor and working-class African American and Latino youth) and the disciplinary domain of power, where the rules that bring about these outcomes are implemented.

One important component of disciplinary power concerns the growing significance of surveillance in seemingly color-blind settings. Historical patterns of color-conscious racism simply sorted kids into segregated schools and treated them differently according to their category. The white schools got more money and better teachers, and everyone had a clear sense of the racial rules. Specifically, people knew their places of inequality and seemingly treated one another with the appropriate amount of domination and deference. But what happens in a society when everybody is technically equal and where sorting mechanisms of this kind are forbidden? In the multicultural school described above, the kids as individuals were all in the same school together. In this seemingly color-blind context, surveillance may grow in importance because the rules can no longer be counted on to assign entire classes of people routinely to their assigned places (by race, in this case). In the above example, African American boys were disciplined when the teacher saw so-called aberrant behavior, but that same teacher may overlook or choose to see differently the same behavior in other children.[48]

When an individual teacher unintentionally treats kids differ-ently, harm is done to kids, yet the responsibility lies with the personal choice of the teacher. Yet legalizing this kind of differential treatment as a matter of public policy for ostensible reasons of public safety means that entire groups of people can be placed under surveillance due to their ascribed characteristics (being socially blackened). For ex-ample, the term *profiling* increasingly refers to a seemingly benign set of behaviors grounded in statistical predictions. One places an entire population under surveillance and then identifies possible criminals or threats to society from that population via their statistical profiles. This shift toward statistical profiling may appear to be non-racial, yet it gains strength from preexisting forms of so-called racial profiling that long have affected African Americans in public spaces. Within this logic, African Americans are not targeted because they are so-cially black; rather they are placed under surveillance because they fit the *profile* of a criminal or a terrorist or a shoplifter, which, statisti-cally, has been proven to be disproportionately African American. Here one need not have a racist intent to produce racially disparate effects. One common defense of such profiling is that being stopped more often by police and by security guards within shopping malls or airports is a small price for some citizens to pay for the greater good of the safety of the larger group. This argument is usually made by members of this larger group. Yet being routinely stopped, searched, and kept under surveillance can be far more odious and ominous if one falls within the parameters of the perceived threat (social blackness).

Practices such as these grow in importance in seemingly color-blind contexts. Under color-conscious racism, social institutions simply passed laws and rules that *openly* discriminated against African Americans and other historically oppressed groups. Implementing overtly racial rules produced racial hierarchy. For example, the rules of racial etiquette required that African Americans in the South defer to whites by stepping off sidewalks to let whites pass, giving whites choice seats on public transportation, and allowing whites to call them by their first name. In a new context, where color-conscious racism has been outlawed, old forms of control no longer work. Instead, in seemingly color-blind contexts, social institutions need ways to move people to their assigned places (discipline them) using rules that are racially neutral but that produce racially disparate effects. The rules may apply to all, but they are differentially applied.

Thinking about social institutions as sites that differentially discipline populations suggests that a seemingly color-blind society may require more complex patterns of surveillance. The power to see and overlook, to greet and ignore, are part of a larger context of surveillance. For example, when I frequent a department store, stand patiently at the counter, and am repeatedly ignored, whereas a five-foot-ten-inch blonde woman breezes up to the same counter and receives instantaneous service, I can interpret this act as one of my being disciplined about my subordinate place as an African American woman. I can disrupt this discipline by polite means (waving a platinum American Express card to demonstrate that I have money to spend), but having to think about incidents such as this *at all* is part of how disciplinary power operates. Each incident may be benign by itself, but when episodes such as these recur to the point where the pattern of racial discipline is evident, I am faced with the choice: What should I do? Is it good for me to ignore this treatment? If I speak up, how should I do it, and will it even make a difference? Situations such as this make me angry; an attitude that places me at risk of being classified as just another irrational, angry African American woman. My anger, in turn, garners puzzlement from people whose race, gender, or linguistic competence exempts them from these practices, and as a result, they never experience these *patterns* of differential disciplinary treatment. Their familiar responses become recast as voices of reason: "See how angry they are all the time? Why are black people so angry? Nobody is doing anything to them—I didn't see anybody lynched last week. They're so oversensitive. They make everything about race. What's their problem?"[49]

If the daily assaults of disciplinary power make me angry, how must people feel who lack protections of money, educational credentials, age, and gender? African American and Latino youth are under constant surveillance. They encounter metal detectors in school that ostensibly make sure that they don't have weapons; they are followed by security in stores and malls; police routinely stop them regardless of what type of neighborhood they are in. Our organizations are much more cognizant of watching certain people, of profiling certain people, of keeping certain groups of people under surveillance, and yet they claim that these tactics are not racial at all.

These are the patterned, subtle, hidden-in-plain-sight assaults of disciplinary power in seemingly color-blind contexts. In seemingly color-blind contexts, the daily, routine exercise of disciplinary power can be largely unintentional and enforced by well-meaning, amiable individuals. Disciplinary power need not be punitive and is often carried out by smiling people. This is what can make it so difficult to spot. Teachers who disproportionately send African American boys to punishment rooms may believe that they are doing the boys a favor. People who simply follow orders and who never think about what the rules might mean exercise disciplinary power, even people who themselves may be disciplined by these very same practices. I was re-minded of this when I observed a smiling, African American restau-rant hostess who politely greeted all customers and then routinely sat the African American patrons in the same, less desirable section of the restaurant. When it comes to upholding disciplinary power, is it enough for any of us to defend our actions with the claim that we were just following the rules?

Despite the seeming dominance of tactics such as surveillance in the disciplinary domain, some people are quite innovative about un-dermining the very policies they're supposed to be upholding, a topic I take up in the next chapter. For example, students and teachers can be quite subversive by appearing to follow the rules, but doing so in a way that actually undermines them. This kind of passive disobedi-ence not only challenges the authority of those who implement the rules, it also undermines the legitimacy of the rules themselves. In this sense, disciplinary power is rarely exclusively top-down, with un-derlings passively carrying the weight of it. Instead, we continually negotiate this domain, often with surprising results.

"I DON'T SEE RACE": THE CULTURAL DOMAIN OF POWER

What justifies these structural arrangements and disciplinary prac-tices? How is it that some people believe so strongly that the status quo is right and other people remain convinced that it's flawed? If America's social institutions are racially rigged, why don't more peo-ple notice? How can so many people claim, "I don't see race," when it is right before their eyes?

The cultural domain of power contains social institutions and practices that create and diffuse society's main ideas. All institutions deal with ideas, yet families, religious institutions, schools, and the media constitute especially important sites where the cultural do-main of power operates. Ideas typically inspire actions, so how we live our everyday lives reflects our beliefs about what is possible, desirable, forbidden, impractical, and true. Ideas can move people to challenge inequality or they can encourage them to submit quietly to their subordination. Actions in the cultural domain of power help justify or challenge the social inequalities of color-blind racism by creating ideas that uphold it or aim to change it.

To be effective, a society that reproduces racism in seemingly color-blind contexts has to convince people that color blindness is such a worthwhile goal that the society must pass laws outlawing color-conscious practices. It then needs to find ways to convince people that, via the legal system, a color-blind society has been achieved. The cultural domain helps accomplish this outcome by both developing a system of beliefs (or ideology) of color blindness and by claiming that color blindness is a reality. For example, a person can now support Martin Luther King Jr.'s dream that we judge one another by the content of our character and not by the color of our skin in theory, primarily because these ideas are taught in school and reinforced in other social institutions. Armed with this belief, a person arguing within the assumptions of a color-blind ideology might claim that U.S. society is now color-blind.[50] They might identify Barack Obama's successful 2008 presidential campaign as evidence that U.S. society is now color-blind. Such people are quite willing to accept that racism is a practice that happened in the past, or in other places, but that it does not happen here and now. In this way, people cannot separate the *ideal* of color blindness, their deep-seated desire that King's dream really has come true, from the *reality* of whether a color-blind society has actually been achieved. Furthermore, their belief in the ideal can be so strong that it becomes a myth of color blindness—people become unable to see racial inequality at all.

What are the main components of the myth of color blindness, and how do they operate in seemingly color-blind settings? First, color blindness and social blackness are deeply intertwined, and both are part of what's being negotiated, manufactured, and imagined in the cultural domain. Ironically, color blindness *requires* people who are visibly of color to be seen to provide evidence for the claim that color no longer matters. One must *see* color to erase it and become blind to it. To function, color-blind racism needs *visible* representations of blackness and brownness simultaneously to claim the universal, social justice ethos of the *Brown* decision while deflecting attention away from the *Brown* decision's failures. Moreover, this visible color is increasingly class- and gender-specific. On the one hand, one cluster of images of people of color include middle-class African Americans, light-skinned Latinos, model minority Asians, and biracial, multiracial, and racially ambiguous individuals in a new group of honorary whites. Many in this assimilated group may be phenotypically of color, but they have the image of being "just like us," or white inside. On the other hand, a cluster of images of socially black people showcase the failures of poor and working-class African Americans, non-English-speaking Latinos, whites in interracial marriages and love relationships, and undocumented immigrants, who constitute a new socially black population. While derived from phenotypical markers of appearance, this is a blackness that is uncoupled from the "one-drop" stricture of biology inherited from the Jim Crow era where having "one drop" of African blood was used to classify people as black.

Second, the myth of color blindness asks us to imagine society as being separated into two spheres—public and private—and argues that under past practices of color-conscious racism, both spheres upheld racism. In other words, prior to the 1960s, people who held racist beliefs could express them freely in their families, churches, Boy Scouts, and fraternal organizations (private institutions); they could also expect that U.S. social institutions would uphold these racist beliefs through policies regulating schools, jobs, and housing (the public sphere). In contrast, in seemingly color-blind settings, people are encouraged to believe that racism no longer exists in *public* social institutions, mainly because African Americans and Latinos possess the formal rights to attend school anywhere they want, to apply for any job that interests them, or to live in the neighborhood of their choice. The myth of color blindness encourages people to see the social institutions of the structural domain as free of racism (there are laws against that); and the practices of the disciplinary domain as regulated by non-racial procedures and rules (such as high-stakes tests or statistical profiling). In essence, an ideology of color blindness upholds the belief that the system is in fact fair because discrimination based on color is now forbidden in *public*.

If this is the case, if the structural and disciplinary domains become identified with a public sphere that is then assumed to be non-racist (for example, color-blind), then where did racism go? Where exactly is it in a seemingly color-blind society? Ruling out the structural and disciplinary domains leaves the cultural and interpersonal domains as sites for explaining any racial disparities that exist. When pointed out to them, most people can see racial inequality, but how they *explain* that inequality differs considerably. Arguing within a cultural framework, racial inequalities need not be explained by *contemporary* racism in the public sphere. Instead they can be attributed to other factors, such as deviant family structure, individual motivation, poor work habits, and inappropriate cultural norms or other cultural remnants of *past* discriminatory practices of the structural and disciplinary domains.

A third core idea of the myth of color blindness flows from the second one. If public institutions no longer cause racial inequality, then why should people (other than those few people who still perpetuate it) take responsibility for fixing it? Dismissing the impact of practices in the structural and disciplinary domains leaves us looking to culture itself and individual values and beliefs as being the primary sources of racism. Thus, people are free to continue believing whatever they want in *private* (in this case, racist beliefs) so long as they do not act on these beliefs in public social institutions. Moreover, this point of view can argue that racial discrimination, for example, may be acceptable in spheres that are seen as off-limits to public oversight.

By law, public institutions must practice color-blind policies. In contrast, individuals are free to hold racist beliefs in private, unregulated settings.[51]

The inconsistent response to racial speech emerges in this interpretive climate. On the one hand, campus speech codes in the 1990s were struck down with the argument that the free speech of individuals needed protection. Despite evidence of direct harm to the African Americans, Latinos, women, and lesbian, gay, bisexual, and transgendered (LGBT) students who reported incidents of what they experienced as hate speech in their dormitories and classrooms, courts refused to censure hate speech. This response suggested that people were free to think and say what they wanted, even virulently racist and sexist speech, so long as they did it in spaces of legal protection; namely, the quasi-family space of the college campus. Moreover, arguments about speech codes gave greater credence to forms of racism that were spoken, an effect that highlighted speech as occurring at the intersection of the cultural and interpersonal domains.[52]

On the other hand, in contrast to the speech code debates, a few simple words of speech can be highly censured. Take, for example, the controversy that surrounded the racial gaffe committed by radio host Don Imus in 2007. During his radio program, Imus characterized the players on the Rutgers University women's basketball team as "rough girls," commenting on their tattoos, with his executive producer responding by referring to them as "hardcore hos." As the discussion continued, Imus described the girls as "nappy-headed hos," and his executive producer remarked that the two teams looked like the "jigaboos versus the wannabes."[53] Imus apologized but eventually was suspended and fired by CBS (MSNBC dropped its simulcast of the radio show). Similarly, in 2006, during a performance at a comedy club, performer Michael Richards was caught on a cell phone video shouting "Shut up!" at a heckler in the audience, followed by "He's a nigger!" to the rest of the audience. Addressing a group of African American hecklers, Richards used the word six times altogether, and also made a reference to lynching.[54] These incidents illustrate how individuals can be publicly censured for saying the kinds of things that many people may say in private, or, in an even more private space, might think but never say out loud. Don Imus and Michael Richards both made the mistake of "seeing" race and using impolite terms to discuss it in public.[55]

The outcome of incidents such as these that occasionally erupt in the public space of color blindness is a racism without racists.[56] In other words, if each individual feels that he or she is not "racist"—and this applies to browns, whites, blacks, honorary whites, social blacks, and all points in between—why would they even think to look for the structural or disciplinary configurations of racism? In a setting where each individual sees everyone else as the source of problems, people do not develop the critical capacity to evaluate their beliefs. The result is a public that seems ever-vigilant about a few words uttered by public figures yet is passive about hate speech in private settings or racial practices in neighborhoods, schools, the government, and other public institutions.

In this way, color-blind ideology masks racial practices in the structural and disciplinary domains and even manages to erase its own culpability in the cultural realm. The ideology of color blindness thus helps manufacture a racism that has virtually no racists, where racism lives on in the realm of ideas but not in everyday life, and where no one really feels responsible for fixing it or even demanding that public institutions try to do so.

Everyone is exposed to color-blind ideology to varying degrees, but it can have different effects on different segments of the population. For example, different arguments and tactics may be needed to convince whites, Latinos, and African Americans that society is in fact color-blind. Here mass media becomes a major factor in producing products for segmented audiences within an overarching assumption of color blindness. In their coverage, news events, television shows, movies, and the morality plays of reality television rarely challenge the assumption of color blindness. Rather, they operate within its assumptions by explicitly depicting images of American society as being far more integrated than it actually is. At the same time, racially and ethnically segmented cable networks belie this seeming integration.[57]

A good deal of mass-media cultural products have been devoted to convincing whites that they are not racist and to explaining the rules of how one can tell the so-called racist whites from everyone else. The frenzy around the Michael Richards and Don Imus incidents accomplished this purpose—people like Richards and Imus were racist because they uttered bad words, and those who never would think of saying such things were by definition less racist than these media figures. Moreover, the speech of Richards and Imus could be recast as "just words"; Richards had a momentary lapse of judgment and simply misspoke. Transforming Imus's transgression into harmless words required a different rationalization. Imus, it was claimed, simply used words that African American kids seemingly say all the time. He was an innocent victim of the excesses of hip hop culture.[58]

The significant impact of powerful ideas such as the myth of color blindness lies in its ability to frame how we see the social relations around us. Take, for example, how ideas about the meaning of race, gender, and ethnicity influence employment patterns in the hospitality industry. Because hotels constitute one important segment of this growing industry, they are also prime places to see how color blindness is manufactured in a context where color-conscious (and gender-conscious) decision making shapes the filling of jobs. In most corporate chain hotels (Holiday Inn, Marriott, Hilton, and so on), I am much more likely to be greeted at the reception desk by a multicultural welcoming team. When I go to the hotel restaurant, the people who serve the meals may be immigrants, typically are ethnically distinct people, and can be either men or women, not predominantly one or the other. They are likely to be brown, but they often speak nonstandard English. Then there is the dirty work of the hotel. I typically see immigrant women from diverse ethnic groups (depending on the region of the country and the actual country) cleaning the rooms. In over twenty years of hotel visits, I have *never* seen a white man cleaning a hotel room—only women, and typically women of color. I rarely get a peek into hotel kitchens, but when I do, the staff members invariably appear to be African American or Latino men.

Through these entire encounters, I've never been sure exactly who is actually running the hotel or who profits from it. Instead, I am treated to a command performance of color blindness by the seemingly endless array of color in the staff, all of whom seem genuinely fond of one another. At the same time, I am witnessing the persistence of a color-conscious labor market that maintains racial hierarchy via race and gender patterns in specific jobs. These same labor patterns are replicated within airports, hotels, and similar settings, only with different players designated as white, black, honorary white, socially black, and all points in between. When we see this pattern repeated so much, it feels natural and normal to have an immigrant woman who speaks little English cleaning your room and a woman of color with impeccable British-inflected English making your room key. Which is more real, the culturally manufactured friendly relations among the staff, or the differential in the paychecks that this racially stratified staff takes home at the end of the day?

The myth of color blindness illustrates the strength of hegemonic ideas, a signature feature of the cultural domain of power. Hegemonic ideas are designed to justify these occupational patterns by convincing us that they are natural because that's the way it is, and because it's natural, there's no way to change it. Hegemonic ideas also shut down dissent and uphold the status quo. For example, many Americans mouth Martin Luther King Jr.'s words that people should be judged by the content of their character and not by the color of their skin, yet these same citizens would refuse to pay for the schools, roads, housing, health care, Social Security, and other public institutions that would enable children of color to be judged by the content of their character. Such color-blind citizens who wrap themselves in a self-righteous morality seem content if their own children are well fed, well dressed, and safe in their local public schools, but they don't concern themselves with other children, especially if they are brown. Ironically, the universalistic language of inclusion invoked by ideas about dreams, character, and color blindness upholds the illusion of racial integration, yet it masks the unequal effects of persisting racial segregation for large segments of American youth. These American patriots claim that they don't see color, yet the burgeoning gated communities in America's suburbs suggest otherwise.

"WHY CAN'T WE ALL JUST GET ALONG?": THE INTERPERSONAL DOMAIN OF POWER

One reason that color-blind racism is so difficult to see, and thus so difficult to challenge, is because most people rely on a commonsense notion of racism that focuses on individual attitudes, values, and behavior. For example, many African Americans become bogged down in endless discussions of "Who is really racist?" and "How can we get white people to change their ways?" Similarly, whites often claim that they are not racist with facile arguments such as "My grandfather never owned any slaves," or the ever-popular middle-class, liberal response, "My [best friend, nanny, housekeeper, gardener, coworker, college roommate] is black, so I can't be racist." When most people think of racism, they envision the interpersonal domain of power populated by individuals who have strong opinions about race and racism. In response, they say, "Why can't we all just get along?"

Ironically, there seems to be *more* attention paid to questions of racial identity in a seemingly color-blind society (where it shouldn't matter) than was paid to racial identity in a color-conscious one. In a color-conscious society, everyone is assigned a place, with most people not thinking to question the categories. Rather, one might try and change the value attached to the category. "Black is beautiful," the signature cry of the 1960s Black Power movement, illustrates this tendency. Or individuals might accept their racial classification but try to reposition themselves within it or distance themselves from it —a typical case being the "exceptional black," whose speech and demeanor distinguish her from ordinary African Americans. In contrast, in a color-blind society, the racial categories themselves come into question. People find themselves in this in-between space of racial uncertainty, where old rules and formulas don't seem to work anymore. The case of Don Imus reflects these new racial dynamics —how could he know for sure that the words he was using would get him into trouble when so many African Americans use the same language?

The absence of preformulated social scripts of what it means to be African American or white or Latino leaves all of us trying to decide which categories apply to us from one setting to the next, and how to present ourselves within different settings. The earlier explanation that I gave of social blackness, honorary whiteness, and the processes of blackening and whitening that accompany them suggest that managing race in contemporary interpersonal relations takes a special effort in a seemingly color-blind context. Color-conscious situations provide more certainty about racial identities but less hope about bettering oneself. In contrast, because they are being renegotiated constantly, seemingly color-blind contexts require more effort but may offer greater hope for individual advancement.

Several things happen in seemingly color-blind environments that have multiracial, multiethnic populations. For one, because neighborhoods, schools, jobs, and citizenship categories no longer contain clear messages as to who belongs in which category, individuals are left more to their own devices to figure out the system of classification. The loosening of social boundaries of all types has left many people asking: "Who am I?" Race is no different. Rather than assuming that the social systems around us give us our identities, we must create identities in situations that change from one context to the next. In theory, this sounds freeing, the cyberspace fantasy of leaving one's body behind and becoming a black woman if one is a white man, and vice versa. But in practice, fluid racial identities can lead to errors (my being accidentally whitened), bad feelings (my resentment that I was classified as white so that the South African tour guide could share her Zulu family story uninterrupted), misrecognition (my colleague's inability to see me), and perhaps even hope, as expressed by youth who refuse to be boxed in by racial categories themselves. The interpersonal domain is riddled with new complexities as individuals try and figure out the new rules of racial etiquette that are needed in seemingly color-blind contexts.

The interpersonal domain of power reveals that the true measure of our docility and/or our rebellion lies in recognizing what I call "social scripts" that are handed to each of us. Based on how we are defined within structural power relations, by how belief systems construct us for others, and by the types of experiences we have had with institutions that strive to discipline us into our proscribed place, we each have some sense of who we should be and how we should understand and treat others.[59] Despite its manipulation by other spheres, the interpersonal domain is the one place where we can think for ourselves and can be responsible for the consequences of our speech and actions. This is a domain of individual choice, of deciding to follow the rules, to break them, or to write new ones altogether.

One reason that we are so fascinated by racial categorization is that our safety and that of our loved ones may depend on it. How can we recognize our enemies in a racial society organized via color-blind practices? A lengthy tradition of thought focuses on this issue—there are lots of everyday rules to help us spot the dangerous one from the "other group," however our own group defines that term. This same tradition of thought provides far fewer clues for answering the parallel question—how do we recognize our allies?

Today's seemingly color-blind context has ushered in entirely new possibilities for human relationships within the interpersonal domain of power. Interpersonal relations can be more complex and satisfying than a simple set of exchanges between people who are already identified as racists and their victims. Instead, the interpersonal domain can be a zone where people seek connections that enable them to be unique. In some ways, the social networking possibilities of the Internet have created a vast new space for people to find one another unhindered by the categories that constrain their everyday lives. This does not mean that the Internet is a free space, but rather that the new technologies that it symbolizes can be used for a variety of ends, including imagining new racial identities.

Despite the possibilities presented by new technologies, when we turn off the computer, we live in real time and space. The question of finding allies in the context of everyday life is far more difficult than typing a term into a search engine. For those of us who cannot escape our everyday lives through air travel or cyberspace, the hard work lies in crafting different kinds of relationships in everyday life.

Surprisingly, in a context of seeming color blindness, finding one's allies need not require talking about race at all. In a context where talk of race is often misinterpreted as creating racism, sometimes it's better to take action rather than engage in endless discussion about the meaning of racism. Let me give you an example of how I managed to spot an anti-racist ally without ever having an extended conversation about race. When my daughter was three or four years old, she attended a multicultural daycare as one of the handful of African American children in her class. She befriended Buddy, a sociable, blond, blue-eyed boy. Despite Buddy's easygoing nature, when Buddy's mother invited my daughter for a play date at his house, I worried. Parents of small children know that worry of sending your child into unfamiliar settings and wondering how they will be treated. This fear can be especially palpable for African American parents. Buddy's family was white, but what kind of white? I had no way of knowing. I had no language to ask this question and considered declining the invitation with a thin excuse and a polite "No."

One small incident changed everything and assuaged my fears about the racial dynamics in Buddy's family. I decided to be more attentive to Buddy, and when I did so, I saw that Buddy brought a bald, black Cabbage Patch doll to school with him. His mother not only sent him to school with a doll (a gender violation for boys), but with a doll that was black and male. Who gave Buddy this doll? He certainly did not buy it on his own. Who allowed him to take it to school? I was amazed to see Buddy walking around school, blond, blue-eyed, and easygoing, just being four years old, dragging his little, bald, black Cabbage Patch doll with him. That's all I needed—I gave my child permission to play at Buddy's house. To this day, Buddy's mother and I have never had one conversation about race. I know neither her motives nor her formal politics. But I do know that, given the community where both of our children were growing up, she took a risk in giving her son a black doll and allowing him to take it out in public. Her behavior concerning how she was trying to raise her child said more to me about anti-racist practice *without words* than the endless speeches and essays that I routinely encounter from my colleagues. Some people have no difficulty talking about anything, even uncomfortable topics such as race. But how many in their everyday lives risk something of value (in this case, their child's possible mistreatment) to challenge social inequalities?

How might we become better risk takers in taking principled stances, even small ones, such as sending our children to day care with seemingly inappropriate toys? Here too, numerous examples exist in everyday life of ordinary people who decided, for whatever reason, that the risk of practicing resistance to some perceived injustice was worth it. Much of African American women's history describes this kind of passionate embrace of principles, not in the abstract, but rather in the daily actions of caring for others (literally and figuratively). More recently, as racial categories dissolve and race becomes more salient in a society with shifting racial rules, others also arrive at this risk-taking place through an ethic of care. White mothers of visibly socially black children often come to realize that fighting for their children's well-being as individuals could not be a solitary endeavor. These mothers certainly had no difficulty categorizing people into racial categories, regardless of how they felt about them; but they also had to learn the meanings of social blackness that were attached to the categories themselves. Caring for their children meant critically analyzing and practicing resistance to racial practices. Often, without knowing it, these people are each other's allies.[60]

Most people who espouse a color-blind ideology do so not because they want to paper over racism, but rather because they want to believe in Martin Luther King's ideal of a color-blind society. They want to live fully human lives in a fair and just society. This is a noble goal. Yet when it comes to questions of negotiating the racial politics of seemingly color-blind settings, we each have to decide where we as individuals are going to plant our energy. Each of us must come to terms with our individual actions in everyday life around a series of issues, including racism. At the end of the day, does it really matter that you have won a debate about the benefits of assimilation or multiculturalism, or that you have convinced your opponent that personal responsibility is more important than structural change? The practices that come from these beliefs are what is at stake, and in this terrain, issues of conscience and personal responsibility can be measured only by what people actually do, not what they think other people should do, or what they themselves might do if someone would only let them.

3

Would You Know It If You Saw It?

Practicing Resistance in a Seemingly Color-Blind Society

Two weeks after the 2008 presidential elections, Barack and Michelle Obama traveled to Washington, D.C., to make plans for their move into the White House. High on their list of concerns was choosing an appropriate school for their two children. Neither Michelle nor Barack Obama had been born to affluent families, and as a result, both saw the significance that receiving first-class educations had meant in their own lives. Like most parents, they recognized the connection of a high-quality education to success in the United States and wanted to provide the best education possible for their children. The Obamas decided to send their children to an elite private school known for its experience with handling the privacy and security of the children of government leaders. They saw this choice as the best fit for what their daughters needed.

Two days before the Obamas' school decision was announced to the press, a fight broke out at Anacostia High School, a Washington, D.C., public school located in a poor African American neighborhood a little over three miles from the White House. As one event in a string of violent incidents in the public schools, the Anacostia fight left five students injured, including three with stab wounds. The day following the incident, a large police presence watched the school, with some officers standing outside the front doors and others patrolling alleys and forcing those hanging out there to move on. Anacostia High School also heightened the sensitivity of its metal detectors to prevent students from bringing more weapons into the school.[1]

These two events, occurring over a three-day period and so close together in physical space, signaled a vast social distance concerning the meaning of race, class, and education in the United States. Together, they raise some important issues about resistance to social inequalities in seemingly color-blind settings and the centrality of education to it. On the one hand, Obama's historic election gave new meaning to the belief that anything is possible in America. His ascendancy to the presidency upholds one core value of America society—namely, that with motivation, talent, and effort, individuals can better themselves and rise to the top. Parents who encourage their kids to aim high, using the phrase "You can do anything and be anything you want in America, including becoming president," now have tangible proof of that assertion. Anything is possible, even for African American children, now that Barack Obama has been elected president.

Anything seems possible, yet is it probable? To examine this question, we must imagine what it must be like for kids who currently attend Anacostia High School and who may be just like Barack Obama, Michelle Obama, or other upwardly mobile, high-achieving professionals were as children. Many poor and working-class kids in city schools such as Anacostia have the same impetus toward motivation, talent, and effort. Most people who teach in such schools know that the talent is there. Yet even the most motivated, talented, and hard-working students may spend their days worrying about their physical safety or hoping that their teachers will show up. Certainly kids want to believe that upward mobility for them via school success is achievable. Realistically, however, how high can they climb using the paths of opportunity that are provided to them in their city schools? Certainly it is possible that any of them may become president, but is it probable?

Herein lies the difference between the importance of the Obama presidential victory as a symbolic achievement within the cultural domain of power and the persisting inequalities of color-blind racism in the structural, disciplinary, and interpersonal domains. It is important to point out that Barack and Michelle Obama could achieve their success because they had educational opportunities that were denied to previous generations of African Americans. Their accomplishments should inspire all kids who prematurely give up on school. Yet it would be a sad commentary if the symbolism of Obama's victory were used to deny opportunities to the large number of kids whose class, race, ethnicity, or immigrant status leaves them assigned to inferior schools. Such thinking substitutes symbolic victories for hard-hitting structural change. Color-blind racism as a system of power is riddled with contradictions such as this.

Given the challenges of recognizing color-blind racism as a system of power, how might one practice resistance to it? Where is resistance today? Would we know it if we saw it? In this chapter, I explore these questions with respect to the domain of education because it is a crucial space for intervention in our society, and because my experience is rooted in it. For proper context, we need to start with a bit of history.

RESISTANCE AND SCHOOLING

Education has been on the front line of debates about the meaning of race in America and, as a result, public school reform often serves as a benchmark of the success or failure of racial progress. Since the 1960s, anti-racist resistance strategies have focused on dismantling racial segregation through a commitment to school desegregation. Armed with a belief in color blindness as a valuable social goal, most of this anti-racist resistance embraced policies of *inclusion* of racial/ethnic students in public schools as an important remedy for the historical patterns of their *exclusion* from many social institutions. Most reformers accepted the idea that color blindness itself constituted a worthwhile social goal and that policies that aimed to foster equal treatment in racially integrated schools would strengthen democratic institutions. People who were dedicated to racial equality and to school reform as central to its realization simply pushed ahead with Martin Luther King's dream.

The specific strategies that anti-racist resistance took during the post–Civil Rights era seemed straightforward because the exclusionary practices that characterized racial segregation were so prominent. One could identify resistance strategies within each domain of power that made some contribution to the overarching goal of school integration. For example, in the *structural* domain, school busing, redistricting, creating magnet schools, and similar policies and programs aimed to diversify student populations. Similar policies with the goal of diversifying the teaching staff included teacher reassignment. Strategies in the *disciplinary* domain focused on diversity training for administrators and teachers so that they could provide more culturally sensitive teaching, work collaboratively in multiracial work groups, and be better equipped to work with parents from different racial/ethnic backgrounds. Desegregation strategies in the *cultural* domain involved rewriting textbooks and similar curricular materials to include the experiences of African Americans, Latinos, and other marginalized groups. The theory was that schools that engaged in these changes would boost the self-esteem of their students of color (the assumption that being of color necessarily brought low self-esteem was questioned less often) and help privileged students better function in a multicultural world. The *interpersonal* domain would improve with these reforms, it was promised, and more sensitive students would go out into the world and bring additional changes. In essence, color-conscious racism catalyzed an arsenal of color-conscious strategies to bring about color blindness.[2]

But how well did these strategies work? And will they work today? Many of these strategies were successful at what they set out to do. For example, today it would be rare to find a social studies textbook that made little mention of African Americans, or history courses that examined only the achievements of white men. Today, more white students attend racially integrated schools than in the past, providing the opportunity to interact with classmates of different racial/ethnic backgrounds. Yet many of these strategies may have reached their useful limits. For example, school busing initially showed great promise to bring about integrated schools because cities and counties with sizable African American and Latino populations also had sufficient numbers of white students to craft meaningful desegregation plans. Now, busing within urban districts to achieve racial integration makes less sense because whites have moved out of urban districts and counties with high populations of African American kids, enrolled their children in private schools, or have pursued other options. In the structural domain, this unofficial resegregation of American public education has left inner-city African American children in schools that are as segregated as those of the 1950s.

Understanding these contradictions is more complex than simply evaluating the effectiveness of tactics. We may need new forms of anti-racist resistance because we confront a new form of racism, which is organized around a politics of *inclusion* rather than one of *exclusion*.

For example, within the tactics of anti-racist resistance to racially segregated institutions, progress could be measured by the degree of inclusion of formerly excluded populations. Thus, for example, if African Americans were visibly included in schools and other settings, then those settings were no longer exclusionary; their patterns of inclusion were evidence of their color blindness.

But we need new standards of success because the problem today is fundamentally different. For one, the problem is no longer *either* exclusion *or* inclusion but rather a more complex history of strides in school desegregation followed by increased resegregation.[3] Fifty years after *Brown v. Board of Education*, it seems clear that the majority of poor and working-class African American and Latino youth continue to attend racially segregated schools. One common practice of color-blind racism in an era of mass media is to divert our attention from patterns of resegregation by overemphasizing relations in desegregated schools. Focusing on the visible inclusion of students of color in some desegregated schools, however important, overlooks the vast majority of kids who will attend racially homogeneous schools in the near future. Racially integrated schools may be a worthwhile goal, but more attention to best practices in education at racially homogeneous schools may be even more important. How do we improve those schools? What might anti-racist practice look like in racially homogeneous schools?[4]

Thinking that sees the solution to past patterns of racism through the lens of simple inclusion is problematic on another front as well. Measuring successful resistance simply by counting the numbers of African Americans and Latinos in various institutions does not allow for the possibility of racism *within* racially desegregated situations. Take, for example, the large amount of attention paid to the question of the racial achievement gap in racially integrated, middle-class schools where white students outperform African American students. Can this gap be explained by student characteristics? Or might seemingly racially neutral institutional practices contribute to these outcomes? How one diagnoses this gap leads to very different analyses of simple inclusionary policies as the solution to past practices of racial exclusion.[5]

Despite these complexities, it is important to ask: How can we learn to practice resistance that is effective in dismantling color-blind racism? Specifically, when it comes to schools, would we know resistance if we saw it?

In response, we might outline a critical analysis to see what new opportunities exist for taking action in contemporary school settings. I suggest that the domains-of-power framework offers a good starting point for this task.[6] In this spirit, the rest of this chapter explores how the domains-of-power framework might be used to catalyze new ideas about resistance in a context of color-blind racism. To guide my exploration, I apply the domains-of-power framework to public schools and schooling in the U.S. context, both in grades K–12 and in the system of community colleges and public universities that are major routes for equity for a large percentage of the population. Rather than examining education primarily as a gatekeeper for privilege, I think we need to think creatively about education as a protector of fairness and a facilitator of equity. Private schools play an important role, but because public schools must take everyone, it falls primarily to public institutions to educate the American public for democratic participation. I remind readers that just as public schools are vitally important to preparing youth, education is central to creating a more informed public. In both senses, practicing resistance might catalyze another kind of public education.

APPLYING THE DOMAINS-OF-POWER FRAMEWORK: RACE, RESISTANCE, AND PUBLIC SCHOOLS

In the following sections, I investigate practices of resistance by drawing upon my own experiences as a teacher, curriculum developer, textbook writer, and college professor. I invite you to use my experiences as suggestive jumping-off points for developing an analysis of your particular situation. Particulars matter, for they may dictate which domain you emphasize and what might constitute the successful practice of resistance in your particular setting. Everyone is different, and everyone is differently situated. People can bring a variety of skills, temperamental strengths, and professional expertise to bear on each of the domains I talked about in chapter 2. Some of us are better positioned to intervene in the cultural domain, others in the disciplinary. Some are very public in their acts of resistance; others work behind the scenes. But I hope as a writer that the examples in this chapter inspire ideas about the range of possibilities for creative resistance across our (troubled but renewable) democracy.

In Table 2, I draw upon my own experiences to apply the domains-of-power framework to issues of race, resistance, and public education.[7]

Table 2. Practicing Resistance: Education and Schools

STRUCTURAL DOMAIN	CULTURAL DOMAIN
• Creating safe and free learning spaces • Frontline action: classrooms as political spaces • ?	• Filters, frameworks, and media literacy • Telling your own story • ?
DISCIPLINARY DOMAIN	INTERPERSONAL DOMAIN
• Cultivating counter-surveillance • Teaching and learning as subversive activities • ?	• Specialized resistance • Hope • ?

Please keep in mind that this diagram is a work in progress—open-ended and not comprehensive. Ideally, constructing this table should be a collective endeavor, with all of us adding our practical ideas, no matter how small, to this larger project of identifying and classifying anti-racist initiatives. Developing this table would then give us a framework for discussion and alliances that might catalyze creativity. I invite readers to help me think through this framework. In chapter 2, I presented racism as a system of power. Here I sketch out some tools that we can use to begin to identify actual and potential practices that work in each domain that may be especially needed in a context of seeming color blindness.

RESISTANCE AND THE STRUCTURAL DOMAIN OF POWER: NO CHILD LEFT BEHIND . . . FOR REAL

When it comes to contemporary education, how might we envision resistance within the structural domain of power? The list of possibilities seems endless. There is a voluminous amount of literature on the reform of school districts, clusters of schools, individual schools, and the broader federal policy climate for schooling. In all cases, reforms focus on revising how districts, schools, and classrooms are organized, as well as the rules that will govern them. Because this is a vast field for taking action, here I focus on two specific structural changes: the first, a brief discussion of the kinds of spaces that kids need; and the second, a look at classrooms as frontline actors in bringing about structural change.

Creating Safe and Free Learning Spaces

Many kids do not need educators to tell them that their schools and neighborhoods are failing them. Poor and working-class kids, especially African American and Latino youth, are already aware of how U.S. society views them. But I think that they do not know what to do about it. For example, listen to the lyrics of Dead Prez's song "They Schools":

> They aint teachin us nothin related to solvin our own problems, knowhatimsayin?
> Aint teachin us how to get crack out the ghetto,

They aint teachin us how to stop the police from murdering us.
And brutalizing us, they aint teachin us how to get our rent paid,
    knowhatimsayin?
They aint teachin our families how to interact better with each
    other, knowhatimsayin?
They just teachin us how to build they s**t up, knowhatimsayin?[8]

These lyrics express the anger of many poor and working-class African American kids about the irrelevance of school in their lives. Groups like Dead Prez may express these ideas, but such beliefs are not unique to Black American youth. Instead, the anger that permeates rap and hip hop reflects a global crisis of socially black youth in countries as diverse as Brazil, Senegal, France, and the United Kingdom, who see no promising future for themselves, either.[9] Faced with societies that are saying to them "We don't need you," they are pissed off. But that place of being pissed off, that place of recognizing and caring enough to try to say something about it, is also potentially a site of organizing, a site of democratic possibilities.

I use the words *place* and *site* metaphorically, but the metaphors are connected to physical spaces as well. Many kids implicitly reject this function of school as a gatekeeper that seems designed mainly to miseducate them, but where can they go in their everyday lives to analyze these ideas? Songs such as "They Schools" may provide ideas that get them thinking, but where in their physical space can kids freely express what is on their minds (and perhaps have those thoughts challenged)? Where can they practice skills of critical analysis and healthy debate? Where would kids find safe spaces where they can talk openly and honestly about ideas that are on their minds?

These questions are best addressed by thinking about space as an institutional phenomenon. Ironically, kids spend enormous amounts of time in the physical space of their schools, yet schools typically suppress this kind of open and honest dialogue. There are, of course, the basics of space: too many urban schools in particular are physically dilapidated. And I do not minimize the importance of physical conditions as expressive of attitudes toward the people asked to inhabit them. But I mean to point to space in a different sense. The worst physical space can be made into a vibrant location if it is, first, safe (a major reason kids skip school or behave as they do in their classrooms is that they think their environment is unsafe); and second, free, that is, a space where they can share unpopular, scary, provocative and, most basically, *political* thoughts and have those thoughts taken seriously and not dismissed out of hand. Kids need ownership over the space. A safe space is one that protects kids from the dangers that lie outside it and where the rules that regulate its internal workings protect them as well. A free space is one where kids are accepted and that defends democratic participation. Safe and free spaces are the bedrock of democratic processes.

Ideally, entire school districts, individual schools, or individual classrooms could be known for this type of space. Sadly, much space that African American and Latino kids occupy is not even safe—they attend dangerous schools in dangerous neighborhoods. Yet while many other schools are safe, they are far from free. Classrooms can be safe spaces, yet many are situated in schools where political opinion is routinely censured. How could it be different? Public schools are largely designed to train students to fit into what already exists, not prepare them to imagine something different. Public schools are not in a good position to create safe spaces for informed critical debate.

Teachers can certainly create isolated, politically active, safe spaces within public schools, even with an uncooperative administration. Simply closing the door and telling kids that one's classroom is a safe space is a fundamental first step. This route is hard, it can be lonely, and it may not be possible. Certainly public schools have many gifted and motivated teachers and students who want to change their classrooms and schools into safe political spaces, yet their hands are often tied.

Those who create these spaces outside public schools, whether in private schools or in community settings, face far fewer restrictions. Yet innovation with space (whose lessons we can imagine in any setting) can catalyze ideas for how to transform space in even the dreariest setting. Let me share three examples of creating safe spaces, each of which fostered free expression.

The first example concerns the free, safe space created by Jocelyn, an African American student at the University of Cincinnati, for her senior honors project in African American studies. When we met to discuss her possible project, Jocelyn told me how, as part of her job in an afterschool program in a local community center, she noticed that the programming for the eleven- to fourteen-year-old girls seemed inadequate. On the surface, they did have a place to go—they were the girls who were not on the street and who were in the community center. But she felt that they lacked a place where they could just talk. Her response was to design a project for African American girls called "A Place of Our Own."[10] For her project, she requested a space in the community center where the girls might go, and she developed a short curriculum to jump-start conversations. Because Jocelyn thought that the girls deserved nice things, she commandeered a sofa from a friend and brought in decorations to make their space pleasant. She realized that, even though the girls had access to one another anytime they wanted, they needed another place of their own that was a safe space for sharing ideas.

Our weekly conversations during the six-week duration of Jocelyn's project were fascinating. Jocelyn reported that at first, the girls were a little quiet; yet when they began to talk, she was surprised at how candid they were about the issues that they faced. Over the weeks, the girls had increasingly frank discussions about their bodies and sexuality. Jocelyn was amazed at the scope and depth of what they discussed, on their own terms. She brought them information when it seemed appropriate or when they requested, but they set the terms of the discussion. She did not come armed with a rigid curriculum of what she thought they needed to learn. Instead, what they needed was a place of their own where they could explore what they wanted. In essence, they turned a safe space into a free space.

A second example comes from another African American student at the University of Cincinnati. Maya, a returning student, was a mother of seven who lived in public housing. She enrolled in my Contemporary Black Women class, and her analyses of the issues that faced U.S. Black women kept her classmates listening with rapt attention. Maya was a powerful figure. Yet one day she arrived in distress because she had just learned that her young teenage daughter was pregnant. After expressing sorrow and anger, she asked, "What can I do?" We had no easy answers for her. Over the next few class sessions, Maya described how many of the girls in her complex also were pregnant. In response to what she had initially seen as her private trouble, Maya invited the girls into her living room to have a space to talk. She reported that at their first gathering, they relaxed and really opened up to one another. She decided to encourage them to keep coming back. In doing so, her living room became a safe and free space for the girls.[11]

My third example comes from my own teaching in the community schools movement of Roxbury, Massachusetts. I taught at a K–8 school that was housed temporarily in an old nursing home while the school's new building was finished. By any standards, the configuration of the space was unsuitable for children—we had to adjust to classrooms that in many cases had been small private rooms for elderly residents. The condition of the space itself was also horrible. My job was to teach African dance to a lively group of fifth- and sixth-grade, poor and working-class African American students. The only space in the entire building that was large enough for dance was an airless, windowless room in the nursing-home basement that someone had painted black.

When I arrived with my tape player (this was before the iPod) and kids in tow, I remember my feelings when I first entered that room. With no windows and its black walls, the room felt like it was sucking the life out of us. But it got worse. There were small pans on the floor with what appeared to be bits of food in them. The custodian who accompanied us told me that the pans contained rat poison, that I should keep the kids away from them. He reassured me, though, that when we were in the room, the rats most likely would stay away. How could I teach dance in this space? How could anyone dare to dance in these conditions?

But dance we did. I asked the kids to stamp their feet as a ritual that we used every time we entered the room. Through our collective sound (the voice created by our feet), we claimed that space as ours, and our sound transformed that space into a space of creativity (as well as scared away any lurking rats!). We put on music, and we danced in that ugly room. Eventually it came to be a safe and free space for us. The imagination and excitement of my students were amazing. By the end of each dance class, we had all forgotten our surroundings. Our safe space enabled us to create beauty in a space that seemed designed to destroy it.

Despite tremendous variability in their goals, pedagogy, and overall organization, one reason that alternative schools of all sorts (both private and some public charter schools) are successful is that they create safe and free spaces for kids. They put the kids in the center of education and develop everything in response to what the kids in front of them actually need. Tremendous variability shapes what kids need, and, as a result, the kinds of safe and free spaces that schools can create are endless.

Frontline Action: Classrooms as Political Spaces

Schools change when people decide to change them from whatever locations they find themselves. School reform can start virtually anywhere and is unlikely to succeed if it is not practiced in multiple locations. But beyond this truism, it is important to point out that classrooms are the bedrock of educational institutions. The model of the classroom that most people envision defines the classroom as an applied setting, a location where teachers transmit to students ideas and theories developed elsewhere. Teachers are technicians who are "trained" to implement someone else's ideas and theories. Teachers are not supposed to challenge the curriculum. Rather their job is to "teach" it. But what if we imagined classrooms as places where all ideas were open to debate, including, for example, those of the textbooks, or of the girls in A Place of Our Own, or (without the profanity) those of Dead Prez. In these kinds of classrooms, the actual materials and texts are less important than how they are used. Safe classrooms, where all ideas are welcome, conflict is practiced and expected, and agreement is not required, become free spaces.

Rather than seeing classrooms as removed from the seat of power, as sites where decisions that are made elsewhere simply flow through them or as sites where everyone merely follows the rules, classrooms are deeply implicated in reproducing the structural domain of power. Practicing resistance in the structural domain requires changing classroom practices, a process that, if we can see it differently, constitutes grassroots political practice. From this perspective, the classroom is already a political space, whether the teacher chooses to recognize this reality or not. Teachers do not introduce politics into seemingly apolitical classrooms by bringing their partisan politics into them. The question is not whether classroom space is political or not, but rather what kinds of politics are practiced there.

The classroom is a dynamic location, an inherently political space where we actively create, revise, research, and debate our own points of view about what we choose to believe and what we choose to reject. These are the exact same skills that will be needed for an educated public that is prepared to uphold democracy. Classrooms are places where we practice workable coalitions or where we practice reproducing skills of hierarchy. When it comes to the structural domain of power, it is tempting to think of structure as something that is fixed and immovable, something that confines our actions. Certainly, this is how structures feel—sometimes like soft beds, but more often like cages. But just as democracy is not a finished product (a structure) but a process, school structures only take on meaning by what people actually do. Thus, structures are in people, in us, and, via pragmatic actions in classrooms, we bring the structures to life.

This is not to say that each individual is free to do whatever he or she wants. A good deal of my discussion thus far has emphasized the constraints of structures. I understand structural constraint. That black, windowless classroom in the basement of a nursing home is my metaphor for structural constraint. Rather, practicing resistance in the structural domain of power means that individuals must decide how to breathe life into the structures that they inherit. Through our decisions, we make and remake the structures. When the kids in my class decided to dance in that room, they did not make the actual structure of the room disappear. Instead, their actions changed the meaning of the constraints symbolized by that basement room.

Classrooms need not be sites of disempowerment. Instead, no matter how challenging, they are places of possibility because teachers and students can make them anew each day. It may appear that those in higher-up positions decide everything, a top-down view of power that is designed to disempower those lower in the pecking order and thus ensure the smooth reproduction of existing structures (in this case, education). But those on top govern only with the consent of those beneath them. If teachers and students did not cooperate, the structures would be different.

Given this significance, what actually happens in classrooms becomes critical because when classroom practices change, the contours of structural domain also change. Because one focus of this book is envisioning democratic possibilities, I have been emphasizing what it might take to envision democratic classrooms. Specifically, what are the potential benefits and pitfalls of developing classroom communities that encourage multiple points of view across what seem to be major differences?

One potential benefit of grounding classroom communities in

dialogues that encourage multiple points of view is that we all practice skills of honing our own points of view. But we do so in a collaborative context where we realize that we do not have all the answers. The major pitfall is that teachers who move too openly or aggressively in this direction may lose their jobs or suffer job-related penalties. I wish that were not the case, but it is. If a teacher encourages criticism and debate in the classroom, this often means that the teacher may be perceived as a traitor to her or his position. In essence, the teacher relinquishes an authority that is based in a fear granted by an unfair system (Dead Prez's view is what many of the kids are already thinking), in exchange for an alternative form of authority, based in respect and granted by students who want to learn what the teacher knows. The goal is worthy, but is it possible to get there from here?

It basically depends on where we start. Some pedagogies that are currently prevalent in classroom communities might be more easily moved in the direction that I advocate here than others. I will use examples from higher education, but the approaches are common. To me, we currently have three predominant and unsatisfying ways of organizing classroom communities. One method concerns the many classrooms organized around the familiar lecturer preaching to passive listeners. This teaching style falls within Brazilian educator Paulo Freire's notion of the "banking" concept of education. In his classic *Pedagogy of the Oppressed*, Freire argues that the banking concept of education upholds social inequality and oppression. Situations where subordinate groups are expected to absorb information from more powerful figures uncritically or "bank" accepted knowledge to spend later on do not equip disempowered people to challenge social inequality. This banking model of classroom practice assumes that students know little and must be filled up with knowledge selected for them by the person in control. Here teachers talk and students listen.[12]

Other classrooms claim to foster dialogue but really create adversarial debates. Freire's work is useful here as well. Freire suggests that dialogue should be central to pedagogies used with subordinated and oppressed groups such as the Brazilian peasants who inspired his ideas. As an alternative to the banking concept, he posits that teachers use a problem-posing concept of education. As Freire's ideas have traveled, the problem-posing dimension has been overshadowed by a focus on dialogue. Yet when the definition of dialogue gets put into practice via strategies of adversarial debates, we are left with the illusion of an emancipatory education with a classroom practice that can be just as damaging as the banking concept.

It took me some time to tell the difference in my own teaching, especially because students have been primed to mistake debates for dialogues. For example, when I once asked my undergraduate students in my Sociology of the Black Community class what they considered a good class to be, they typically cited examples of arguments or debates. But here's what they meant: A good classroom discussion aims to produce winners and losers, the exact same skills that have fostered partisan politics overall. Kids already know how to do this—in the U.S. context, a good debate aims to silence one party so that the other can be declared the winner and the other the loser. Ironically, many of us view classrooms organized around adversarial debate as typifying "free speech." I ask: Why go to a school at all if you already know what you think? Why listen to anyone if you already know everything that they think as well?

In contrast, heated debates where the goal is to understand the perspective of the other can be far more productive. Neither party should harden his or her own position. Instead, the goal is active listening, so that each participant reconsiders his or her point of view in light of a different perspective. We need not change our minds, only deepen our perspective. Here, the possibilities of engaged conversations are endless. I have been teaching for more than thirty years, yet individual students always say or do something that surprises me. I continue to learn from them.

A classroom that encourages multiple points of view must protect unpopular speech, but it must also help everyone understand why an individual might believe certain things. Conflict often results in trying to have dialogues across differences, not just of experience, but also across the very real differences in power among people that exist within all classroom communities. I remember the struggles that Nick, one young white man enrolled in my Sociology of the Black Community class, had in discussing race with African American students. Black students in the class felt comfortable enough to express anger about the incidents of everyday racism that they routinely encountered. While Nick tried to understand the institutional structures of racism, he was floored by their anger, and questioned it. Serious conflict ensued, with some students yelling that others simply didn't understand.

In class discussion one day, someone thought to ask Nick how many African Americans he knew. Nick offered, "Not many," but he admitted that he had many long conversations with his family's African American maid, and that she had never expressed any such anger to him. Over time, my students came to share the kinds of experiences that led them to their beliefs. Nick, for example, simply could not imagine his family's maid ever being as angry as his classmates. At that point, many of the African American students came to see that Nick could talk only about what he knew, and that what he knew was framed by his experiences in a racially segregated (all-white), affluent environment. Moreover, what was true for Nick was also true for each and every one of them. African American students, for example, could not speak in one voice. Instead, each individual could speak only from his or her own experiences, just as Nick was forced to do. Some were angry, while others were not angry at all. When more people came into the discussion as the class evolved, the dialogue continued, still heated at times but not through the lens of adversarial debate where we began.[13]

What will be required for developing such classrooms? How do we ground our classrooms in democratic processes skilled in working with heterogeneity, conflict, and resistance from the students we most want to reach? Ideally, as the example of Nick and his class-mates suggests, we each need to see the partiality of our own point of view and develop empathy for the point of view of others. No one individual possesses all the answers. No one individual can even ask all the right questions. More importantly, developing skills of active listening to understand another's point of view is crucial for develop-ing empathy.[14]

Let me give an example of how developing empathy differs from simply acquiring more knowledge about the unknown. Reading the works of other women of color in the United States gives me a sense of the types of connections that exist among African American women and Asian American women. But it also gives me a sense of why U.S. Black women's point of view is partial. For example, Amy Tan's classic book on Chinese and Chinese American women, *The Joy Luck Club*, resonates with themes that pervade the work of African American women writers. Mother-daughter relationships, domestic violence, racial-ethnic identity, generational differences, and the constraints and contributions of culture permeate Tan's fiction. By reading Tan, I realize how differently positioned she is than I am in discussing these issues. I read her works because I want to hear her point of view so that I can develop empathy for Chinese and Chinese American women's experiences. I do not read her work as if she were the best expert on motherhood. I do not read her work to prove her view of motherhood wrong, or to prove mine right. To me, we each have a partial point of view and we need each other's partiality to make more sense of our own. When it comes to understanding motherhood, I need to engage Tan's point of view, the ideas in African American women's writings, the points of view of the teen mothers in Maya's living room, and many other sources of information.

People are not naturally good at empathy—you have to practice it—and what better place to practice it than in classrooms? Class-rooms are places where people practice dialogues across differences in power generated by structures of race, class, gender, and sexuality, and in this sense, they are essential to practicing resistance against these structures of power. We can't remake another group's experience by collapsing it into our own, but we can use our own experiences to imagine what a different group has experienced, thinks, and feels. Thus, empathy is based on an informed imagination, one grounded in a certain level of self-knowledge and self-awareness.

Developing the empathy needed to move individuals toward dialogues, coalitions, and alliances requires that we understand our own position. Our own position is never finished and we cannot understand our own position in isolation. This is why we want African American kids to learn their history—not so they can replace false images of themselves as thugs and "hos" with equally false images of themselves as kings and queens that they can lord over others. Rather, self-knowledge that catalyzes empathy should better prepare them for coalitions and alliances with people whose experiences resemble theirs, yet differ. With this foundation, they are better able to use their ideas and knowledge to empathize with other individuals (and groups) who may be similarly affected by inequality. Rather than seeing their experiences as disconnected, they come to identify points of similarity and divergence between their aspirations and those of others.

In a classroom, the answers we give matter less than the questions we ask. Big, important questions rarely have short, simple answers. Rather than masquerading as being a place that has all the answers, the classroom can be the place to hone the questions and bring the best ideas of kids to bear on provisional answers. Some answers will appear to be true by most in the group and, on that day, become the most objective truths. Yet when people in safe and free spaces come to understand that they are making truth instead of consuming it, the rules of the game change. As Alice Walker maintains, "[W]hat is always needed in the appreciation of art, or life is the larger perspective. Connections made, or at least attempted, where none existed before, the straining to encompass in one's glance at the varied world the common thread, the unifying theme through immense diversity."[15] Claiming one's own position and developing empathy for those of others, not shouting the loudest or falsely believing that one's own point of view is the best, is the condition of being heard. Via these activities, we change the structures that contain us.

RESISTANCE IN THE DISCIPLINARY
DOMAIN OF POWER: LIE DETECTORS

Resistance to color-blind racism in the disciplinary domain of power can take a variety of forms—from individual covert disbelief, to individual covert actions, to individual overt actions, to collective overt actions, to collective rebellion. We know less about this resistance in this domain than others because, to be effective, it often must conceal its own operation.

The disciplinary domain of power describes the ways that people use the rules and regulations of everyday life to uphold the racial hierarchy or to challenge it. The disciplinary domain encompasses two sets of behaviors—how the rules of organizations regulate who can say and do what, and how people actually carry out these rules in their day-to-day behavior. Disciplinary aspects of color-blind racism in the classroom might include rules that reward African American students who reject any mention of race, and differential application of rules to students based on their race. The disciplinary domain of power focuses on the dynamics of how individuals and organizations exercise power—in other words, how people enforce and/or resist rules, the techniques and practices of organizations that regulate populations.

Youth often do not submit willingly to school discipline, even when their resistance jeopardizes their academic school success. For example, a four-year study of African American adolescents in a Washington, D.C., inner-city high school paints a compelling picture of the complex ways that they resisted school discipline that tethered school success to racial assimilation.[16] Similarly, the Latino high school students who walked out of school in March 2006 as part of what grew to be a national protest against anti-immigration policies also indicate the willingness of youth to break rules when they see the stakes as being high.[17]

One mechanism of practicing resistance in the disciplinary domain is to encourage kids and parents to develop more sophisticated skills of countersurveillance. If surveillance is a major strategy for achieving social control, how might countersurveillance be a tool of resistance? Moreover, the goal of teaching and learning is to get kids to fit into the existing system, yet fitting into a color-blind situation, especially a situation that is organized around forced assimilation, is typically fraught with difficulties. Suppose we challenged this basic goal of education? In the following sections, I examine these two themes of practicing resistance in the disciplinary domain; namely, (1) cultivating skills of countersurveillance as a way to practice resistance within school settings; and (2) broadening the idea of teaching and learning from that of passing on a repository of knowledge to one of teaching and learning as activities that subvert this objective.

Cultivating Countersurveillance

As we have seen, surveillance is a mechanism of control that helps keep color-blind racism going. When people feel that they are being watched, they often behave differently. Surveillance is based on the idea that groups with more power have more authority to watch those with less power. Sometimes social position is enough to grant one person the liberty to place others under surveillance. Teachers and school administrators have the power to place students under surveillance, evaluating their behavior and handing out social rewards based on their observations. Gender, race, and similar systems of power grant the members of the dominant group authority to place members of a subordinate group under surveillance. Thus, men can stare at women, often offering unsolicited comments about women's dress, demeanor, and appearance. In contrast, few women take these liberties with men.[18] There is a difference between looking at someone and placing them under surveillance. Surveillance is a technique of modern power relations.[19]

Countersurveillance occurs when less powerful groups reverse these relations and place the more powerful under surveillance. Socially black people, for example, can watch back, gaining valuable ideas about racial power relationships that can be used for a variety of purposes. In this sense, countersurveillance can be a critical tool of resistance for members of oppressed groups. For example, countersurveillance occurs if I am your slave, servant, or student and, as a result of this structural relationship, you have the right to watch, supervise, and discipline me. You may be watching me because you think I'm going to poison your soup, steal the silver, or misbehave and disrupt the class. But surveillance goes both ways. In the course of watching you from my structural position of relative powerlessness (as a slave, servant, or student), I see things about you that routinely escape your attention. I learn your vulnerabilities by watching you, knowledge that may be useful to me in navigating the unequal power relation that joins us.

Often countersurveillance is essential for reasons of safety. To avoid danger, less powerful people can become incredibly conscious of and vigilant within potentially dangerous surroundings. Most women understand how surveillance and countersurveillance affect the use of physical space. Women and men have different notions of physical safety. Where is it safe to walk and not walk? What time of day can I walk? Should I walk alone or with a friend? These are questions that women are much more likely to ask themselves than men. Oppressed people can also use tools of countersurveillance for varying political ends. Terrorist groups also routinely use these same skills of countersurveillance—as was the case with the 9/11 hijackers, who lived in the United States unnoticed for many years, learning the ways of America before taking their dramatic action.

In the examples that follow, I describe how developing countersurveillance can be an effective tool for teachers and students who wish to practice resistance in the disciplinary domain. In school settings, contemporary tools of surveillance are more sophisticated than past practices; everyone is watching everyone else, a core feature of social control in contemporary societies. Thus, skills of countersurveillance learned in school settings can become useful in a wide range of situations.

I first learned lessons of countersurveillance during my long years of education in the Philadelphia public schools. Over the years, it became clear to me that my teachers did not like me, primarily because they did not think I belonged in their classrooms. I didn't even have to open my mouth; they had little interest in what I had to say. As one of the few African American students in the top tracks in my middle school and high school, I became increasingly silenced in their classrooms, the price of my public school education. Yet, with hindsight, beyond gaining a top-notch technical education, I learned far more from those with power over me than they ever learned about me. In some ways, being ignored turned into an advantage for me. Despite years of covert and occasionally overt silencing—recall my "What does the flag mean to you?" vignette from chapter 1—I had years to practice the skills of countersurveillance.

Kids need not undergo years of quiet suffering to hone their countersurveillance skills. Teachers can be proactive in developing skills of countersurveillance in kids and yet do so within the norms of acceptable practice for their institution. This is one important lesson that subordinates often learn—one can follow the letter of the law but perform it in such a way that you bend it to your own agenda. Principals, teachers, bosses, and store managers can tell you the rules, but it is extremely difficult for them to micromanage every detail of how an employee chooses to follow those rules.

"Lie Detector," one of my favorite classroom exercises, illustrates how teachers can cultivate a form of active listening that underpins countersurveillance. I once asked my sixth-grade class to listen carefully to a ten-minute lecture I was about to deliver on President Abra-ham Lincoln. I told them that I was going to tell them three "lies." Their task was to raise their hands when they thought they heard a lie. Using a standard "just the facts" tone, I began my lecture with some unassailable facts: for example, the day and place of Lincoln's birth, and the date he was elected president. In my (boring) rendition of Lincoln's life, I stated, "One of Lincoln's major accomplishments was that he freed the slaves." At this point, many hands went up. I stopped my lecture so we could discuss this point. The hand-raisers yelled out, "No, he didn't. No, he didn't. We know he didn't free the slaves." Other students were puzzled, saying, "I thought he freed the slaves—he didn't free the slaves?" This was a great starting point—not everyone agrees on what is the truth.

Every time even one hand went up, I stopped my lecture and we discussed why we thought I told a lie or not. I recall one especially heated exchange, one where only a few hands went up. The remain-ing students looked at the few hand-raisers in amazement: "Why are your hands up—everybody knows that this is true." Because the mi-nority hand-raisers stood their ground, we discussed the whole notion of minority opinion. Just because the majority of people believe some-thing doesn't necessarily mean that it is truth.

As this lesson continued, one girl finally protested the entire assignment in frustration, blurting out, "Miss Hill, this is silly. We know *you* wouldn't lie to us!" This was the teachable moment. I re-sponded, "I may not willingly or knowingly lie to you, and I may love you dearly. But I may still pass on lies to you because I don't know any better." This exercise challenged one fundamental rule of classrooms. When we ask students to listen to lectures and take notes, we basi-cally require that they remember or record nuggets of truth. Here I was asking my students to listen to and to take notes on nuggets of lies. No wonder this girl was upset.

That particular class session was fascinating to me, mainly be-cause, with hindsight, I now see it a way of practicing anti-racist resistance. It was scary for these sixth-graders to confront the idea that truth and lies are not fixed ideas, and that so-called facts reflect the point of view of whoever has the power to define them. But it was also freeing, because the students began to practice thinking about themselves as part of this process of sorting ideas into categories of truth and lies. This exercise also had the bonus of practicing incorporating multiple points of view, the benchmark of democratic learning communities. In the "Lie Detector" exercise, each individual had an opportunity to vote by raising his or her hand and expressing his or her opinion.

The skills of countersurveillance practiced through exercises such as "Lie Detector" need not be publicly named. I could (and did) say to the students that certain so-called facts about Lincoln would be on the standardized test. If they wanted to pass, they needed to give the "right" answers. But I could also say to them that they were free to disbelieve, to listen to every word from every teacher (including me) as a potential lie. Each one of us can bring skills of critical thinking to any situation. Schools operate by identifying truth, packaging it, and by hiring people to discipline kids to accept it. Often teachers want to catalyze resistance by replacing their own more "truthful" version of the truth while leaving the processes intact. Stated differently, they want to change the content of education (cultural domain) without changing the disciplinary practices that uphold their own power. Practicing resistance in the disciplinary domain requires disrupting the everyday assumptions that uphold disciplinary power. For example, instead of replacing one truth with another, disrupting disciplinary power might mean teaching kids to listen for lies instead of truth.

Developing the ability to "read" the social cues of a range of social situations illustrates another dimension of the benefits of becoming skilled in countersurveillance. Reading social cues requires that we think about literacy much more broadly than reading books, analyzing media, or learning new languages, even in school settings. Countersurveillance might catalyze more sophisticated communication skills that enable kids to understand what kind of situations they are in, to "read" the situations in terms of what's appropriate and what's not appropriate, and to adjust their behavior accordingly. To me, reading social cues reflects the intersection of countersurveillance and a form of literacy.

Many teachers deal with this theme of reading social cues as a form of literacy but have few frameworks for how to think about it. Teachers typically view this aspect of student behavior as "disciplining" them to obey social norms that remain unstated. Within the disciplinary framework, kids who curse, don't take their hats off in class, chew gum, wear clothing that is too tight, too loose, too short, or too low-cut, or in other ways fail to adhere to a code of conduct, are being "bad." Rather than evaluating these behaviors within an imposed moral framework of good and bad, I suggest that we place these behaviors within a literacy framework and ask what we want students to learn by changing their behavior. The goal is not to be trained into appropriate behavior. Rather, treating the reading of social cues as a form of literacy enables each individual student to decide for himself or herself the ways in which he or she wishes to respond to them. Highly perfected skills of countersurveillance are essential to this task.

Through fashion and clothing, people send out social cues that others must "read" to figure out power relations. Status, authority, and real, tangible rewards are routinely associated with how people dress. Yet the power relations that underlie clothes as social cues for power are not naturally absorbed. They must be learned, and schools and teachers are often on the front line of negotiating these issues. Take, for example, the dilemma I faced several years ago concerning my scantily clad teaching assistant. This particular student had a large bust and showed up to teach wearing a tube top and a miniskirt. I thought the students were never going to be able to concentrate if she went into class dressed like that, and I struggled to find the right words to say to her. For me, this was not a moral situation that labeled her as a bad or loose woman based on her attire, and I was worried that she might take anything that I said that way. Instead, I evaluated her clothing choice in the context of how her ability to read (and misread) important social cues might affect her professional success. I asked, "Do you think that your outfit is appropriate for teaching?" "Oh, Dr. Collins," she replied, "I have a sweater." That made sense until she took out an itty-bitty sweater that barely covered her shoulders. This was a step in the right direction, but we definitely were not there yet.

Situations such as this can be difficult for teachers and school personnel because legally, we should not micromanage people's clothing choices. Kids often interpret this unsolicited advice about their clothing choices as unwanted meddling in their private lives and need for personal expression. Often, they resent it because the advice is given within judgmental, moral frameworks of right and wrong. Instead, I suggest that a range of classroom behaviors would be better approached through the social literacy framework of helping kids read social cues. They are already watching one another, a form of surveillance. Rather, the issue is the values that they attach to certain social cues, such as clothing and speech. For kids, the consequences of not being able to read the social cues of the power relations in school settings can be damaging. For example, a high school teacher shared the example of a dark-skinned, Dominican girl who, despite her good grades and popularity, was repeatedly sent home by school officials because of what she was wearing. They found her clothing to be sexually provocative, yet they could offer no clear reasons for why that was so.

At a fundamental level, kids need practice at reading the social cues of their own classrooms and school settings and their home communities. Being able to detect lies and read social cues, skills developed through the active listening and watching needed for countersurveillance, can catalyze cultural competence in "reading" multiple social situations. Here, being able to move among multiple situations and translate becomes the gold standard of educational competence. In her study of the school success of minority kids, sociologist Prudence Carter categories the kids she studied into three groups: kids who tried to fit into the school culture by erasing their minority culture (mainstreamers); kids who rejected school norms in favor of their minority culture (noncompliant believers); and kids who moved comfortably between school culture and their home cultures (straddlers). In contrast to assimilation models that suggest that the mainstreamers would experience more school success, Carter found that the straddlers did best.[20] Thus, kids with finely tuned skills of countersurveillance may better prepare them to detect, manage, and influence the social cues in situations where they are expected to assimilate, or where skills of multicultural translation may be valued, or where a *mestizaje* ethos is emerging. Skills of multiple literacy would better position them to determine the appropriate communications patterns and behavior, not just in situations where different languages are spoken but also where different social cues stem from different systems of ideas that in turn reflect unequal power relations.

Teaching and Learning as Subversive Activities

How might we think about teaching and learning as subversive activities where teachers engage in sophisticated ways of appearing to discipline kids but at the same time encouraging them *not* to fit in? How might kids develop effective skills of fitting in yet learn to challenge the very terms of their participation? Is it possible for both teachers and students to buy into the disciplinary processes of schools without selling out? Clearly, this is not easy to do.

I think that the most sophisticated teaching that I have seen (and hopefully tried to do) aims for a place in between outright rebellion (which can get kids put out of school and teachers fired) and pressuring kids uncritically to fit into a system that teachers often see as fundamentally flawed. To do this, the hidden curriculum itself becomes the curriculum to be unmasked and taught (reading and evaluating social cues), with the formal curriculum (learning Abraham Lincoln's biography for the standardized test) serving as cover for this more subversive perspective. Moreover, seeing the classroom as a frontline political space and helping people practice empathy by engaging multiple points of view lay the groundwork for subversive teaching and learning.

In a mass-media-saturated environment, kids often arrive at school with far more information than did kids of prior generations. Hip hop culture in particular often equips some kids with a critical consciousness on education itself (for example, Dead Prez fans). When kids figure out that teachers are using their voice of authority to uphold a hidden curriculum that reproduces inequality, they can see teachers as all part of one huge conspiracy of lies. I am a believer in truth-telling, but I also know that truth-telling can carry substantial risk. In this context, perhaps teachers need creative instructional techniques that deliver skills of fitting in without buying in, of being critical as an indicator of not selling out.

Let me share a classroom example of how rejecting the hidden curriculum became part of the first class that I ever taught on African American women. My students were seventh- and eighth-grade African American girls at a tough, inner-city middle school, ironically named the Martin Luther King Middle School. We all entered the building through one door that was manned by a very large African American male security guard. The door had no handle on the outside, so latecomers had to bang on it to call him to let them in. The halls were patrolled by a stick-carrying assistant principal, a fact that I discovered the day when he yelled at me and demanded my hall pass. I dreaded leaving my classroom for fear of running into him. This was the carceral school prior to the era of metal detectors.

How were kids supposed to fit into that setting? How could I stand in the front of the classroom and uncritically defend those practices, especially when teaching a formal curriculum centered on African American women's resistance to racism, sexism, and class exploitation?[21] My students may have appeared to be submissive, but they were fundamentally angry and frequently rebellious. This fact became apparent the day that one girl stood up and threw a chair at another over some small infraction. When that chair whizzed by me, I realized that the traditional techniques of teacher training that I learned in the storied halls of the Harvard University Graduate School of Education—for example, the standard, middle-class dialogical model of "Let's get in a circle and discuss topic X to death"—were just not going to work with these girls. We needed to do something different. There was no way that they could understand the content of my lessons (namely, African American women's intellectual and political traditions) without understanding and possibly subverting the school that had us all on lockdown.

The first thing that I had to do was create a safe classroom space, much like the spaces that Jocelyn created through her A Place of Our Own project and that Maya created in her public housing living room. I had to create a learning community that was a safe space in a school that really wasn't particularly safe, even for me. To establish this space, I closed my classroom door and said, "I have to tell you the truth. I want to teach you this material, and to do that, we need a space where we can be honest with each other. I want to create a safe space where what happens in here, stays in here. If you say anything that is off-the-cuff, it goes no farther than this room." They listened, yet they struggled with what I said next: "If I say things that are a little off-the-cuff, and if any of you decide to report me, I'm going to deny it. You know what this school is like—they will believe me before they believe you, even if I am lying. I'm doing this because we need a space where we can all speak freely, including me. In order to say the kinds of things that need saying, we will need to watch each other's backs, all right?" That part of the speech got their attention. They were silent, so I pushed on. I explained my fundamental classroom rule: no one could interfere with anyone else's learning. My job as a teacher was to explain and enforce this rule.

I am not advocating that teachers tear up their credentials and try to pal around with their students. I am saying that meeting the needs of students can require choosing to subvert the rules rather than blindly upholding them. In this situation, my students could not begin their education about African American women without thinking about and talking about themselves as young African American women. But how were they to do this? They had so little practice at speaking out loud about the realities of their lives. How would I move them toward a classroom where multiple points of view were expressed and everyone was heard? I decided to start this process by asking them to tell the story of their own lives. Yet telling these stories out loud, giving full testimony to what you really think in public, can be dangerous, as was the case in the school that my students attended.[22] Plus, they had no practice doing it.

Faced with this dilemma, I encouraged my students to keep journals, to testify in private.[23] I provided the journals and set aside classroom time for journal-keeping. I required that they write something in their journals each session, but they did not need to use the entire time writing. They could choose to sleep, think, or look out the window, but they had to put at least some words to paper. I told them that I would not grade their journals—I wouldn't even read them. Instead, I would look at them from afar just to see that they had written something. I just wanted them to have a place where they could talk to themselves.

I want to be clear that I am not sharing this story as an example of a technique that I advocate using with all groups at all times. Rather, in the context of the repeated silencing that these girls had undergone, this technique worked with this particular group of learners. My students were adolescent African American girls living in an inner-city neighborhood who felt that nobody had any interest in what they had to say. The lesson that they needed to learn was that other people's interest in what they decided was important to them was irrelevant (even sympathetic teachers). What mattered was that they were important enough to themselves to care what they themselves thought. Regardless of what other people thought, their lives should matter to them.[24]

Several of my students did invite me to read their journals, and to this day, I remain humbled by their courage. My class contained a high percentage of girls who were quick to talk but slow to trust. I did have an opportunity to read their journals, and was fascinated by what they said. For example, one girl wrote about the use of the term *black:* "Black, black! Look at all the terms that go along with Black. They're all bad or ugly!" She then compiled a long list of all the negative uses of the term—black sheep, black magic, and a few that I had not considered. This student basically unpacked denigrating racial language and images that have been used to justify racism. Then she got angry in response to her own journal entry. Subsequent entries were filled with profanity—but then, it was her journal; these were her thoughts, an analysis of her experience.

She wasn't the only one—many of my students were angry and therefore were well along the path of deciding to disbelieve the main tenets of their public school education (recall my Flag Day experience). But the tools that they found available to them were either outright rebellion (for which they were always getting into trouble) or seeming submission. Many had thought rebellious thoughts before, but they needed more choices about how to manage it. For many, learning how to subvert the system while being disciplined by it was very helpful. For teachers and students alike, engaging in this kind of subversive activity requires finding one's own voice and becoming bold enough to criticize one's surroundings in ways that are effective. In this case, the journal exercise in the classroom where we colluded to break the rules involved using the power of the written word to talk to ourselves and then to one another. Teachers and students alike need more safe places where we can take risks such as thinking unpopular thoughts and engaging in unpopular action. That is what we managed to do in that particular classroom. Kids began to find their own voices to talk about things that were really important to them.

RESISTANCE IN THE CULTURAL DOMAIN OF POWER:
CULTIVATING MEDIA LITERACY

Schools and mass media constitute two increasingly interdependent sites that are especially central to the cultural domain of power. Both are concerned with the power of ideas—creating them, sharing them, and critically analyzing their meaning and effects. Yet schools now contend with an increasingly influential mass media that affects not only what happens within schools but also trends in broader society. Schools are sites of learning, yet the media constitutes a second or even a first school for a considerable segment of youth. African American youth, for example, can no longer as readily depend on a deeply textured web of families, churches, fraternal organizations, school clubs, sports teams, and other community organizations to help them negotiate the challenges of racial inequality. Mass media fills this void, especially mass media that markets black popular culture and that seemingly addresses African American tastes.[25]

A new color-blind racism that relies on the centrality of ideas, ideology, and culture in constructing and contesting racial meanings and practices has been helped by the growing influence of the mass media and popular culture. The films, music, magazines, music videos, television shows, and images produced by the global entertainment, advertising, and news industries present color-blind racism as natural, normal, and inevitable. For example, global mass media circulates images of black femininity and black masculinity and, in doing so, ideologies of race, gender, sexuality, and class. It is very important that we make sense of the cultural complexities of color-blind racism where, for example, Black American youth culture is celebrated, yet actual African American kids who create that culture experience discrimination in their everyday lives (this is a large part of what they rap about); where racial vocabulary has disappeared (it's not chic to tell racial jokes), yet everyone knows what certain words really mean ("welfare queen" and "inner-city" as code words for socially black);

where, until the ascendancy of Barack Obama, gifted and accomplished African Americans with American last names like Rice, Powell, and Thomas occupied visible positions in government only dreamed of by African Americans who encounter barriers to voting; and where the seemingly best job in poor and working-class African American and/or Latino neighborhoods may be low-status, low-wage work in the service industry, the global drug industry, the black culture industry, the sex work industry, or the military (which lately has included dangerous tours of duty in Iraq and Afghanistan).[26] Because mass media and popular culture now assume such importance, acquiring media literacy constitutes an increasingly important dimension of practicing resistance in the cultural domain.[27]

New technologies and the ascendancy of mass media hold numerous opportunities for resistance. Some thinkers suggest that youth are already using the media to practice resistance *outside* school-based settings. For example, some variations of hip hop might express the political opinions of socially black youth who feel shut out of the system.[28] This suggests that the generation that has come of age within a media-inflected environment sees new ways of using the media for political purposes. When it comes to media literacy among youth, schools are more likely to be following trends than setting them.

Cultivating media literacy need not be confined to school-based settings, but it should become increasingly prominent there. In particular, cultivating media literacy among youth so that they can develop their own critical analyses of their neighborhoods, schools, families, and friends, as well as the media messages that they confront on a daily basis, constitutes a vitally important form of resistance. Schools may become sites where students practice skills of media literacy that they can take with them in their everyday lives.

The overarching goal of media literacy should be to help youth move from being passive consumers to active creators of knowledge. Being able to analyze media messages and images is important, but becoming media-literate also involves understanding the reasons that various forms of media replicate the patterns that they do. Specifically, it is important to understand the corporate culture behind the image of popular media; that is, understanding that what is being portrayed is not necessarily "real" (particularly in hip hop) but rather a carefully calculated and packaged commodity.[29] What are some core ideas for developing media literacy?

I use the interrelated terms of *filters* and *frameworks* as core ideas to develop media literacy through the practice of critical thinking. Briefly put, filters are the shortcut lenses that we use to view the world. We cannot see everything at once, so we filter what we see and hear, primarily by selective viewing (a filter that obscures our field of vision, much like covering one eye at the doctor's office to eliminate the input of the other eye). Filters work to help us quickly navigate the seemingly seamless sights and sounds of contemporary mass media. YouTube, the explosive growth of video, and the ability to download rich media via MP3 players and cell phones all speak to this simultaneously visual and oral nature of mass media. Filters serve as cognitive shortcuts that enable us to process information quickly (however erroneously). Basically, filters allow us to Google the mass of information in our everyday lives.[30]

In contrast to filters, frameworks refer to the interpretations that we give of our filtered and therefore partial view of the world. Frameworks can be simple classification systems or they can provide interpretations of the world; for example, the difference between systems of classification in libraries that enable us to find the specific Chicano studies book that we need, and an explanation of why Chicano studies books, once classified, should be included in the library. Some frameworks are virtually identical to filters, whereas others are more analytical and theoretical. For example, my earlier discussion of the domains-of-power framework was designed to assist readers to bring a more analytical framework to color-blind racism and other contemporary systems of inequality.[31]

We often notice frameworks when we are in new situations where old frameworks do not work or work less perfectly than before, or where we cannot figure out the framework. I was reminded of this during a visit to a bookstore in a small Southern city. I enjoy visiting bookstores, in part to see in what sections they shelve my books—Sociology, African American Studies, Women's Studies, or Cultural Studies. I also visit them to see the stable and shifting categories that are used to categorize books. This bookstore really threw me. As I walked through the store, I could uncover no apparent order, no pattern that I could discern. Books were on the shelves that did not appear to belong together. The store felt chaotic, yet that experience helped me see how reliant I was on store categories as frameworks for how I thought about books.

Filters and frameworks typically work together in shaping social meaning. Take, for example, the construct of social blackness that I use throughout this book. There is no one definition of social blackness that applies in all places at all times. Rather, the filters that enable us to categorize people in races (whether we see race) and our frameworks of interpretation (how we categorize and evaluate what we see) together produce social blackness. Social blackness is highly correlated with skin color, but this is not its origin. Instead, the power to define race lies in the power relations of the context as organized through filters and frameworks and not necessarily in the biology or the culture of any specific individual. These relations of social blackness may be especially well suited to the visual nature of contemporary consumer culture as well as the needs of contemporary color-blind racism.

In the following sections, I explore specific techniques for cultivating media literacy via a dual strategy that encompasses: (1) recognizing the interactive nature of the filters and frameworks that are encoded in the content of what kids see and the filters and frameworks that they, as consumers of media, bring to their media experiences; and (2) writing your own story where we validate our own filters and frameworks and create new ones. Together, these strategies should help people move from being passive consumers of media to developing their own independent interpretation of media to, for many, becoming active creators of it. They equip people to practice resistance in the cultural domain of power.

I focus on specific techniques as a window to understanding the broader array of critical thinking skills that are necessary for media literacy. These techniques can be developed in a variety of ways—through immersion in unsupervised media activities such as posting messages to community bulletin boards, blogging, posting videos to YouTube, participating in social networking sites, and so on; through school-based initiatives such as those I explore below; and/or through alternatives that we have yet to conceptualize. I am less concerned with specific activities that can be used to teach these skills (although I do provide suggestions) than I am in focusing attention on the links between critical analysis and media literacy.[32]

Filters, Frameworks, and Media Literacy

Because media is part of the lived experiences of young people today to a much greater degree than of previous generations, critically analyzing this relationship between media-generated filters and frameworks and their own filters and frameworks becomes vitally important for youth. Filters and frameworks shape what we see in all aspects of our lives and our interpretations of what we perceive. Yet when it comes to mass media, youth have had far less formal, school-based experiences that help them analyze mass media. In this context, sounds and images of visual media can take on an aura of "truth" because pictures seemingly depict "reality" and the narration that accompanies images sounds believable.

One important component of media literacy is recognizing the connections between the filters and frameworks that are encoded in media content (for example, the origins, organization, and social meanings of images of African American youth) and the filters and frameworks that African American youth, as consumers of media, bring to their media experiences. For example, poor and working-class African American girls may perceive and interpret media images differently than middle-class African American men, or working-class white women, or Latina lesbians. Moreover, the filters and frameworks that each individual brings to his or her media experiences reflect far more than identity categories of race, class, gender, or sexuality. Political perspective (feminist women may view mass media images of African American women differently than conservative women), region of the country, or even the setting where a person experiences a media product (watching a video through one's phone versus watching with a group of people in a bar) influences the filters and frameworks that an individual brings to a media product.

This may sound complex, and it is. But this complexity also makes for endless, interesting, open-ended opportunities to share the various forms of seeing media products, especially in classrooms that encourage the free exchange of ideas. Through classroom examples, I want to focus on three elements of this process that might serve as good starting points for practicing resistance by cultivating media literacy. They are: (1) the notion that what you bring to the act of "reading" media shapes how you read that media; the message is not intrinsic to the film, video, or other product, and, instead, each person creates the meaning based on what she or he knows; (2) for oppressed groups, recognizing the alternative filters and frameworks from one's own experiences can be a useful and empowering source of knowledge; and (3) one can craft new interpretations of social reality to challenge what is accepted as authoritative truth. To illustrate these ideas, I draw your attention to two classroom examples.

My first example comes from my experience teaching a social studies unit on South Africa under apartheid to a group of lively seventh- and eighth-grade African American kids. This example focuses on the small area of looking for contradictions between what one knows, how what one knows shapes what one expects to find, and explaining the discrepancies. In looking for visual material, the only film that I could afford on our meager budget was a free film produced by the South African Film Board under apartheid. After I previewed the film, and before showing it to my students, I distributed demographic information to them about the South African population—the percentages of "blacks, whites, coloreds, and Indians."[33] I asked, "Based on the information about the South African population that I have given you, what would you expect to see in a government film about South Africa?" They were quick to show off what they had learned. They confidently stated that they expected to see many black people because the majority of the population was black. Then I showed the film. There were three black people in the entire film: two black men who were working at the South African Stock Exchange manually changing the numbers, and a black woman who was sitting on a park bench minding a white child.

My students' jaws dropped open. "That can't be right," they said. "That makes no sense—where are the black people?" Then they started asking the kinds of questions that teachers who encourage critical thinking relish: "Who wrote this story? Whose film is this? Who selected the images that are in this particular film?" In our classroom discussion about the film, it was clear to my students that the film excluded black people—and had to try pretty hard to do so, given the large black population of the country. My students were especially interested in the reasons that this had happened. For many, it was the first time that they had been encouraged to move beyond the stance of passive recipient of truth that seemingly is incorporated in documentaries. Moreover, they were able to critique the film because they had prior research and "facts" to back up their point of view. Furthermore, they depended on knowledge outside their own experience to contest the depiction of South Africa in the film.

When it comes to media literacy, one of the most difficult aspects of teaching is to see the invisible structures that shape what we see and hear. A first step in seeing those structures is to help learners identify their own knowledge base and bring it to the act of seeing and hearing media. This is an important first step, if only because it begins to break down widespread assumptions of truth and fiction. Indeed, the hardest thing to see is what's not in the film—what's missing. Unless you think to look for what's missing, you don't notice what's missing, particularly if the text is very smooth and carrying you along with the images that you see. What I did with my students was to encourage them not to be passive consumers, but to question the filters and the frameworks of the South African Film Board. I did this by helping them value their own filters that they brought to viewing things; namely, their own knowledge concerning what they expected to see.

My second example comes from a class of third- and fourth-graders that I taught in an inner-city school with a limited budget. Here the process focuses less on the filters and frameworks that viewers bring to their media experiences (as was the case with my fifth- and sixth-graders, who used their new knowledge to challenge the voice of authority) and more on the skills of doing a close textual analysis of how media products are constructed. This school used filmstrips that teachers routinely showed to impart information. Students were encouraged to learn information from the filmstrip. Teachers today often use documentaries in a similar fashion. We ask students to view the documentaries as simple recordings of seemingly truthful experience rather than analyze how documentaries present themselves as voices of authority. Basically, we often teach our students to be passive consumers of the ideas in the filmstrips or documentaries, failing to encourage them to question the frameworks that these ideas reflect.

The beauty of those old-fashioned filmstrips was that the sound track and the filmstrip were not presynchronized. Unlike the seamless productions of today, the teacher had to change each slide manually when the sound track gave an oral cue. I routinely found myself showing images that did not match the voiceover. My seeming mistakes revealed that sight and sound were not naturally joined. Rather, they were grafted together, with the teacher showing the filmstrip providing the technological link. Rather than seeing this slippage as an unfortunate consequence of teaching in a school with no money, I decided to use this technology differently. I wondered what would happen if I *explicitly* separated the sound track and the images; in essence, if I took away the frameworks (provided by the narration) for how we were to see the slides (preselected images using the producer's filter) from the filmstrip itself. What would we actually see in the absence of the narrator's voice of authority? Would the interpretive framework provided with the filmstrip still work?

For the students, I turned off the sound and showed them the entire filmstrip (without any text). The only words were the title of the filmstrip on the first slide. I divided the students into small groups and asked each group to construct a script using only the actual title and the images that I had shown them. Because there was no official story that they were supposed to figure out, all scripts would be equal. Their stories simply had to make sense of the pictures that I had shown them. We then viewed our filmstrips and compared what we created. Their stories were far more interesting than the official one. They asked each other many questions about their respective stories. I marveled at how similar their stories were in spots (some images were pretty unambiguous) and how they differed so dramatically in others. The meaning was not embedded in each picture; rather, the scripts gave us filters and frameworks for how we might see the images. I finished the exercise by showing the filmstrip with its official narrative turned on. This sparked another round of discussion.[34]

Part of developing media literacy is practicing critical analysis on various forms of media, typically by bringing what one knows to the act of seeing and listening. These two small examples illustrate the type of critical thinking within the burgeoning field of media literacy. Media literacy projects have a wealth of pedagogical suggestions for how to teach kids to "read" multiple forms of media.[35] Contemporary technology provides endless opportunities to practice this kind of critical thinking about crafting one's own authorial voice and placing it in dialogue with others. If I were doing the equivalent of my filmstrip exercise today, I would encourage students to mix up the images or question why these images and not others were selected, or ask them carefully to examine the components of any one image. Sophisticated visual media, such as video, television, documentaries, and feature films, all lend themselves to this kind of close textural reading and analysis.

With older students, films provide an excellent opportunity to explore this complex, interactive process of analyzing media-generated filters and frameworks and developing a critical eye on the filters and frameworks that we bring to our media viewing. This kind of close, textural analysis also illustrates the fine line between fiction and nonfiction, between a documentary and a feature film. In some sense, they are both fiction. If we are willing to use feature films in classrooms (rather than seeing them, as some teachers do, as a reward for some other desired behavior), they can be rich texts for getting at multiple points of view, for identifying the difference between the story and the frameworks that created that story, and for analyzing how the filmmaker, through the use of camera angles, shot choices, and lighting, encourages viewers to see some things and not others. When one adds an analysis of sound tracks and music, one can see the links between cultural products such as films and the social context that produces them. Here, classrooms can provide an invaluable opportunity for cultivating these skills of media literacy because by providing safe yet structured spaces for expressing opinion, they give kids access to the alternative ways that their classmates can see the same thing.

Telling Your Own Story, Building Mediated Communities

Being able to analyze media messages and images produced by others is important, but equally significant is gaining the skills to create one's own media products and finding ways to share them with others. The overarching goal of media literacy should be to help youth move from being passive consumers to analytical interpreters to active creators of knowledge.

Writing the story of your own life is an exercise in empowerment. With young children, this move to tell their stories is fairly straightforward. Children who are learning to read can write simple stories about their lives, illustrate them with their own artwork, and share them with one another.[36] But the more embedded we become in media environments, the more we encounter the stories of other people. Inequalities intervene such that it becomes more difficult for marginalized youth to tell their stories.

I think that individuals and groups who decide not just to react to the cultural products of others, but also to create cultural products of their own, practice resistance in the cultural domain. In this regard, films can play a vitally important role in a context of color-blind racism that depends on manipulating the visual, that surrounds youth with a media-saturated environment, but that also provides far fewer places for analyzing its own operation. Because youth lead such segregated lives, media fills in the gaps. Take racial segregation, for example. Many kids remain marooned on racial islands of people just like themselves, but visual media can help them see beyond their everyday lives. Films present kids neither as heroic figures nor as tragic victims; they show human beings trying to cope with the circumstances of their lives. Given the history of dehumanization that has been part and parcel of racism, this is an important contribution. Instead of viewing documentaries, feature films, and television as entertainment where one can passively peek into the lives of others, teachers can use visual media to educate kids about shared social issues and shared humanity. Moreover, the media can be used to develop empathy.

Films that challenge prevailing representations of socially black youth can go a long way to reverse dehumanizing depictions of them. Let me discuss two examples from independent cinema that collectively challenge the dehumanization of socially black youth, who are routinely presented as two-dimensional figures. The film *Tsotsi* focuses on a young man who is a throwaway kid in the new, post-apartheid South Africa. Through his demeanor and behavior, Tsotsi is clearly a thug. But this particular film humanizes Tsotsi, neither glorifying his violence nor evoking sorrow for him as a victim. The film works in a different register than either of these familiar responses. He is still a scary young man, but the whole notion of a thug who is simultaneously alien and human encourages viewers to examine the society that we have created for him. We see the content of his character in the context of his conditions. One scene sums up the film for me— a scene of drainpipes that have been brought into a South African township for a new sewer system. It has taken so long to build the sewer system that street kids moved into the pipes as housing. Tsotsi grew up in those pipes. When we question why we get certain types of behaviors from certain types of kids, we would do well to remember Tsotsi.[37]

The Brazilian film *Cidade de Deus* (*City of God*) also illustrates how feature films can provide useful texts for critical analysis. *City of God* became the highest-grossing foreign film of 2003 in the United States, grossing over $7 million in the United States and over $27 million worldwide. One noteworthy feature of this film concerns its production. The vast majority of the cast were not professional actors and instead came from real-life *favelas* (ghettos), and in some cases, the City of God *favela* that was depicted in the film. In making the film, the directors hand-picked approximately a hundred children and recruited them into an actors' workshop. In contrast to more traditional methods (for example, studying theater and rehearsing), the street youth focused for several months on simulating authentic street war scenes, such as holdups, scuffles, and shootouts. To create an authentic, gritty atmosphere, the youth were encouraged to improvise.

This film aggressively challenges the dehumanization of socially black youth on two levels. First, the use of actual *favela* children in the making of a fictional account of a real setting blurs the boundary between fiction and nonfiction and thus makes the boundary itself suspect. Second, despite the level of violence to which they are exposed and in which many participate, the children in the film are human, not statistics. The film participates in a tradition of creating space for oppressed groups to tell their own stories, and in doing so, to begin the process of public political self-definition. Who better to represent the *favela* than its members? This is quite different than the commodified version of black ghettos that is manufactured by global corporate media.[38]

As I have stressed throughout this chapter, simply creating new media content is not enough. Without attending to the business end of media structures, films of greatest interest to youth may never get made and, if they do, may not be seen by anyone. Here the Internet brings new possibilities for both telling new stories and distributing them. In this regard, alternative mechanisms for the creation and distribution of media offer new opportunities for practicing resistance in the cultural domain of power.

The tools for this kind of use exist. Top-down structures that dictated what constituted news and fashion alike have been disrupted by technologies that enable kids to blog, video, text-message, and make films. New video technology has rapidly expanded the ability of people to make their own films, from the shorts that are posted on YouTube to the types of independent films discussed above. Moreover, new distribution mechanisms mean that many more people have access to the cultural products of others. Short videos are readily available on YouTube and Netflix, and downloading films online gives people access to film libraries far larger than those available at brick-and-mortar video stores.

Youth are not simply the beneficiaries of these trends, although the digital divide means that they do not all benefit equally.[39] In many cases, they initiate these developments. Youth use the media differently. I am most intrigued by the emergence of mediated communities; namely, projects that combine real spaces where youth come together (the kinds of physical safe spaces discussed earlier in this chapter), with virtual spaces organized via social networking on the Internet. When these spaces take on a political agenda that is more than being spaces of critique and instead use the mediated community to link the local and global, new democratic possibilities emerge.

Take, for example, the political actions of Words, Beats, & Life, Inc., a mediated community that combines virtual and physical dimensions.[40] The Words, Beats, & Life initiative illustrates a fusion of a cybercommunity (the group does business over the Internet) with traditional brick-and-mortar communities of grassroots organizing (the safe-space model explored earlier in this chapter), to produce a hybrid (*mestizaje*) community adequate for their political project. Based in Washington, D.C., for its brick-and-mortar, grassroots community activities, the initiative sponsors a D.C. urban arts academy for children, conducts workshops as part of its university project, and is forming a hip hop business incubator.[41] Its virtual community reaches people through its Web site as well as its *Global Journal of Hip Hop*, a peer-reviewed journal used in numerous hip hop and popular culture studies courses around the United States. The journal was developed as a venue to publish up-and-coming and established scholars from around the world who write about hip hop culture and community. Overall, groups such as Words, Beats, & Life provide a provocative site for practicing resistance in the cultural domain of power.

RESISTANCE IN THE INTERPERSONAL DOMAIN: WE CAN EACH DO SOMETHING

In a much-quoted line from his "I Have a Dream" speech, Martin Luther King Jr. hoped that in the American democracy that his civil rights activism was working so hard to deliver, his children would be judged not by the color of their skin but the "content of their character."[42] In the decades since King issued this clarion call, the belief in fairness has become official government policy. King was right—we should not judge people by the color of their skin. But the implications of King's full vision are often lost by ignoring the implications of the very name of the March itself—it was a March for Jobs and Freedom. In short, we cannot judge people by the content of their character without knowing the context of their lives. This means developing empathy for the contexts of their everyday lives. More often, this requires doing the same for our own.

The example of King's life suggests that practicing resistance in everyday life might require following one's conscience as a measure of the content of one's character. In the post–Civil Rights era, we retain the vision of King's dream of color blindness, but we also realize that challenging color-blind racism requires some form of sustained, principled action. As James Baldwin points out, one of the problems of education is that "precisely at the point when you begin to develop a conscience, you must find yourself at war with your society. It is your responsibility to change society, if you think of yourself as an educated person."[43]

Sometimes practicing resistance as an educated person feels like being at war with American society. Certainly the mainstream press far too often depicts cultural critics and rebellious youth alike in this fashion. But practicing resistance in everyday life might mean holding fast to ethical principles that help us see our responsibility to change society. When it comes to practicing resistance against racism, becoming an educated person might mean seeing one's actions as embedded in all domains of power. In other words, when joined to an individual commitment to practice resistance in the first place, the structural, disciplinary, and cultural domains of power provide a useful way to see how our everyday actions in the interpersonal domain take on great significance. In brief, we can each do something.

Because the domains-of-power framework catalyzes complex and robust understandings of resistance, it also enables each of us as individuals to decide where and how we want to practice resistance. Some people move comfortably among the domains of power, but I think that most people do best when they develop practices of *specialized resistance* that are tailored to their talents and skills (artistic talents, mathematical ability, verbal skills, and so forth); to a field of emphasis (for example, education, health, and neighborhood development); and to the domain of power where they can be most influential. This notion of specialized resistance within the domains-of-power framework helps us avoid the danger of picking specific action strategies such as boycotts, picketing, and writing editorials and assuming that these constitute the most radical or only forms of resistance. Instead, the domains-of-power framework suggests that individuals can engage in specialized resistance *within* a domain of power as well as *across* more than one domain. Specifically, anti-racist activity might occur in a variety of locations that are connected in a synergistic fashion. A comprehensive view of resistance would look for characteristic forms of resistance in all four domains. Rather than evaluating each domain, it would instead begin to search for links among them so that specialized resistance in particular domains would benefit from understanding what was happening in other areas.

This focus on specialized resistance creates space for us to see our *individual* behaviors as inherently political and to review our relationships and everyday decisions in the context of racial politics. Take, for example, how the assumption that African American teachers should work with African American kids might affect a teacher's decision to accept a teaching job in a primarily white, affluent, suburban district, or a primarily low-income, African American neighborhood. Most people would assume that the choice to work in the African American neighborhood constitutes the more "political" choice, primarily because the needs are so great in urban districts. But specialized resistance in the interpersonal domain is far more complicated than this. Because both settings are inherently yet differently political, they each have different needs that in turn offer different ways to practice resistance.

Kids in underfunded urban schools need quality teachers. It would be nice if these teachers were people of color, but the focus on race misreads the nature of the real need. Too much emphasis has been placed on finding role models for African American kids at the expense of finding quality teachers, regardless of their background. African American kids in urban schools need teachers who care about them—that is the bottom line. They need teachers who possess a culturally sensitive understanding of the obstacles their students face; who are not afraid of their students, no matter how big they are or how aggressively they talk; who set high, attainable standards for students, push them harder to reach them, and then celebrate when kids accomplish what they thought was impossible for them, to their amazement. These are teachers who refuse to patronize African American kids but who will treat them like they are just as smart as any kid in an affluent, white, suburban district. This is very difficult work, and each individual who takes on this kind of commitment needs to be honest about whether he or she *can* do it or, more importantly, *wants* to do it. Being African American within this population of skilled, committed teachers is a bonus, not a qualification for practicing resistance.[44]

Teachers in underfunded urban schools, by necessity, specialize in certain kinds of resistance. The context that they are in mandates it. In a similar fashion, teachers in well-heeled districts or private settings may also face the consequences of being on the front line of race and education, but they encounter these general issues in particular forms. Regardless of class and racial background, specialized resistance by individuals in suburban districts or in private well-heeled schools will necessarily take a different form than that of teachers in city schools. Here, the issue is not to choose which arena offers the most important venue for all individuals but rather to ensure that individuals value what they are doing as a form of practicing resistance. They need not come into contact with one another to respect each other's characteristic forms of activism.

Thinking expansively about resistance, as the domains-of-power framework counsels us to do, may seem freeing at first glance. But freedom of choice tempered by conscientious decision making and carrying the responsibility to think and act responsibly can be intimidating.[45] One potentially scary dimension of the domains-of-power framework is that by suggesting that actions are limited only by our unwillingness to see possibilities within and across all four domains of power, we are confronted by our own culpability for colluding with what we see around us. Here, the internal space of consciousness matters. For example, if we believe that things are hopeless before we even begin, and that strategies will not work before we try them, then we collude with the ongoing patterns that we claim to oppose. This may provide the illusion that we are doing the right thing, but it really turns us into the people who have bought into fatalistic ideas that foster our docility. We become the people who have sold out, even while mouthing the latest religious, liberal, progressive, or conservative point of view. The far more responsible, and difficult, path lies in never forgetting to ask the question, is buying in selling out? from one context to the next.

The ways in which I practice resistance have changed over time and have matured from one setting to the next. I am fundamentally a teacher. This is how I conceptualize my scholarship, my pedagogy, and my advocacy. I have spent many years in many types of classrooms and have taught every grade from kindergarten to graduate school. I write in multiple forms of language (from the colloquial to the highly technical) and publish my work in diverse venues as one way of practicing resistance. Early on, I became convinced of the power of literacy, whether reading picture books when I was six years old, to "reading" the social cues around me in my public school education, to teaching my students to engage in a close textual reading of films. I recognize that ideas matter and that we must access every available resource to practice resistance.

I see what I do as a form of intellectual activism. Many of my students and colleagues have had difficulty seeing their work in political terms. They see politics as somehow lying outside the classroom door and the ivory tower. But, as should be evident in this book, inequalities (in this case, racial inequality) are produced within the educational system, just as schools are essential to inequality's survival. Schools are also frontline spaces for working for social justice. In this context, every idea matters, hence the concept of "intellectual activism." That's my terrain of struggle in everyday life. That's my form of specialized resistance. What will be yours?

4

Somebody's Watching You
To Be Young, Sexy, and Black

Associated Press: You got some criticism for naming your energy
  drink Pimp Juice.
Nelly: I don't think they understand. They hear the word, and they
  think, "Oh, my goodness," but you're not protesting Coke and
  Pepsi, and they have caffeine and stuff that is addictive and stuff
  that can harm you if you drink that. Pimp Juice has none of that.
  It's good for them. Sometimes you have to wrap it up in bad so
  they can get the good out of it. If you understand me, it's not
  even my angle. My son might come in and get two As and a B,
  and be like, "Man, I pimped that test!" . . . It's just different these
  days, it's just lingo, it's just slang.

  "Nelly Is One Hot Commodity" (2004)[1]

Hip hop superstar Nelly may be on to something when he notes, "It's
just different these days." Nelly identifies bona fide shifts in popular
culture where words gain new meanings. Nelly claims that if his son
came home with good grades and celebrated by saying, "Man, I pimped

that test!" he wouldn't be bothered. Why would Nelly criticize his son's use of language or, for that matter, anything else? Nelly is doing well during these "different" days. Nelly sold 15 million copies of his first two albums, and his popular sports drink, Pimp Juice, did so well that the Associated Press titled its interview with him "Nelly Is One Hot Commodity." According to Nelly, times have changed, and he has simply changed along with them and benefited from those changes.

But part of the difference that Nelly identifies may also be caused by his behavior and by the actions of similar African American youth who have become celebrities in hip hop culture. In a climate where one-upmanship can mean increased profitability, Nelly is controversial. He is the one who, in his popular music video "Tipp Drill," swiped his credit card through a woman's buttocks, an action that catalyzed picketing by Spelman College students when he wanted to visit their campus. Brushing off their complaints as a personal affront to him, he replied, "I think everybody is most upset about the credit card issue, but she said do it! This is a grown woman that told me, 'Go ahead, do it.' I never forced any of these girls to do anything. This is a job, they agreed to do it, they knew everything that was into it and these girls would be doing it whether Nelly was shooting a video or not." The women in his music videos were just doing their jobs, and Nelly was doing his—a simple business transaction.

Nelly's behavior and beliefs are not especially unusual. What makes his behavior stand out is that he is watched by millions of people when he engages in it. Youth know who Nelly is because they can watch him (or archival footage of his videos when he is no longer as popular) on music videos, Web sites, DVDs, Black Entertainment Television (BET), iPods, and similar sources. New technologies have made Nelly and similar celebrities readily accessible to large numbers of people. Nelly is a young African American male, a member of a group that garners a disproportionate share of surveillance without any media assistance. Nelly on the street would be placed under surveillance in a range of settings, his anonymity becoming part of what entitles people with more authority than he has to watch him. Yet the irony here is that Nelly now gets paid (quite a bit) for being watched, his fame granting him an individuality that he might never acquire without his celebrity status.

In this media-saturated environment, the fact that we watch Nelly should come as no surprise, because, when combined with new technologies that foster greater undetected surveillance, watching is increasingly a dimension of everyday life. This concept of *watching* has multiple meanings and connotations. For one, it references the many social institutions that now keep people under surveillance to deter unruliness, disobedience, or crime. The benign surveillance that my African American middle school girls faced from the stick-wielding assistant principal (as I described in chapter 3) seems quaint when compared to metal detectors, permanent guards with weapons, and the often-intrusive searches that students face in many contemporary inner-city schools. Techniques routinely targeted to African American kids and other seemingly undesirable groups have spawned new forms of surveillance within U.S. society in response to ever-greater, yet intangible, threats. In this sense, we are all being watched; we watch one another as a mechanism of control and, in this way, mutually police one another.[2]

Watching also refers to how many American citizens experience mass media, a passivity of watching that resembles how some people watch soap operas or game shows. In a culture that bombards individuals with mass-media spectacles and peppers them with a stream of advertisements, passivity constitutes one defense against media overload. Here, we are expected to watch, uncritically consume, and enjoy the images that flow through our television sets and computers. Some populations are seen as being more easily duped by these relations than others. Specifically, African American youth are often conceptualized as a marginalized, powerless, and passive population buffeted by the market forces of global capitalism.[3]

Watching need not be negative. Another iteration of watching refers to the situation of caring for, the meaning of phrases such as *watching over* and *watching out for*. Childhood should be a time of being cared for or "watched" in a mindful way. Adults should watch over children by shepherding them and protecting them from dangerous situations. Who watches out for kids like Nelly when they are children? Do they learn to watch out for themselves and, as a result, come to see the world as a series of threats? More of this kind of watching might catalyze another type of society, one where people cared more for one another and for our democratic institutions.

The phenomenon of Nelly is situated within these spaces of watching, those where people are placed under surveillance at convenience stores and bank machines, in airports and store dressing rooms, on YouTube, by other people, traffic cameras, and nanny cams; where consumers passively watch a hugely influential mass media that shapes our ideas and behavior about which candidate to support and which shoes to wear; and where people watch out for one another in ways that nurture, protect, and teach. African American youth serve as an interesting entry point, and paradox, for exploring these various meanings of surveillance and watching. On the one hand, this youth population is intensely watched, held in a constant state of vigilance and suspect, by social institutions such as law enforcement and stores. On the other hand, African American youth endure *a lack of* institutional care, to the point of neglect, as is too often the case with many institutions that do not watch out for their best interests.

In this chapter, I center on African American youth to shed light on the power of the media to shape complex ideas about race, culture, and sexuality within relations of global capitalism.[4] Because African American youth live within the borders of the world's preeminent superpower, their experiences provide lessons for many other groups. The chapter is divided into four parts. The first part examines how the relationship between social blackness and consumerism creates a specific place for youth. *Social blackness* references who gets identified as being black in an economy (in this case, advanced capitalism that relies on consumerism) and how they are used by that economy. The second part introduces the black culture industry and the global sex-work industry as two growth industries of contemporary capitalism. The third part examines African American youth's placement at the convergence of these two industries. The fourth part returns to the theme of practicing resistance by suggesting how African American youth and their allies might engage in a twofold project of critical analysis and taking action.

SOCIAL BLACKNESS, CAPITALISM, AND YOUTH

Some years ago, one small story in my local newspaper caught my attention. The article reported that when an African American basketball celebrity released his new gym shoe, numerous inner-city kids cut school to go to the store to be first in line to buy them. The shoes cost over $100, an amount that even I wouldn't pay for gym shoes. How did these kids get the money to pay for these shoes? Moreover, how did kids come to want those particular shoes so much? What were they buying, and buying into, by purchasing those shoes?

We often dismiss events such as these with generational analyses that kids will be kids. Many of us have witnessed kids who camp out overnight to snare concert tickets and video games. Others suggest that poor families are to blame when African American and Latino kids engage in similar behaviors: "Those kids come from bad families. They don't have any role models. If they had Mamas and Daddies who told them what to do, they wouldn't be out there throwing their money away on gym shoes." I think that these arguments miss the point. My guess is that many of those kids have wonderful, hard-working parents who preached the significance of going to school and the value of a dollar. But the kids chose something else. Something else was going on.

Events such as these have convinced me to investigate the significance of the mass media (television, radio, and print) as central to the economy. The media manufactures ideas about race, gender, sexuality, class, and nationality, but a sizable part of its function concerns its centrality to how contemporary capitalism works. In short, the media helps get your money out of your wallet and into somebody else's bank account. As a generation, youth are frontline actors in this particular process. We can see how adults are targeted for subprime mortgages or credit cards with hidden fees and exorbitant interest rates, but we overlook the centrality of youth within the consumer economy. We like to think that youth who have no money or very little money are not involved in consumerism and thus are not targeted as a lucrative consumer market. However, I think that something else is going on that speaks to the intersection of social blackness (race), consumerism (class), and how African American youth might be positioned in these relations (age). That's where I want to start this analysis.[5]

In chapter 2, I introduced the notion of *social blackness* as a category of contemporary racial politics. My goal was to show how blackness, whiteness, and similar categories (and by implication, race itself) are not identity categories rooted in biology, but rather the way that they reflect relations of power. The best way to think about social blackness is to conceptualize it as a place to which people are assigned in the power hierarchy, not as an identity that people are born with. Within this conceptualization, rather than starting with a group of people who are assumed to be black and then studying the place that they occupy in a given society, one starts with the power relations that construct place itself (in this case, how racism limits the opportunities of some groups and privileges others within a given place such as a city, region, nation, or continent) and then looks at which people are routinely assigned to those specific places. A socially black population refers to any group that is oppressed or "blackened" in a specific social context of racism as a system of power.[6]

Under color-blind racism, especially in a global context, social blackness has become more diffuse and therefore less easily understood. For one thing, one can no longer say that racism affects *only* people who are biologically classified as being of a denigrated race, for example, people of African descent, indigenous groups, or Asian populations. The seeming bond between racism and biology has been loosened. Currently, it may be more accurate to say that racism creates socially black people, broadly defined, who are disproportionately of African descent. Biology matters, but it does not determine racism.

Social blackness is a global phenomenon that takes different forms across different societies. Groups that are not of African descent often serve as the proxy "black people" of their respective societies; here, social context is key. Thus, in areas of the United States that have few African Americans, Latinos and indigenous peoples are treated as the "social blacks" (become proxy "black people"); in New Zealand, the Maori population can occupy the place of the "social blacks"; in India, it's the Dhalit; and in contemporary France, the *beurre* youth of Parisian suburbs can be the "blacks."[7] Social blackness is not a permanent status, yet when bound to biological markers such as skin color, hair texture, and facial features, it can appear to be. Individuals and groups can move in and out of the category of social blackness. For example, after 9/11, many Middle Easterners in the United States found themselves redefined as a socially black category. A graduate student recounted a story of two of her friends, one Indian and one Iranian (both born outside the United States), who have been called "sand niggers" in the United States.[8]

Despite the seeming fluidity of the process, individuals and groups rarely become socially black by choice. Thus whites in the United States do not become socially black when they enjoy and identify with music, dance, and other expressions of African American culture. Instead, this is a case of, in the words of Greg Tate, whites who want "everything but the burden."[9] Rather, social blackness is an assigned category that is part of the power relations of that society, not a personal identity category that is optional.[10]

In the United States, being assigned to a socially blackened or "denigrated" space is strongly correlated with being of African descent.[11] Historically, places of social blackness were seen as being exclusively and uniquely occupied by people of African descent. In earlier periods, such as slavery or Jim Crow segregation, African Americans encountered intense surveillance. Thus, much attention was paid to keeping African Americans in their place and watching them to ensure that they did not escape. In contemporary U.S. society, African American youth is the population most closely stigmatized by the power relations of social blackness. Remnants of this type of policing of social blackness persist today—random police stops of African American youth to inquire what they are doing in certain neighborhoods, including their own, fall under these patterns of watching youth to sustain social blackness. Welfare policy could be seen as a gender-specific example of social blackness—poor women *as a category* were socially blackened via state surveillance and control (control over reproduction/marriage/right-to-work or care for a child—these mechanisms of control were all linked to women's ability to receive benefits) and racial ideology (welfare queens). This blackening affected poor white, Latino, and African American mothers alike, yet African American women were most prominently depicted as the face of welfare.[12]

While I want you to remember the conceptual distinction of social blackness as a form of racism that can apply to any group, it is equally important to stress that African Americans, as a specific population group with almost four hundred years of history in the United States, have disproportionately borne the brunt of racism. Thus, African Americans are the "social blacks" of America. This statement may seem unnecessary to make but it gets at racism as a system of power and its role in creating race, not just reflecting it. Social blackness is about unequal power relations brought about by racism, both in the global context, within specific countries and regions, and among racial/ethnic groups.[13]

Social blackness clearly serves a political purpose. Specifically, classifying poor and working-class youth as socially black makes it more legitimate to watch them and place them under surveillance. But why blacken people at all? This argument about the political nature of social blackness as part of racism goes only so far. Why is social blackness still needed? Who benefits from its continuation?[14]

Here I think that it is important to detail not only how processes of social blackness reproduce racial disadvantage, but how social blackness is implicated in reproducing poverty and economic disadvantage. The contours of social blackness are tightly tied up with the needs of advanced capitalism in general and consumerism in particular. This is the case in the United States as well as in a global context.

Social blackness is all about finding one's assigned place, and the place to which socially black people are assigned is one of poverty. Each society has its poor and disadvantaged groups who are black metaphorically, if not literally. Again, the lived realities of poor and working-class African American youth provide a unique window through which we can examine the persisting economic inequalities of contemporary capitalism. Because work has disappeared, many African American urban neighborhoods provide few jobs for *adults*, let alone teenagers.[15] Many young adults work low-paid jobs in McDonald's, Burger King, Kentucky Fried Chicken (KFC), and other fast-food establishments, yet these jobs typically provide few benefits and a limited future. At the same time, because many young African American men in particular have been incarcerated, employers will not hire them. In this context, many teenagers, both boys and girls, choose either to join the military or to work in the illegal drug industry, which seem to be, for many, the only employers in town.

This large and seemingly intractable population of inner-city African American youth who lack access to legitimate jobs constitutes a political conundrum for American policy makers. Because non-incarcerated African American youth possess citizenship rights, employers can no longer compel them to work for no pay or for very low pay. Black American youth faced with few viable employment options often earn their living not through legitimate work (the steady, albeit poorly paid, jobs held by their parents and grandparents), but rather through other means. Military jobs that remove them from their neighborhoods, employment in the drug industry, continued dependence on people with income (parents, girlfriends, and/or the welfare state), and hustling (for example, exploitation of one another through pimping) constitute important sources of income for poor and working-class Black American youth.[16]

The growth of the punishment industry illustrates how African American men are exploited. They are turned into commodities that are necessary for maintaining prisons as consumer markets.[17] As one prisoner describes it:

> I cannot go on strike, nor can I unionize. I am not covered by workers' compensation of [sic] the Fair Labor Standards Act. I agree to work late-night and weekend shifts. I do just what I am told no matter what it is. I am hired and fired at will, and I am not even paid minimum wage: I earn only one dollar a month. I cannot even voice grievances or complaints, except at the risk of incurring arbitrary discipline or some covert retaliation. You need not worry about NAFTA and your jobs going to Mexico and other Third World countries. I will have at least five percent of your jobs by the end of the decade. I am called prison Labor. I am the New American worker.[18]

In essence, African American men's commodified bodies become used as raw materials for the growing prison industry.

It is very simple—no prisoners, no jobs for all the ancillary industries that service this growth industry. Because prisons express little interest in rehabilitating prisoners, they need a steady supply of bodies. If KFC found chickens in short supply, their profitability would shrink, or even completely disappear, and they might even close. KFC's corporate sponsors have little interest in extracting labor from its chickens or in coaxing them to change their ways. Rather, the corporation needs a constant supply of cheap, virtually identical chickens to ensure that their business will remain profitable. In this way, prisons use the bodies of unemployed, unskilled young African American men (and increasingly, women), the virtually indistinguishable bodies that populate corners of American cities. The focus is less about appropriating the labor of incarcerated African American men (although this does happen) than it is about finding profitable uses for their bodies.

To remain profitable, corporations face additional problems. Corporations rely not only on cutting the costs attached to production, but also the constant need to stimulate consumer demand. Sustaining relations of production requires not only a steady supply of people to do the work and a steady supply of raw materials (for example, KFC needs chickens), but also ever-expanding consumer markets. Keeping the U.S. economy going, for example, requires that Americans shop. Ideal consumer societies are those where people feel compelled to shop, even if they don't actually consume, eat, wear, view, use, or need what they purchase. For example, addictions of all sorts—branded items, luxury items, and so on—are profitable for those who supply or "deal" in these products.

Similarly, ideal consumer societies are also those where consumers are in debt. In this case, the guaranteed consumption is of money itself, as the usurious rates of local check cashing enterprises ensure. Just as the production side of capitalist economies requires ever-expanding supplies of labor and resources for production, so too does the consumption side require ever-expanding consumer markets. Thus, the consumerism of contemporary capitalism must constantly recruit new consumers.

In the same way that people do not naturally work and must be encouraged or compelled to do so, people do not naturally engage in consumerism without prompting. Media is essential in stimulating this kind of consumerism (for instance, the use of Joe Camel to encourage smoking, or at least smoking a particular brand). Most market demand for products and services stems not from needs but rather from seemingly unmet desires. In this context, physical addictions create ideal consumers. If young consumers become addicted to tobacco, alcohol, drugs, or similar products, they can be counted on to keep consuming, despite the health risks. As the repetitive behavior of shopping addicts suggests, the ideal consumer is one who is addicted to consumerism itself, never mind the actual product or service consumed.

These emerging patterns of social blackness and the pressures on U.S. consumers place African American youth at the center of a series of new challenges. Particularly when we consider the ever-expanding role of the media as a driving force within consumer society, we see how African American youth are at the crux of discussions about power and wealth in a global context.

In chapter 2, I introduced the idea of poor and working-class African American youth as being on literal lockdown within structural relations of racial segregation, managed by disciplinary practices of surveillance.[19] Ghettos, prisons, dead-end jobs, and other features of being on lockdown suggest that African American youth seemingly have few options and no future, and thus are unimportant in a growing global economy. Moreover, no longer are African American youth only on lockdown by way of their limited opportunities and racially segregated neighborhoods. These are the material conditions of being on lockdown. Today, the depiction of young black people in popular culture is another growing important component of lockdown. In this context, watching African American youth perform so-called authentic blackness within popular culture venues (such as Nelly's Pimp Juice) helps manufacture ideas about social blackness that in turn stimulate consumerism.

Looking at a surplus of young African Americans who do not

want to work at McDonald's, do not want to be exploited in prison or who do not want to deal with the welfare state, corporations find it attractive to involve this group in consumption activities. How does the U.S. political and economic system absorb the large numbers of youth who are assigned to this category of social blackness in its growing industries? Conversely, how do African American youth who find themselves in this surplus population negotiate these new consumer relations?

WHAT DO YOU SELL WHEN THERE'S NOTHING ELSE TO SELL?

Many people believe that because African American youth cannot get legitimate jobs, they have nothing to sell in consumer markets. But in a mass-media consumer culture, African American youth might be well positioned to sell images of black culture within U.S. popular culture. For one thing, a stereotypical black culture has long been a marketable commodity in U.S. consumer culture, with the marketability of black popular culture tapped well before the unprecedented explosion of hip hop in the 1980s and 1990s.[20] For another, African American culture and youth culture have been intertwined since the rock and roll era. As Grace Palladino points out, many white teens "wanted to be Black at least on Saturday nights."[21] Rock and roll—initially a white, teenage version of rhythm and blues—became primarily associated with age, not race, and ushered in a demographic shift that permanently altered popular culture.[22]

African American youth may be well positioned in relation to another, albeit more controversial, trend. In a consumer culture that relies on sexuality to sell products, sexualized images of young African American bodies may be especially marketable. Images of black teenage girls in skintight skirts and tops and shirtless boys in baggy pants who grab their crotches can be used to sell products and, as a result, get people to consume more than they need.[23] In this sense, bundling together ideas about black popular culture with issues of sexuality by seeing the bodies of young African American women and men as the site of their convergence might constitute a hot commodity. When Nelly swiped his credit card down a black woman's buttocks in his "Tipp Drill" music video, he invoked both of these meanings.

One of the best ways to get at these complex ideas about race, culture, sexuality, and consumerism is to examine two increasingly interdependent industries where African American youth can find work—namely, the black culture industry and the sex-work industry. Both industries have storied histories in the United States, yet neither is routinely examined as an industry within the structural domain of power.[24] Instead, both are routinely classified as cultural practices at best, if not as matters of individual, personal choice.[25]

The black culture industry has a long history, yet its contemporary contours are something quite new. In the 1990s, the pressures to turn black popular culture into a commodity that had long permeated American mass media became incorporated into global mass-media venues. New technologies (digitalization) enabled industry officials to commodify more precisely African American culture and market it globally through new distribution mechanisms (Internet, cable television, iPods, cell phones, and so on). The content of this highly marketable, commodified black culture draws heavily from the cultural production and styles of urban African American youth. The unprecedented explosion in popularity of the hip hop industry points to how an African American aesthetic and lived (urban) reality (and fantasy) were simultaneously expressed by artists and packaged for sale. Industry executives profited from hip hop—but so did the artists themselves.

The shift from color-conscious to color-blind racism required new justifications, and changes in the content of what was deemed to be authentic black culture reflected this shift. Because racial desegregation in the post–Civil Rights era needed new images of racial difference for a color-blind ideology, class-differentiated images of African

American culture became more prominent. In the 1980s and 1990s, long-standing depictions of African Americans as overwhelmingly poor and working-class became supplemented by new images of an African American middle class. The cultural practices of poor and working-class African Americans were routinely depicted as being "authentically" black, whereas the practices of middle- and upper-middle-class African Americans were less so. Poor and working-class African American characters in popular culture (TV, music, movies, and so on) were portrayed as being more authentically black. Moreover, their refusal to assimilate so-called American values meant that they best remained in the ghetto.

In contrast, because middle- and upper-middle-class African American characters lacked this authentic black culture and were virtually indistinguishable from their white middle-class counterparts, assimilated, propertied African Americans were shown as being ready for racial integration. Many middle-class African American kids resisted this trend. Instead, they became consumers of hip hop culture because they saw it as the only way to be authentically black. Embracing the music, following the fashion trends, and keeping up with the latest slang all became ways for them to express solidarity with what they saw as an authentic black culture in the seemingly color-blind era. Thus, the black culture industry helped rework ideas about class and race.

This convergence of race and class within the black culture industry also sparked changes in the treatment of gender and sexuality. Representations of poor and working-class authenticity and middle-class respectability increasingly came in gender-specific form. As femininity and masculinity became reworked through this prism of social class, a changing constellation of images of femininity appeared that reconfigured African American women's sexuality and helped explain the new racism. In this context, representations of African American women and African American men became increasingly important sites of struggle.[26] At the same time, African American women and men used these same sites within black popular culture to resist racism, class exploitation, sexism, and heterosexism.[27]

Resembling the black culture industry, the sex work industry also has a long history, and its contemporary contours are also something quite new. The sex-work industry constitutes one rapidly growing, worldwide industry where people are finding jobs and where consumer markets are rapidly expanding.[28] Spurred on by new communications technologies that enable people to see images of a variety of sexual commodities, as well as new travel technologies that open up the world for tourists, the global sex-work industry constitutes an important and growing part of global market economies.[29] The sex-work industry is organized through various ways of selling a commodified sexuality: either one's actual body, or images and representations of one's body, used in marketing, film, videos, music (including rap) and so on. In essence, the expansion of the sex-work industry has been a crucial catalyst and consequence of consumerism.[30]

When I talk about the sex-work industry, I want to be clear that I am not making a moral argument. I am neither censuring sexuality itself nor forms of sexual expression that some people find objectionable—for example, sexuality outside of marriage, gay and lesbian sexual expression, and sex work itself. These issues are moral decisions that are best left to individual conscience.[31] Instead, I am making a *political and economic argument* about the marketing of sexuality under consumerism and the patterns of participation of youth, specifically African American youth, in this industry.

Let me briefly sketch the contours of this expanding global industry. The sex-work industry encompasses a set of social practices, many of which may not be immediately recognizable as sex work. By far, international trafficking of women and girls for the purposes of prostitution has received the lion's share of media attention, but I want to point out how far-reaching the sex-work industry really is. Jobs that are associated with the global sex-work industry include (1) commercial sex-work positions, such as as sex workers (prostitutes) and managers (pimps) who participate in the delivery of actual sexual services; (2) ancillary personnel in the criminal justice system who profit in some fashion from the existence of the industry (police, lawyers, prison guards, and so on); (3) those in industries where sexuality is often part of the product for sale, such as the entertainment industry of strip clubs and massage parlors, or segments of the hospitality industry where sexuality itself is not directly marketed but implied (vacation destinations); and (4) those in mass media that advertise and market sexuality through venues as diverse as television, music videos, and movies ranging from soft- to hard-core pornography.[32]

To use a colloquial term, *pimps* are managers in the sex-work industry. Most people think about the pimp relationship as a relationship of domination between a heterosexual man and a heterosexual woman. But if we look beyond the interpersonal relations, we might also see this relationship as a potentially lucrative occupation whose members do not routinely declare their earnings or assets to the Internal Revenue Service. There may also be a hierarchy of pimps. Some pimps (sex-work managers/sex traffickers) are so high-placed in the global sex-work industry that they need not directly supervise actual sex workers. They may not actually be sending people out on the street; instead, they may be making the decisions about this entire sex-work industry. In contrast, other pimps may be part of a street-level, cottage industry.[33]

To focus solely on the actual *behavior* of commercial sex workers by condemning their behavior in moralistic terms—the case of calling women sex workers "whores"—misses the structural forces that organize this industry, the disciplinary practices that encourage young men and women to participate in it, and the cultural practices that shape consumer demands for sexual services of all sorts. Instead of focusing on the morals and values of individuals, we might recognize that, like other social institutions, the global sex-work industry takes specific forms across the four domains of power, and that many people participate in and profit from its current organization.[34] This global industry reflects conditions of global capitalism that is perpetually in search of new products and consumer markets and that has to advertise and market its products to foster consumerism. Given the scope of the global sex-work industry, we need to think expansively about the many ways in which youth are participating in it.[35]

Now I return to my original question: what do you sell when you have nothing else to sell?[36] Instead, their actual bodies become commodities that fall under the control of others. Today, newly industrializing countries struggle to find employment niches in the global economy yet frequently find the best niches taken. Consequently, in some countries, turning women's bodies into commodities, primarily through sex tourism, sex workers near military bases, and other forms of "pimping" women, becomes one way to foster national economic development and international capital accumulation.

Young African American women and men who lack high school and college degrees may not be able to get the best jobs in the U.S. economy. Yet this population remains essential to new consumer markets, both as suppliers of a stereotypical, sexualized black culture that is bought and sold, and as a consumer market that eschews investment and other wealth-building strategies. What are young African Americans encouraged to sell?

AFRICAN AMERICAN YOUTH, THE BLACK CULTURE INDUSTRY, AND THE GLOBAL SEX WORK INDUSTRY

In the late-twentieth-century and early-twenty-first century, the high visibility granted to rap and hip hop within American media and culture refocused attention on poor and working-class African American youth in ways not seen since the 1960s. During this period, hip hop that seemingly represented authentic black culture and the poor and working-class African American youth who created it became big business.[37] Drawing upon societal perceptions of black culture and wider cultural norms of sexuality, African American youth participated in the sex work industry primarily in three different ways: (1) as workers used to produce racially specific images of commodified sexuality; (2) as commodified images used to sell products within global consumer markets (that is, the ubiquitous "ho" and pimp); and (3) as consumers of their own images and the products associated with them. Here I examine this process by exploring how sexuality has grown in importance in treating both the culture and actual young African Americans as commodities.

In essence, hip hop culture and actual African American youth of varying genders and from varying class backgrounds are now caught up in a burgeoning, skills-differentiated, culturally inflected segment of the sex work industry, one that extends far beyond traditional forms of paid commercial sex-work. Young African Americans may participate in the sex-work industry, not primarily as commercial workers as is popularly imagined (for example, the ubiquitous prostitutes and pimps depicted in Western media), but rather as individuals whose jobs as advertising executives, performers, sports attorneys, songwriters, and producers depend upon marketing and selling representations of commodified black sexuality. Nelly need not be a pimp—he can play one.[38]

Despite the range of youth who are drawn into this industry, poor and working-class African American men and women, their bodies, their images, and their music and dance, are vital to the industry's profitability. Like their socially black, global counterparts, poor and working-class African American youth face meager job prospects. Yet unlike socially black youth in other nations, African American youth have something to sell that garners value in a media-inflected global marketplace: namely, the seeming authenticity of U.S. Black culture itself. In a wealthy country like the United States, a barrage of consumer goods is marketed to African American youth via the trappings of hip hop consumer culture. In this context, many see the need to "get paid" not simply as the cost of survival, but also engage in conspicuous consumption as a marker of class status.[39] In essence, representations of their bodies often serve as symbols of a sexualized black culture. This phenomenon in turn places African American youth in the peculiar position of commodifying their own culture. Black American youth may claim a space of individual freedom within black cultural production, yet this freedom remains pinioned by sexualized representations of young black bodies. These images glorify yet obscure the actual pain of being young, socially black, and American. No longer young, gifted, and black, the mantra of a generation that preceded them, contemporary African American youth are young, sexy, and black.[40]

A closer look at the specific experiences of young African American women sheds light on these social relations. Young African American women's encounters with the sex work industry follow distinctive patterns. First, young African American women are well represented in mass-media representations of sex work. Through its imagery, hip hop culture naturalizes and normalizes social relations of sex work by invoking and fine-tuning the historical representation of the black jezebel to the contemporary black "ho."[41] Whether she sleeps with men for pleasure, drugs, revenge, or money, these sexualized social scripts about African American women as potential or actual "hos" constitute modern versions of the jezebel, repackaged for the needs of consumer society.

At the same time, young African American women are far more protected from actual commercial sex work than their global counterparts. Because African American girls possess American citizenship, they cannot be as easily trafficked as poor women and girls in other countries. Girls are typically trafficked *into* the United States, not out of it. Moreover, African American girls' access to education and social welfare programs provides alternatives to commercial sex work. These factors may account in part for the virtual absence, with some exceptions, of research on African American adolescent girls and sex work (as compared to sustained attention to the sexual practices of African American teen mothers, whose pregnancies are of great interest to the state).

This does not mean that young African American women's involvement in sex work is confined to sexual stereotypes in the mass media. Rather, the changing contours of African American civil society may provide new venues for sex work. In the global context, commercial sex work is not always a steady, full-time activity but may occur simultaneously with other forms of income-generating work, such as domestic service, informal commercial trading, or office work.[42] In a similar fashion, African American girls may seek out multiple sources of income, one of which is sex work. The activities of the seemingly ubiquitous divas, gold diggers, "video hos," and "video vixens" of hip hop culture may not be labeled sex work or prostitution.[43] Restricting the concept of sex work to paid prostitution and to the image of the streetwalker may obscure the various ways that young African American women's bodies and images are commodified and then circulated within the sex work industry.

How do the gender- and age-specific sexual scripts advanced within hip hop culture carry U.S. Black popular culture to global audiences? How do these scripts shape actual social relations within a global sex work industry? In essence, poor and working-class African American girls seemingly confront a similar set of challenges as their global counterparts; however, they do so within the American context. Here, their rights as American citizens shield them from deportation and provide partial alternatives to commercial sex work; specifically, social welfare services. Yet welfare is not enough to make ends meet.[44] In this context of scarce economic opportunities, sex work may garner supplemental income. For example, take the sexual histories of one group of young, Southern, rural, and poor African American women reported in a *New York Times* article on HIV/AIDS.[45] Some women reported that they started having sex at very young ages, almost always with older men, and that they could not persuade their partners to use condoms. They described an informal sex-for-money situation, where nothing was negotiated up-front. Rather, unstated assumptions where women who engage in casual sex with men expect to be rewarded with a little financial help, perhaps in paying the rent, or in buying groceries, held sway. From the outside, these behaviors may seem to be morally lax, yet the impoverished African American women who engaged in sex-for-money relationships desperately needed the money, especially if they had elderly parents or dependent children. The consequence of this less formalized sex-for-material-goods situation was often tragic. Pressures to engage in this informal sex work may be tied to the rapid growth of HIV/AIDS among poor, heterosexual African American women.[46] In the context of their lives, many African American women feel that because they had so little control over other aspects of their lives, sex work of all sorts provides survival.[47]

Placing existing research in a context of the sex work expected of young African American women also sheds light on how media-circulated sexual stereotypes of young African American women as "hos" might operate. For example, the various forms of sexual violence visited upon African American women have received substantial scholarly attention.[48] Rejecting the stereotypes of overly sexualized African American girls, research on African American adolescent pregnancy finds that many pregnancies were unplanned and the fathers were much older than the mothers.[49] Some evidence exists that sexual abuse at the hands of older African American men may be interpreted by young African American women as just the cost of "being a black woman." In this sense, rape and sexual assault become coded as unpaid sex work, another element of the naturalization and normalization of sex work for young African American women.

These examples suggest that, for reasons of survival, many young African American women resign themselves to using their bodies in formal and informal ways as one source of material support. They may not be streetwalkers in the traditional sense, but they may view their sexuality as a commodity with potential value. Beliefs such as these can become difficult to disrupt in the context of a powerful mass media that defines and sells images of sexualized black women as part of a seemingly authentic black culture. Representations of sexualized young black women are a staple product of many hip hop artists. In this context, if one is repeatedly depicted as a "ho," taking the next step of "getting paid" for sex work demanded by boyfriends, baby daddies, athletes, rap stars, relatives, and strangers makes sense.

Black male involvement in the sex work industry may involve less direct sexual exploitation of African American men's bodies and more sexual images of black male bodies within hip hop culture.[50] Young African American men also sell a commodified sexuality— a shirtless, muscle-bound, tatted-up, pants-sagging male sexuality that seems influenced by prison culture.[51] The black prisoner's body in hip hop—sexualized representations of black men as rapists, thugs, hustlers, pimps—is relevant; this is a lawbreaking, prison-destined population that, via its captivity and the violence this seemingly generates, becomes a sexualized commodity. Given this dismal situation, it is no wonder that many young African American men without prospects of making it as professional athletes aspire to be rappers so that they too can "get paid" and avoid the military and the exploitation of both the prison complex and the drug industry.

Some thinkers take issue with the common belief that African Americans make poor ethnic entrepreneurs. Instead they suggest that young African American men engage in a version of "bootstrap capitalism" that sells authentic black music to global markets in much the same way that ethnic entrepreneurs opened restaurants to sell ethnic food. Taking a far less sanguine view, others focus on the moguls at the top of these hip hop empires, seeing them as condoning impractical forms of upward social mobility that are blocked for the majority of poor and working-class African American youth, and behaving as downright hustlers who help maintain a black, urban plantation so that they can become rich.[52]

Regardless of your point of view, hip hop is big business. Jay-Z topped Forbes.com's 2007 inaugural Hip Hop Cash Kings list of the top-earning people in the business. In 2008, he ceded the throne to Curtis "50 Cent" Jackson, who raked in $150 million in twelve months—almost twice what Jay-Z made.[53] In this context, the growing centrality of the icon of the pimp within hip hop culture (in particular, the proximity of this image to sexualized images of African American men as rapists and hustlers), as well as to a "clean" association with authentic black culture (versus the violence of the thug), raises interesting issues concerning how African American men might profit from their placement in the black culture and sex work industries. In essence, whereas young African American women face sexual stereotypes of the "ho," an image that conjures up sexual service, young African American men may be faced with the stereotype of the pimp, an image that symbolizes sexual prowess, business acumen, and power. Interestingly, these are the very same qualities that define the hip hop mogul. The dynamic of "pimping" means to hustle, fool, or otherwise extract something of value from a seemingly willing source. Pimping is a relationship of dominance and control that can shape young African American men's relationships with women and with one another.

In the context of a powerful global mass media, African American men's bodies can be turned into commodities (the case of the prison industry), and the pimp emerges as a positive image whose power rivals that of legitimate businessmen. Hip hop culture is widely recognized as male-defined, and at the center of this space of black masculinity, the representation of the pimp looms large. Recognizing the value of commodified black culture, many African American rap stars have started their own record labels, clothing companies, and more recently, sports drink divisions. Their desire lies in tapping the profitability of a huge global consumer market of youth who purchase the rap CDs, sports drinks, gym shoes, and clothing lines of hip hop culture.

Are "pimps" the poor man's version of the hip hop mogul? Where might these two images converge? Perhaps it's this move to converge the images that enables the fused pimp/hip hop mogul to remain "authentically hood"; that is, not only authentically black, but also authentically "of the ghetto," despite the fact that he is a millionaire. This is the challenge for successful rappers. Russell Simmons constitutes the epitome of the hip hop mogul "sans pimp"—he is respected in the industry but definitely does not promote a "tough" or "hood" image. Perhaps it's this move to create a sexualized pimp persona that enables the rich rapper to talk about the devastation of the ghetto without seeming out of touch as he retreats to his multimillion-dollar home in the Hamptons. Here, the rapper's ability to hustle and pimp his way out of the ghetto (which includes pimping women along the way) is evidence that he is still "authentic" enough to be able to rap.[54]

Overall, the contemporary synergy between the black culture industry and the global sex work industry plays out in gender-specific ways. These gender-specific versions of sex work within hip hop via images such as the "ho" and the pimp point to contemporary patterns of a commodified and increasingly sexualized black culture. These trends converge to structure a new place for young African American women and men, one that provides jobs for some, enormous wealth for others (rap stars, hip hop moguls, industry executives, and so on), and continued economic exploitation (poverty) for far too many.

Take, for example, the 2003 release of Pimp Juice, Nelly's sports beverage that I discussed at the beginning of this chapter.[55] Claiming that Pimp Juice is a benign energy drink, its official Web site describes it as a "healthy, non-carbonated energy drink possessing a tropical berry flavor" (see, for example, www.letitloose.com). Despite Pimp Juice's claims that its vitamins and 10 percent apple juice signify health, its typical display near beer and other alcoholic beverages within African American corner stores, as well as the yellow-and-white design of its can that resembles a popular beer (albeit in a smaller container), suggests something else. Initially marketed within African American neighborhoods, by 2004 Pimp Juice was disseminated by sixty distributors in thirty-two states and eighty-one markets. Pimp Juice had gone global. According to its distributor, because Pimp Juice was flying off the shelves in the United Kingdom, the Caribbean, and Mexico, the manufacturer planned on selling the product in Australia, Japan, China, and Israel, and recently launched the brand in France and Sweden. Not only did Nelly's song "Pimp Juice" help resurrrect the concept of the pimp, but ironically, because he owns the company that manufactures the beverage, he also profits from its sale.

Pimp Juice (the product) arrived with its own sound track. The lyrics of Nelly's song "Pimp Juice" make it clear what pimp juice really is and who constitutes its target customer. Nelly opens his song by boasting that because his woman wants him only for his "pimp juice," he needs to "cut her loose." He then moves on to describe the power seats, leather, and sunroof of his "pimpmobile." When "hos see it," according to Nelly, they "can't believe it." Nelly knows their game and tells them to dust off their shoes so as not to dirty his rug. For those who still don't get it, Nelly ends his song with a rousing definition of pimp juice: "Your pimp juice is anything, attract the opposite sex, it could be money, fame, or straight intellect," he croons. Always an equal-opportunity kind of guy, Nelly proclaims, "Bitches got the pimp juice too, come to think about it dirty, they got more than we do." By itself, "Pimp Juice" is just a song. Yet when coupled with the music video of Nelly representing a pimp, and mass-marketing campaigns that put cans of actual Pimp Juice in corner stores for young African Americans to buy, the circle is complete. When Black American youth spend $1.89 for one can of Pimp Juice at the corner store in their racially segregated neighborhoods, with Nelly's song "Pimp Juice" playing in the background, what exactly are they consuming?

This one product illustrates the increasingly seamless relations among the commodification of black bodies (the resurrection of the sexual scripts of pimp/prostitute within hip hop culture), struggles between corporations and hip hop capitalists in search of new consumer markets (rap star Nelly's apparent aspirations to become a hip hop mogul), the expansion of new consumer markets (how Pimp Juice is marketed to African American consumers and global youth markets), and potentially new systems of control within African American civil society (African American women's participation in sex work).

PRACTICING RESISTANCE: JUST SAY NO?

When confronted with the seeming ubiquity of cultural products such as Pimp Juice, how might African American youth critically analyze practices such as these? Moreover, what can they do? Is it enough to just say no? The political challenge for all youth assigned to places of social blackness certainly involves rejecting these assigned places and finding a new place and purpose in the world. But how does one do this?

The act of rejecting cannot be a simple refusal, an uncritical "no." Simple refusal to take one's place (in this case, the place of social blackness) may result in having no place at all. People who are faced with this seemingly forced choice of *either* buying in and therefore selling out, *or* opting out and therefore failing to challenge the status quo, can become dispirited and pessimistic that things will ever change. In this context, practicing resistance requires envisioning a new place outside these narrow options and taking steps to get there.

The analysis that I develop below refers to the particular case of early-twentieth-century African American youth. But it is important to remember that this case of African American youth as a socially black population in the United States taps the broader issue of how race, class, gender, sexuality, and nationality converge to produce similar yet specific "places" for all youth. I examine what practicing resistance might mean for African American youth and their allies. Yet this argument is by no means unique to young African Americans. Rather, I encourage you to build upon this argument and expand it to other groups, as well as to fine-tune this argument for different segments of the African American youth population. I also encourage you to remember the many ways of practicing resistance discussed in chapter 3.

I see two dimensions that African American youth and their allies who wish to practice resistance might consider in responding to their assigned place of being young, sexy, and black. One dimension is to analyze their assigned place critically. Without being dedicated to assessing one's place critically, it becomes virtually impossible to respond to it, let alone change it. Socially black youth may be assigned to a place, yet classification need not mean acceptance.[56] Critical analysis lets you know what you are dealing with. Beyond critical analysis, an equally important dimension of practicing resistance is to take responsibility for developing appropriate action strategies. Socially black youth who experience the pain of negotiating their assigned place realize that they cannot simply think oppression away. Taking action shapes what we think, and what we think affects what we do (or don't do).[57]

CRITICAL ANALYSIS: KNOWING YOUR PLACE

When it comes to practicing resistance, African American youth are surrounded with numerous media examples that can be used for critical analysis. For example, what is the significance of Nelly's marketing of Pimp Juice, the product, and pimp juice, the metaphor? Is this just a harmless product? What does the example of African American youth and Pimp Juice reveal about the relationship between social blackness, advanced capitalism, and the media? How are African American youth—especially poor and working-class African American youth—placed on lockdown? Peeling back the surface view of how Pimp Juice is marketed might reveal new pressure points for reform, contestation, creating alternatives, or outright rebellion.

Let me now reposition this one example of Pimp Juice within (1) the earlier frame of the domains-of-power framework that I developed in chapter 2; (2) the ideas about practicing resistance from chapter 3;

and (3) some of the main ideas that I have examined up to now in this chapter. Thus far, I have spent the bulk of this chapter spelling out the emerging assigned place for African American youth.

Table 3 maps how a constellation of factors work together to shape the assigned place for African American youth and their allies.[58] It illustrates how the assigned place of African American youth reflects structural features of contemporary capitalism that limit job opportunities in some industries while creating them in others (black culture and sex work); disciplinary practices that place actual U.S. Black youth under surveillance in physical spaces (such as ghettos, prisons, or schools) and in media spaces (such as the marketing of hip hop culture); cultural practices that manufacture and circulate images of Black American youth culture as a source of authentic blackness and that are sexualized (pimps and "hos"); and an interpersonal domain that potentially interferes in relationships among African American youth. Moreover, this example suggests that many young African Americans go *willingly* to this assigned place, because their conscious collaboration, unconscious participation, or both is required for this entire system to work.[59]

To start a critical analysis, I see several provocative directions that African American youth and their allies might pursue to develop a critical analysis of a phenomenon such as Pimp Juice. For one thing, the example of Pimp Juice reveals some of the new forms of economic exploitation that have been handcrafted for African American youth. Pimp Juice in all its manifestations is designed to separate young African Americans from their money. Moreover, it does so in a sophisticated fashion that routinely hides this function. When we focus disproportionately on how African American youth are depicted in the media, we neglect the real story of who is making money. In essence, African American youth are exploited to consume commodified images of themselves, activities that foster their continued economic exploitation. The sophistication of this process emerges from sophisticated marketing mechanisms of consumerism and the centrality of the media. Specifically, the Pimp Juice beverage is

Table 3. Critical Analysis of Your Place:
African American Youth and Lockdown

STRUCTURAL DOMAIN: ORGANIZING LOCKDOWN	CULTURAL DOMAIN: JUSTIFYING LOCKDOWN
• African American youth participation in the converging black culture and sex work industries • African American youth as new consumer markets	• Manufactures "Pimp Juice" as one image of African American masculinity • Manufactures the "ho" as one image of African American femininity • Justifies watching youth of different genders and classes for reasons of entertainment and social control (dual meaning of *watching*)
DISCIPLINARY DOMAIN: REGULATING LOCKDOWN	INTERPERSONAL DOMAIN: UNCRITICALLY ACCEPTING LOCKDOWN
• Institutions have socially black, African American youth under surveillance • African American youth use gender to watch (police) one another • African Americans used as passive consumers of "Pimp Juice" products and images	• Pimps/"hos" as a template for normalized gender relations in African American communities • Rejection of this template could be interpreted as rejection of black culture; adds to pressure of consumer conformity

targeted to young African American consumers with an eye toward generating a profitable, guaranteed African American consumer market. The placement of the product in small stores in African American neighborhoods, the ways in which the can of Pimp Juice looks like a can of beer, and the introduction of sports energy drinks in general all reflect the need to expand consumer markets. Here one also sees the connection between consumerism and debt, the relation between style and social class status.[60]

Another provocative direction that African American youth and their allies might take in critically assessing cultural phenomena such as pimp juice and the Pimp Juice beverage as its tangible product concerns the impact of consumer addictions on the leadership capacity of youth. Uncritical participation in consumerism, especially if it becomes addictive, ultimately fosters passive citizens and people who are unable to lead. The example of how the Pimp Juice beverage is sold to African American youth as a specific consumer market illustrates how the relationship between consumerism and addiction is cultivated. If kids can become addicted to this product, they will continue to consume it. The Pimp Juice product invokes notions of symbolic power; namely, the belief that if one expresses the stylistic trappings of power (on credit), one actually possesses real power. Kids with a can of Pimp Juice can access the seeming power of the pimp, even if some had to scrape together the money to buy the drink itself. In the U.S. context, real power lies in corporations and the government, not in the individual choice of consuming a can of Pimp Juice.

The example of the cultural phenomenon pimp juice also illustrates the changing relationship between African American culture and politics, and thus a critical analysis of these changes might catalyze new ideas for practices of resistance. Historically, the music of African Americans (here used to signify a broad range of cultural practices) emerged from the honesty of lived social conditions.[61] Capitalism has found ways to package forms of African American cultural expression in ways that market a commodified black culture to a broader audience.[62] For example, the blues sung by performers in Mississippi Delta speakeasies in dialogue with Southern African American audiences differs from the blues sung by performers to whites in The Blues Alley. It differs not just culturally, but also politically.

Hip hop faces a similar set of challenges. Old-school hip hop more closely resembles the early phases of a new cultural form. In contrast, its current expression exemplified by Nelly's "Pimp Juice" (and Pimp Juice) illustrates the successful appropriation of African American culture for profit. According to M1 from Dead Prez, "Hip Hop is programmed by the ruling class. It is not the voice of African or Latino or oppressed youth. It is the puppet voice for the ruling class that tells us to act like the people who are oppressing us. Who's to blame? The schools, the media, capitalism, and colonialism are totally responsible for what Hip Hop is and what it has become. But we didn't intend on that. Hip Hop was a voice just like the drum, the oral tradition of our people."[63]

In essence, African American youth and their allies who develop a critical analysis of the political and economic underpinnings of hip hop as a business might see new avenues for practicing resistance. The possibilities here are legion. In today's rap music, images of African American youth as young, sexy, and black are broadcast and sold globally—mostly to suburban whites. These images reinforce rigid class, gender, and racial lines that reproduce existing power relations. They justify white fears and allow cultural arguments to take precedence over social justice arguments—that is, the pimps and "hos" are responsible for their own oppression because of their deviant and destructive behavior. What might happen if whites simply stopped buying hip hop, or if some whites were more vociferous in their criticism of the gutting of the political voice of young African Americans? What if more white youth became bona fide political allies of Black American youth by rejecting these pressures?

Another route here concerns the connections between the control of hip hop (its messages, production, and distribution) and youths' ability to exercise political power in the U.S. multicultural, multiethnic democracy. Here, it may be no accident that gangsta rap skyrocketed at the same time that more political forms of rap waned; or that BET was sold by African American entrepreneur Bob Johnson to Viacom—a company owned by Sumner Redstone, a strong supporter of George W. Bush.[64] To analyze hip hop as a crucial source for the changing relationship between African American culture and politics, African American youth and their allies might consider the ways in which affluent, conservative whites who decry the likes of Nelly in public make huge profits in private from hip hop images of the gangsta, pimp, and "ho," and then use these images to mobilize their constituencies against the bad influences of hip hop (symbolized by "Pimp Juice"). When the political argument was framed in cultural terms such as these prior to 2008, conservatives usually won elections.[65]

A critical analysis of all manifestations of the cultural phenomenon pimp juice can catalyze many ideas for resistance to the political and cultural practices detailed above, as they affect broader U.S. society. But a critical analysis can also be developed for relations that are internal to African American communities and, in doing so, reveal ways in which young Black Americans can change their everyday behavior. It is no secret that one of the most emotionally intense issues that confront African Americans pivots on questions of gender and sexuality. Thus, yet another provocative direction that African American youth and their allies might take in engaging in critical analysis concerns the power of media images such as Pimp Juice to influence the relations between and among African American men and women.

What happens when African American boys see the image of the pimp as a template for African American masculinity? What might be the effect on African American girls of identifying with the commodified sexuality of the "ho"? What are the implications of using the relationship between the pimp and the "ho," one of gender dominance and subordination, as the template for heterosexual gender relations within African American communities? If the template of the pimp/"ho" becomes embedded in social relationships as the template for normal gender relations, it installs a system of mutual policing that is difficult to upend. Moreover, because the power relations are embedded in a cultural product, rejecting the pimp/"ho" framework amounts to the perception of rejecting authentic black culture and can lead to charges of assimilation, or selling out for not buying in.[66]

Sex work may be permeating the very fabric of African American communities via new configurations of production and consumption in ways that resemble how sex work has changed the societies of countries in the Caribbean, Africa, and similar developing regions. Caribbean societies that depend heavily on tourism recognize how important sex work can be for struggling local economies.[67] The reconfiguration of the sex work industry within poor and working-class African American communities has shaped the domestic relations within such communities generally and the gendered relations expressed within hip hop culture in particular. Both women and men experience these trends, but here I focus on young African American women as a site of intensified race and gender commodification to build a more general case that also might apply to young African American men.

What we have here is a fascinating and dangerous cycle for African American youth, complete with the use of high-tech media and a sound track that accompanies their subordination. This example of Pimp Juice illustrates how the various domains of racism as a system of power intersect in creating a specific place for African American youth and install a series of mechanisms for making sure that not only are they relegated to this place, but that they go willingly to it, if at all possible. When viewed as a seamless whole, it can be difficult to see places for resistance. But a critical analysis of the parts of the whole (such as the case described here of Pimp Juice within a domains-of-power framework) provides a different view. If there are multiple sites of oppression, so too are there multiple possible sites of resistance.

TAKING ACTION

Gaining a critical perspective is one thing, but where should one start to take action? Social institutions are differentially suited to this task of critically assessing one's place and taking appropriate action strategies to challenge it. When it comes to African American youth, schools and the media (with their varying relationships to popular culture) constitute sites that are dedicated to teaching youth about their assigned place and helping them get there. Because these in-stitutions are designed to teach youth their place, it stands to rea-son that schools and the media will be important targets, if not sites, of political activism for youth. Classrooms that are frontline politi-cal spaces (where teachers perfect countersurveillance, engage in subversive teaching, and foster media literacy), combined with kids who gain a critical eye on their own situation, can have powerful outcomes.

Table 4 suggests some potential practices of resistance that might occur within and across several domains of power. Note that there are empty bullets where you might fill in your own suggestions, large and small. For now, I call your attention to the cultural domain of power, the site where ideas are created and resisted, as a vitally im-portant place for African American youth and their allies to practice resistance.

When it comes to questions of practicing resistance, schools and the media may share a similar purpose, but they also differ in some significant ways. In schools, youth struggle in several domains—the pecking order of the school system itself, which routinely assigns African American kids to the worst schools (the structural domain); school rules that regulate youth actions (the disciplinary domain); and the cultural norms that permeate the formal and not-so-hidden cur-riculum (the cultural domain). In schools, much of this is worked out through direct interpersonal relationships between teachers, princi-pals, and other authority figures. Schools are devoted to surveillance and regulation.

Table 4. Taking Action About Your
Place in Many Sites: Youth

STRUCTURAL DOMAIN	CULTURAL DOMAIN: EDUCATION AND THE MEDIA
• Vote, vote, and vote. • Talk about politics in youth groups, especially gangs. • Know your rights. • ?	• Develop media literacy, especially regarding TV, film, videos, and so on. • Use the Internet for political organization; develop innovative Web sites, blogs, YouTube videos, and chat rooms. • Build political communities through social networking sites such as Facebook. • Create progressive music and dance. • ?
DISCIPLINARY DOMAIN	INTERPERSONAL DOMAIN
• Excel in school. • Complain to the right people and make them listen. • Reject being a passive consumer of "Pimp Juice" products and images. • ?	• Reject dehumanizing scripts: can pimps/"hos" love one another? • Embrace revolutionary love as a template not only for normal gender relations, but for normal human relations. • ?

In contrast, the media does not come with the disciplinary baggage of schools, nor is it as formally structured as a social institution. Given its power to educate, contemporary mass media is surprisingly unregulated. This lack of regulation cuts both ways. Like schools, the media justifies the poor treatment of socially black youth; for example, violence against youth depicted as entertainment. As the case of the cultural phenomenon Pimp Juice illustrates, the media is also a powerful site for creating cultural norms. Yet the media can also serve as a site of resistance, especially for youth who are armed with the technological tools to use it and who see their use of the media as a form of taking action that is informed by their critical analyses.

Given the media's centrality to producing and contesting social meanings of race, gender, class, and sexuality, why would we be surprised that youth choose the media as one important site of their politics? Given the centrality of popular culture for African American youth, especially its overlap with the sex work industry, it stands to reason that, for many, the cultural domain constitutes an important and prominent place where youth practice resistance.[68]

If you have read this chapter with an eye toward developing resistance strategies, by now you should have many ideas for paths that you might follow. The possibilities for resistance within the domains-of-power framework are infinite. But I do want to share one more example of what one committed individual can do when armed with a critical analysis and a clear sense of what needs changing. This example illustrates the significance of specialized resistance in a media context. It also speaks to the theme that we can do something, individually and collectively.

Because so much of this chapter has emphasized the centrality of the media, I want to end with a discussion of how one young African American woman used the media to practice resistance. The case of Pimp Juice illustrated how mass-media technologies were used to construct and assign African American youth to their place. Specifically, the image of Nelly, the visual of the Pimp Juice can, the icon of the pimp in popular culture, and the sound track of the song collectively produce a powerful visual icon that simultaneously produces profits for the makers of Pimp Juice and that potentially influences consumer behavior. These relationships are effective primarily because watching and surveillance have become such a crucial part of disciplinary and cultural domains of power—we passively watch music videos and are disciplined through our uncritical consumerism.

In contrast to this mass-media example, Aishah Simmons's *NO! The Rape Documentary* draws upon similar media technologies, yet in multiple oppositional ways. As an incest and rape survivor, Simmons experienced the kind of violence that can occur in African American communities when African Americans uncritically accept the pimp/"ho" template. Young African American men who admire the strength, leadership skills, and sexual prowess attributed to the pimp can also perceive African American women as objects to be taken, used, exploited, and raped. That is one outcome of relationships among individuals who view each other as objects to be used rather than as fully human people. Sexual violence such as rape flourishes in this climate. In this sense, an image of Nelly holding his can of Pimp Juice by itself is benign. Yet the absence of a critical analysis of patterns of meaning created by a large number of images such as these is problematic.

Given the complex history of African Americans regarding rape and sexual violence, as well as barriers that the public schools face in trying to address these topics, the media becomes an obvious site to begin to disrupt the pimp/"ho" template for African American gender relationships. Recognizing this, Simmons founded AfroLez Productions, described as an "AfroLez femcentric" multimedia arts company committed to "using the moving image, the written and spoken word to address those issues which have a negative impact on marginalized and disenfranchised people."[69] Simmons spent eleven years (seven of which were full time) to produce, write, and direct *NO! The Rape Documentary*. Recognizing how big corporations shape the content of what is actually produced and distributed, Simmons wanted control over her product, and she raised all the money herself. With creative control, Simmons was able to explore the international reality of rape and other forms of sexual assault through the first-person testimonies, scholarship, spirituality, activism, and cultural work of African Americans. Simmons conceptualized *No!* as a black feminist educational organizing tool to be used in the global movement to end violence against women and children.[70]

Simmons's documentary aims to engage people intellectually and emotionally in an experience that leaves them changed. In contrast, contemporary consumer culture asks us to suspend our capacity for critical thinking and watch the images go by. Yet much is at stake when we fail to tell the difference between media treatments of sexual violence whose purpose is to entertain us and to sell products, and those whose aim is to catalyze critical analysis. In this case, we need only compare Simmons's *No!* to Nelly's videos, such as "Pimp Juice." The content of both of these examples of visual media take a stand on how African American youth are assigned a place at the intersection of the black culture industry and the sex work industry. Yet where Nelly's smooth endorsement of Pimp Juice beckons his consumers to say "yes" to this place, Simmons responds with a resounding *No!*

Certainly Simmons's documentary produces important content by using new technologies to practice resistance in the cultural domain of power. But equally significant is Simmons's intended use of *No!* She made the film not simply to share information about a hidden social problem but also to catalyze discussion, analysis, and action. The relationship that Simmons hoped she would have with *No!*'s viewers suggests an especially crucial point about the use of media in practicing resistance. Resistance is not embedded exclusively in the *content* of any particular movie, music video, or documentary—there is nothing that is inherently more truthful about a documentary than a feature film or a Nelly video. Rather, practicing resistance occurs in the *process* of how media is produced and received. Critical analysis applied to Nelly's videos might prove to be an especially valuable exercise, in part because these images are so widespread in hip hop culture.

Who produced a cultural product and for what end are important parts of the equation. But what we as viewers bring to the experience of watching media also lies at the heart of the power of the media to shape complex ideas about who is young, sexy, and black. When it comes to your relationship with the media, what are you watching? How are you watching it? Who's watching you?

Afterword
The Way Forward: Remembering Zora

> They tell me this democracy form of government is a wonderful
> thing. It has freedom, equality, justice, in short, everything!
> Since 1937 nobody has talked about anything else.... The radio,
> the newspapers, and the columnists inside the newspapers, have
> said how lovely it was. And this talk and praise-giving has got
> me in the notion to try some of the stuff. All I want to do is to
> get hold of a sample of the thing, and I declare, I sure will try
> it. I don't know for myself, but I have been told that it is really
> wonderful.
> —"Crazy for This Democracy" (1945), Zora Neale Hurston[1]

African American folklorist Zora Neale Hurston was never known
for holding her tongue. In her satirical essay "Crazy for This Democracy," Hurston points out the contradictions between the American
commitment to democracy and how its African American citizens
had not yet benefited from it. African Americans had long possessed
citizenship rights and thus were beneficiaries of democracy, yet race

and class oppression had routinely stripped them of the rights of first-class citizenship. Hurston's piece appeared at the end of World War II, in the aftermath of the defeat of Nazi Germany, arguably one of the most harmful racial regimes of all time. Despite continued practices of Jim Crow segregation, Hurston did not counsel abandoning the idea of democracy in the United States; rather, she situated her critical analysis in the space between democracy's promise and practices.[2]

The post-9/11 context presents similar contradictions. The United States confronts the challenge both of remaining committed to the ideal of democracy and developing more effective strategies of bringing it about. Using race and youth as bellwethers for analysis, I explored in the previous chapters of this book some of the multifaceted challenges that accompany this dual work of envisioning democratic possibilities and crafting effective strategies for achieving it. Specifically, I explored the complex terrain of contemporary color-blind racism along with possible ways to practice resistance across its domains of power. I also examined challenges that pivot on issues of race, capitalism, and the media, especially as they affect youth whose lived experiences and opportunities have been profoundly affected by their placement in intersecting systems of ethnicity, social class, gender, citizenship, and sexuality.[3] More generally, throughout this volume, I have argued for the need for another kind of public education not only for youth, but also for the American public itself.

Here, I return to the larger question that catalyzed this entire project: How might another kind of public education enable us to envision new democratic possibilities? I center my discussion by showing how the idea of visionary pragmatism might prove helpful in this regard. In chapter 2, I presented a critical analysis of contemporary racism by applying the domains-of-power framework. In chapter 3, I sketched out how people might practice resistance using this same domains-of-power framework. Together, these chapters map out a critical analysis of what needs to be done and provide signposts to how this approach might catalyze other kinds of public education. In contrast, the idea of visionary pragmatism provides us with yet another tool to use in any domain of power in service to principles that we decide are important.

People who embrace visionary pragmatism think critically about the challenges that they face in their everyday lives and believe that they can take action to address them. Zora Neale Hurston certainly lived her life this way, in the context of very difficult times, and reviewing her ideas and actions may help each of us decide where we want to direct our energies.

Zora Neale Hurston walked a fine line in her intellectual work and in her life. On the one hand, she consistently engaged in provocative critical analysis about the democratic promises and practices of American society. She routinely pointed out the failures of democracy when it came to its African American citizens, poor people, and women and argued that democratic ideals would remain compromised so long as these and other groups remained second-class citizens. At the same time, as she satirically points out in "Crazy for This Democracy," Hurston remained committed to democratic ideals. She did not bring an uncritically patriotic, celebratory frame to democracy. Rather, she cast a critical eye on it. Her education did not prepare her to be a passive consumer of democratic ideals but rather demanded that she be an active citizen via participation in and engagement with social institutions through which democratic ideals are accomplished.

We see how Hurston rejected the pressures toward passivity and conformity, but exactly how did she negotiate this tension between her critical analysis of the ravages of racism and her continued commitment to American democratic ideals? How did she manage to take action in her everyday life without being consumed by anger, fear, unwarranted optimism, or apathy? How did she keep visions of new ways of being alive in ways that afforded her practical strategies for action?

Here, African American women's traditions of visionary pragmatism shed light on Zora Neale Hurston's capacity to persist within and transcend the challenges of her times. Two elements of visionary pragmatism are especially significant. On the one hand, people who embrace visionary pragmatism believe in taking principled stances that should guide behavior. Zora Neale Hurston's ability to be visionary and outspoken during a time when African American women were expected to be neither stems in part from her predilection to take principled stances—in this case, about the meaning of democracy. Visionary pragmatism consists of choosing to commit to *principles* that can be used to guide human action.[4] Many principles can provide this guidance, but in this book, I have emphasized the principle of democracy. I have invited readers to commit to democratic ideals.

On the other hand, people who embrace visionary pragmatism do not simply live in the sphere of abstract principles. Instead, they make pragmatic choices in specific social contexts. Because Zora Neale Hurston saw how the vision of democracy was incomplete without pragmatic actions that breathed life into it, she took action by speaking out and breaking the conventions of her times. In this book, I examine the many ways that people can practice resistance in school settings. I have also invited youth to engage in political behavior by developing media literacy skills that will enable them to cast a critical eye on their own cultural practices, such as chapter 4's analysis of race, sexuality, and hip hop.

Visionary pragmatism is the combination of both of these elements. All pragmatic choices are honed by the principled stances that we take in specific social contexts. With this particular vision, or this particular way of looking at the world, everyday life is something that is rooted, grounded, contingent, dynamic, and holistic. It is characterized by infinite opportunities to engage in critical analysis and take action. In everyday life, principles and actions give life meaning. It matters which particular principles one stands for. Depending on what kind of social context you are in, you have the opportunity, if not the responsibility, of seeing how specific principles manifest themselves. For Hurston, for example, democracy was a major preoccupation because racism and sexism limited her participation in it. The challenges of her specific social context catalyzed her choices around how to act; she practiced resistance by disbelieving, doing alternative research, and studying people who at that time were not seen as having anything valuable to contribute.

Part of this whole idea of visionary pragmatism is a creative tension between vision and pragmatism. What emerges is that pragmatic actions shape the vision, and the vision shapes pragmatic actions. If you do not have a vision, you are stuck in the here and now, with no hope and no possibility. This certainly can be the case for African American youth who passively accept images of themselves as pimps and "hos" and act accordingly. But it is also the case for educators who are quick to explain why something won't work. Kids and adults who are addicted—to acquiring material possessions; to using alcohol, tobacco, or drugs; to watching mindless, escapist television; to shopping—live lives that lack vision, even a personal vision for themselves.

A lot of people live their lives like this. Many of us know those people. Many of us *are* those people. It will take a concerted effort to encourage people to feel passionately and act responsibly in a context that preaches both, yet supports neither.

Here is where education becomes invaluable. Education can foster skills of critical analysis that will enable us to see the patterns that enhance or retard the principles we embrace. In this book, I have presented a critical analysis of contemporary color-blind racism. I believe that this new form of racism retards our ability to further democratic processes and that a critical analysis of its organization—the domains-of-power framework—will equip us to develop new ideas. Education can also foster skills that empower us when we want to take action. In this book, I placed a heavy emphasis on multiple forms of literacy, whether it is reading social cues across many different situations or engaging in sustained analysis of how new forms of media uphold new forms of power.

Through critical education, whether school-based or through other means such as the media, we can encounter the ideas and visions of others. Take, for example, the words of Martin Luther King Jr., delivered as part of his historic speech at the 1963 March on Washington for Freedom and Jobs:

> I am not unmindful that some of you have come here out of great trials and tribulations. Some of you have come fresh from narrow jail cells. Some of you have come from areas where your quest for freedom left you battered by the storms of persecution and staggered by the winds of police brutality. You have been the veterans of creative suffering. Continue to work with the faith that unearned suffering is redemptive. Go back to Mississippi, go back to Alabama, go back to Louisiana, go back to the slums and ghettos of our northern cities, knowing that somehow this situation can and will be changed. Let us not wallow in the valley of despair. I say to you today, my friends, so even though we face the difficulties of today and tomorrow, I still have a dream. It is a dream deeply rooted in the American dream.[5]

I quote this passage at length because it is so different from the standard presentation of King's dream, shorn of social context, a free-floating signifier of color blindness. King presented a vision to an audience that needed one, and he did so in a way that invited action.

We cannot attend the March on Washington, but education can place us in dialogue with the ideas of people who counsel both vision and pragmatic strategies of achieving that vision. If denied the opportunity to hear and read the ideas of figures such as King, or to see pictures of the sole student staring down tanks in Tiananmen Square, or to engage in conversations via social networks in mediated communities, we can easily remain without a vision and be denied the skills to realize a vision even if we could develop one.

Embracing change lies at the heart of visionary pragmatism. Because so many people perceive change as dangerous, we must ask what necessary tools might better equip people to live in the dynamic and contingent worlds that are informed by visionary pragmatism. Here again, Zora Neale Hurston provides insight. In essence, Hurston worked in the field of popular culture, yet one that was not yet inflected through mass media and technology, and during a time when communities were not so vastly changed. But the issues were the same. Hurston's life's work foreshadowed many contemporary issues of telling one's own story and using new forms of media to do so. As a trained anthropologist and folklorist, Hurston devoted her career to recording stories, dances, songs, and practices from African Americans in the South, allowing them to tell the stories of their own lives. Hurston did not ask her informants to translate their lives in response to her questions. Rather, she lived among African Americans in the South, striving to record the power of voice and the power of image as advanced within this population. She believed in the power of the voice, not just the authoritative voice of the books that told her what African Americans were like, but in the authority of the speaker him- or herself, who can live life with dignity and be treated a certain way. She believed in the power of telling one's own story. She recognized the significance of African Americans as cultural creators, the notion of claiming the voice of authority for one's own life, as well as the significance of using that voice to challenge authoritative knowledge. In this sense, the issues that she identifies in claiming the voice of authority, the right of oppressed people to tell their own stories, may be helpful in thinking through the political issues associated with media literacy and how media literacy might catalyze pragmatic strategies for envisioning democratic possibilities.

Achieving multiple forms of literacy equips us with the tools to analyze critically the ideas and practices of contemporary society. But achieving multiple forms of literacy also prepares us to be active creators of that same society, to engage in practices within a framework of visionary pragmatism. We need not be passive consumers of any set of ideas or practices. Armed with an analysis of how things work (the domains-of-power framework to guide our thinking), we can act differently in our everyday lives.

This idea of visionary pragmatism might also help us conceptualize another kind of public education. One can see how the practices that shaped Hurston's work and life were visionary in the context of her times. Hurston states, "I'm crazy for this democracy," yet she simultaneously questions what it means. Because democracy speaks to all social groups, especially youth of color, democracy cannot be a finished product but remains a work in progress. Stated differently, democracy is more than simply a system of beliefs. It is a set of processes and practices that are continually responding to the challenges of a particular time and place. Democracy is never finished. When we believe that it is, then we have, in fact, killed it.

Some wonder why I continue to work in education. Why is this a site of hope for me? I remain hopeful because I remain optimistic about the possibilities of youth. As anyone who has spent any time around kids will tell you, kids frequently think the unthinkable and do the unexpected. Kids naturally think outside the box (for evidence, go talk with some preschool teachers, or better yet, go talk with preschool-age kids). Sadly, our job as educators has been to encourage, manipulate, or force kids to fit into their correct boxes and to adjust their expectations for themselves accordingly. I think youth are still open to ideas. Because they see things differently, they create some real possibilities. As an educator, I recognize that the kids are coming through American social institutions regardless of what I do; because of that, what I say and do may be vitally important for the

next generation. To me, what has to change is that the next generation hears new cultural messages about what's possible for them.

I also remain hopeful because, following Hurston, I practice a
version of visionary pragmatism that has and, I hope, will continue
to shape the worldview of oppressed people. Visionary pragmatism
is essential for sustained, principled political resistance. Visionary
pragmatism embraces the vision that deep-seated change is possible,
and in particular, that we can move beyond color-blind racism to
something else. Visionary pragmatism also advocates for developing
pragmatic strategies to bring change about, in my case working with
and on behalf of youth. Because I concentrate on education, both
its school-based dimensions and its media-based manifestations, this
is the part of the interpersonal domain where I most practice resistance. I think that each of us who works in education (particularly
public education) needs to find ways to talk about what we can do differently. Rather than describing our actions through the frameworks
of reform and fitting in, we need to find ways to talk about our work,
in many cases our life's work, and tell a sustained story of practicing
resistance.

A Note from the Series Editor

The Simmons College/Beacon Press Race, Education, and Democracy Lecture and Book Series, a collaborative effort of Simmons College and Beacon Press, annually brings to Boston a prominent public figure to deliver public lectures on the topic of race, education, and democracy. These lectures form the basis for a book published each year by Beacon Press.

The series aims to reestablish in the public imagination the historic connection between public education and the possibility of a robust democracy, against the backdrop of the issue of race in America. It aims to create a location for a sustained, public conversation about the purpose of education in a multiracial and multicultural democracy. It aims to create a place for individuals to examine critically what should happen in school—if school is to prepare the young for the democracy, if school is to be the place where a new common culture, predicated on difference, is created and recreated. It aims to create a location for Americans to examine what is required of schools, the country, and the citizenry if the young are to be educated for self-government, when definitions of what is real, who is of value, and who are members of the nation are daily constructed and worked out in media.

Racial ideology continues to present a significant threat to Horace Mann's vision of public education as the great equalizer and to the belief of Frederick Douglass and other formerly enslaved Africans that education was indeed the pathway from slavery to freedom. The Simmons College/Beacon Press series aims to help strengthen the relationship between education and the democracy, with a broader vision of who members of the democracy are, while unapologetically introducing race into this discourse.

The series is aimed at a broad audience: educators; concerned citizens; civic, religious, and business leaders; parents; students; and community activists. The lectures and books present educational issues in all their complexity, yet in a manner that is readily accessible to a wide audience. The series proceeds on the assumption that public education is at the center of American public life, and that discussions about critical educational issues need to occur in the public sphere and draw Americans from many different backgrounds into thoughtful, informed, and complicated conversations.

We hope that these lectures and books will spark a new energy and excitement about education and the necessary role it must play in democratic life, and create a general audience of readers for critical educational scholarship.

Theresa Perry
Series Director
Professor of Africana Studies and Education
Simmons College
Boston, Massachusetts

Acknowledgments

This book would not have come about without the gracious invitation from Theresa Perry at Simmons College to participate in the "Race, Education, and Democracy" lecture series. I have known Theresa for many years and marvel at her steadfast dedication to social justice initiatives. I want to thank her for her contributions to this project.

Special thanks go out to Valerie Chepp, my research assistant in the Department of Sociology at the University of Maryland, College Park, whose help was invaluable. Valerie handled the bulk of the research and administrative duties for this book, casting a keen editorial eye on this entire project, occasionally tracking down obscure references and helping me better understand contemporary popular culture. I also want to acknowledge the support of sociology graduate students Kendra Barber at the University of Maryland, who did an excellent job of researching ideas for chapter 2; and Michelle Burstion at the University of Cincinnati, who provided important insights into hip hop culture for chapter 4.

This book has benefited greatly from the efforts of a top-notch team of people who worked on this book at Beacon Press. Andy Hrycyna, my editor for this project, was awesome. This entire project was on such an extremely tight schedule that I wanted to throw up my hands in frustration. But Andy possesses that magic combination of being an encouraging coach and a drill sergeant. The book was completed in large part due to Andy's valuable editorial eye and his uncanny knack of e-mailing me just when I was about to fall behind schedule. I would also like to send out a special thanks to Susan Mc-Clung, who copyedited the manuscript. As most authors know, a good copyeditor can greatly enhance the quality of one's writing and this book benefited from being in such good hands.

Albert Hill, my father, Roger Collins, my spouse, and Valerie Collins, my daughter, each provided unique forms of support for this project. Because I am not your typical daughter, wife, or mother, I am extremely grateful that I have a family that recognizes and respects this reality. I also want to acknowledge the contributions of people whose support (often unwitting) helped me finish this book. I value my conversations with Dee Erby, whose caring, thoughtful, and diligent attention to the issues detailed in this book reminded me of exactly the kind of citizens we all might aspire to be. Special thanks to Heidi Schultz for keeping my feet tapping, and to Candy Marshall, Sharon Struewing, and Kelly Leon for reminding me to "woo" on a regular basis.

Finally, I want to thank the participants in the four lectures that I delivered in spring 2008 at Simmons College. Many in the audience cared deeply about the issues here. Through their consistent and diligent work in offering the kind of public education that I study here, they reminded me how important and demanding social justice work can be. I have given many talks in diverse venues, yet the audiences who attended the Simmons lectures were inspiring to me. In that spirit, I dedicate this book to all the teachers, students, parents, neighbors, and school personnel who get up every day and, through their dedication to kids, strive to foster another kind of public education.

Notes

PREFACE

1. (Carson and Shepard 2002, p. 85).
2. The combination of a series of weakened democratic parties and the continued decline of the German economy paved the way for the public's acceptance of the Nazi Party's program.

I. WHAT DOES THE FLAG MEAN TO YOU?

1. Let me say a bit here about my use of language. In this volume, I continue to struggle with pressures not to capitalize the term "Black," a convention more often used by African Americans as a term of group self-identity, as with, for example, Puerto Ricans and Jews, and a convention that I have followed in my earlier work. This battle to capitalize a term of self-identification (as was the case with earlier struggles to capitalize *Negro*—a successful struggle) wears me down. In this volume, I use the terms *African Americans, Black Americans,* and *U.S. Blacks* to refer to this specific, historically created population. In contrast, I use lowercase terms—*brown, black, white,* and, occasionally, *yellow* and *red*—to signal how race as a system of power creates racial categories. I see these lowercase terms as associated with racism, and its power to whiten or blacken

groups and to choose color as a significant feature of lived experience. I will often use the term *socially black* to highlight this usage. For an analysis of these issues, see my discussion of social blackness in chapters 2 and 4.

2. John Dewey and the works of the American pragmatists come closest to the democratic ideals espoused in this volume. For representative work in this tradition, see Dewey (1954), Dewey (2004), and Westbrook (1998). Influenced by this tradition, selected African American and Latino thinkers have also turned their attention to the theme of democracy. For work in this tradition, see Marable (1993), Guinier and Torres 2002), Marable (2002), and West (2004).

3. For Dewey and Addams, see Dewey (1954), Dewey (2004), and Addams (2002). For classic African American thinkers in this tradition, see Cooper (1892) and Du Bois (1979).

4. Sociologist C. Wright Mills's classic work *The Sociological Imagination* explores the need for social scientists to contribute to democratic projects (Mills 2000b). Seidman describes this impetus: "I would like to see sociological theory regain its focus on public debates and issues. Instead of being driven by narrow disciplinary conventions and disputes, theorists should seriously try to address the key social and political debates of our time, and in an accessible language. Theorists need to recover the moral impulse at the heart of social theory, and to see themselves, once again, as public educators engaging the issues of the day." (Seidman 2004, p. 2)

5. For an accessible discussion of how globalization is changing American culture, see Ritzer (2004).

6. For overviews of these histories, see Takaki (1993) and Glenn (2002).

7. (Woodson 1933, p. 84).

8. (Freire 1970).

9. In his classic work *The Souls of Black Folk*, Du Bois describes this notion of double consciousness as the result of living behind the veil, another prominent metaphor for U.S. race relations (Du Bois 1979).

10. See, for example, Dorothy Smith's notion of women's ways of knowing as foundational to a feminist sociology (Smith 1990, pp. 11–28).

11. An expansive literature explores the oppositional nature of African American culture. For one representative work, see my analysis of Afri-

can American women's intellectual traditions (Collins 2000). This notion of oppositional culture and alternative ways of knowing has been studied in many groups. For classic works in this genre, see Scott (1990) and Scott (1985).

12. For Du Bois's discussion of "double consciousness," see Du Bois (1979). See also my extended discussion of practicing resistance in school settings in chapter 3, especially my analysis of oppositional culture.

13. Sociologist C. Wright Mills's discussion of "the personal troubles of milieu and the public issues of social structure" is relevant here (Mills 2000b, p. 8). Mills states, "[T]o be aware of the idea of social structure and to use it with sensibility is to be capable of tracing such linkages among a great variety of milieu. To be able to do that is to possess the sociological imagination" (Mills 2000b, pp. 10–11). In this sense, Mills's concept of sociological imagination resembles the ideas I present here. In *The Power Elite*, Mills criticizes American public education on this very point—that it fails to teach students to see their personal troubles as part of larger social issues. Doing so would help students to see the relevance of their issues for their communities as well as how social issues in their communities affect them (Mills 2000a, p. 318). In this sense, the ideas of Dead Prez discussed in chapter 3 about the failures of public education reflect both dimensions of Mills's model: Dead Prez look to their own personal experiences to identify and analyze social problems. They also identify schools as one important site where those problems are created.

14. The assimilation model, developed from the experiences of white ethnic immigrants, has been the predominant model. For a classic work in this tradition, see Glazer and Moynihan (1968).

15. Historically, various ethnic groups attained full citizenship rights by assimilating mainstream values about race. For analyses of how Jewish, Italian, and Irish people all became more assimilated into a white American identity, see Brodkin (2000), Ignatiev (1995), and Guglielmo and Salderno (2003).

16. Color-blind racism can thrive within an assimilationist framework. This foreshadows the ideas in chapter 2. Assimilation can be seen as a situation of cosmetic diversity, tokenism, and within the parameters of an emerging color-blind racism.

17. The field of multiculturalism is vast. For a good overview, see Goldberg (1995).

18. (Takaki 1993). Takaki's volume traces the histories of groups that are routinely collapsed under ethnic terms such as *Latino* or *Asian*.

19. For an overview of the emergence and use of the term *mestizaje* in Latin American societies, see Miller (2004).

20. Hybridization describes it as "[s]ocio-cultural processes in which discrete structures or practices, previously existing in separate form, are combined to generate new structures, objects, and practices. In turn, it bears noting that the so-called discrete structures were a result of prior hybridizations and therefore cannot be considered pure points of origin" (Canclini 1995, p. xxv). For a discussion of the history of this term, see Young (1995). Another theme concerns cycles of hybridization: "we move historically from more heterogeneous forms to other more homogeneous ones, and then to other relatively more heterogeneous forms, without any being 'purely' or simply homogeneous" (Canclini 1995, p. xxv).

21. This term is drawn from anthropology and has been applied to religious practices (see Leopold 2004). For example, studies of African American religious practices identify the fusion of West African belief systems and those of the Catholic Church. Santeria and voodoo both are syncretic religions. The whole notion of the original religions would remain intact, but there is also a new one that has been expanded and built upon that. So the whole notion of a syncretism is a kind of creative merging that doesn't necessarily devolve or destroy the original religions, but in fact creates yet another *melange,* another mixture. Jazz is also referred to as a syncretic cultural formation, one that is a fusion of African and European influences to create an American music (Ward and Burns 2002).

22. The language of the Sea Islands has been studied as a Creole language, as has Ebonics, or black English. For an analysis of the Ebonics debate, see Perry (1998).

23. These ideas clearly overlap. Some would argue that fusion is not new. In visual arts, for example, the work of Picasso and Gauguin foreshadowed fusion. The nuance here is the fusion of sounds and movement, a fusion that was difficult to capture prior to new technologies of recording and

the Internet as a mechanism for diffusion. For an analysis of contemporary debates in world music, see Haynes (2005).

24. (Miller 2004).

25. (Berry 1994).

26. For various discussions of race and the American welfare state, see Quadagno (1994), Katz (1989), Neubeck and Cazenave (2001), Gordon (1994), and Edin and Lein (1997). For a discussion of the use of racially coded language within welfare discourse, see Lubiano (1992) and Zucchino (1997).

27. This attack was largely achieved through racially coded language. The justification for such policies also appears to be racially neutral, yet the language used to explain the policies remains loaded with sedimented racial meaning. For example, a phrase such as "welfare queen" invokes an African American recipient of welfare. Ronald Reagan's "states' rights" speech, delivered in Philadelphia, Mississippi, soon after the 1980 Republican National Convention, constitutes another example of this phenomenon. On the surface, the phrase supports rights of self-governance and seems to be racially neutral. But when delivered in the historical context, where the term *states' rights* was a clarion call for defending racial segregation, the term can take on new meanings.

28. For a discussion of privatization, see Feigenbaum, Henig, and Hamnett (1998). In an October 1, 2007, article titled "Subcontracting the War," the *New York Times* argued against privatizing the war in Iraq due to lack of governmental oversight and accountability. "Census Counts 100,000 Contractors in Iraq," published in the *Washington Post* on December 5, 2006, illustrates our huge reliance on private contractors. In a related example, the push toward charter schools in public education seemingly relies upon this same impetus toward privatization. The main idea is that charter schools will encourage choice, innovation, and competition, thus behaving as enterprises in the private sector. See, for example, *The War Against America's Public Schools: Privatizing Schools, Commercializing Education* by Gerald W. Bracey (Needham, Mass.: Allyn & Bacon, 2001).

29. (Williams 1995, p. 25).

30. (Tatum 2007; Boger and Orfield 2005).

31. (Holmes 1995).

32. (Goldberg 1993, p. 196).

33. Interestingly, the term *Crips* stands for "Community Revolution In Progress."

34. Youth are defined as being between the ages of eighteen and twenty-nine. See CIRCLE's press release at http://www. civicyouth.org/PopUps/ PR_08_inequality.pdf.

35. The question of generational differences and their role in politics is an emerging area. For provocative accounts of the possibilities of a new politics from the hip hop and post-9/11 generation, see Kitwana (2002), Bynoe (2004), Connery (2008), and Goff (2008).

36. See CIRCLE's press release at http://www.civicyouth.org/PopUps/PR _08_inequality.pdf.

37. http://www.freemaninsitute.com/douglass.htm.

2. SOCIAL BLACKNESS, HONORARY WHITENESS, AND ALL POINTS IN BETWEEN

1. Examples of the tragic mulatto character can be found in films such as *Imitation of Life* (1934 and 1959) and *Pinky* (1949). The three films deal with a main character who is a tragic mulatta with an African American mother (grandmother in *Pinky*) and an absent white father. Both characters attempt to pass as white. *The Human Stain* (2000) features a similar tragic mulatto character who decides to deny his African American family and pass as white. He became a professor and kept it a secret until he was accused of being racist because of his reference to absent African American students as "spooks."

2. http://www.cnn.com/2007/POLITICS/01/31/BIDEN.OBAMA/, accessed November 21, 2008.

3. I assume that the guide (correctly) identified me as non-Zulu based on my style of dress and comfort with my fellow tourists. She did not ask me if I were Zulu but could clearly see that I am of African descent. I compare this experience to pressures that people of color often face to assimilate into white settings by downplaying any cultural differences. In these settings, everyone seems to go out of his or her way *not* to talk about race.

4. The use of the rhetoric *whitening* within Latin American politics as a

mechanism for describing upward social class mobility ("Money whitens") captures these dynamics. The higher one's class position, the more likely one can become white. Yet money alone is insufficient—certain behaviors must accompany the higher social class position for whitening to be successful. For discussions of racial discourse in Brazil, see Fredrickson (2001), do Nascimenta and Nascimento (2001), and Twine (1998).

5. Specifically, current pressures to alter phenotypical characteristics through cosmetic surgery and pharmaceuticals—for example, bleaching creams that promise lighter skin, contact lenses to change eye color, and plastic surgery to achieve the perfect body—all occur within a context of racial valuation. Achieving honorary whiteness may not simply be a matter of cultural alteration—physical alteration may also be at play.

6. (Tate 2003). For example, activities such as being able to name hip hop artists, to dance to hip hop and rhythm and blues, and to move into an inner-city neighborhood can all be seen as cool.

7. Historically and currently, white women bear the brunt of these social norms. Historically, "white" could be maintained as a pure biological category only by strictly monitoring the sexual behavior and marital choices of white women (Collins 2004). With the loosening of gender norms (a parallel development to color blindness), one can see a similar need to identify and manage the gender and sexuality of white women, whose behavior is seen as regulating racial borders. In this context, white supremacist literature contains numerous examples of this tendency to paint white women who have sexual relations with African American men as "race traitors" or as being "blackened" by this experience. See, for example, Daniels (1997) and Ferber (1998).

8. To clarify, the phrase *system of power* refers to a way of organizing power relations that might range from extreme egalitarianism to systems of vast social inequality. Because extreme egalitarianism is rare in modern Western societies, the systems of power that most interest me have been those that reproduce social relations of domination and subordination. One dimension of systems of power concerns the content or type of domination and subordination. For example, racism, sexism, heterosexism, and capitalism are all specific systems of power that have similar characteristics in how they organize social relations of domination and subordination. Another dimension of the concept of systems of power

concerns the mechanisms or processes by which power is organized. The processes that most interest me in this volume are democratic processes, or systems of power that aspire for democratic inclusion.

9. I'm thinking of racial etiquette here, such as the case of Emmett Till, who was murdered because he violated the segregated space of the South. See sociologist Robert Park's classic discussion of racial etiquette in *Race and Culture* (Park 1950, pp. 177–88).

10. For more on this decision, consult Bell (2004) and Bell (1980).

11. Several debates characterize claims about the African American middle class, most stemming from definitional issues. For example, criteria such as income, occupation, educational achievement, and homeownership all factor into discussions of who is in the African American middle class. For representative works, see Lacey (2007), Feagin and Sikes (1994), and Patillo-McCoy (1999).

12. For discussions of upward social class mobility, see Cole and Oman (2003). See also "Getting a Decent Middle-Class American Education: Pursuing Advantage in Schools" in *The Hidden Cost of Being African American* (Shapiro 2004). In this work, Shapiro discusses the pursuit of a good education by poor and working-class families as well as middle-class families who purposely try to leverage educational advantages for their children.

13. Barack Obama is the first African American presidential candidate to win the Democratic nomination, and only six African Americans have run for president in the history of the United States. Obama won 29 states, in addition to Washington, D.C., and Guam, winning 2,206 delegates and 441 superdelegates. For an interactive map of the primary results, see http://www.washingtonpost.com/wp-srv/politics/interactives/campaign08/primaries/.

14. According to an August 2008 census press release (http://www.census.gov/Press-Release/www/releases/archives/income_wealth/012528.html), 21.5 percent of Hispanics were in poverty in 2007, up from 20.6 percent in 2006. Poverty rates remained statistically unchanged for non-Hispanic whites (8.2 percent), African Americans (24.5 percent), and Asians (10.2 percent) in 2007. Among racial groups and Hispanics, African American households had the lowest median income in 2007 ($33,916). This compares to the median of $54,920 for non-Hispanic

white households. Asian households had the highest median income ($66,103). The median income for Hispanic households was $38,679. Citation: U.S. Census Bureau (August 2008). *Household Income Rises, Poverty Rate Unchanged, Number of Uninsured Down.* Retrieved September 25, 2008, from http://www.census.gov/Press-Release/www/releases/archives/income_wealth/012528.html.

According to an October 2008 census press release (http://www.census.gov/Press-Release/www/releases/archives/facts_for_features_special_editions/010849.html), the poverty rate of people who reported they were American Indian, Alaska Native, and "no other race" reached 27 percent. See U.S. Census Bureau (October 2008). *American Indian and Alaska Native Heritage Month: November 2007.* Retrieved September 25, 2008, from http://www.census.gov/Press-Release/www/releases/archives/facts_for_features_special_editions/010849.html.

15. According to a Centers for Disease Control and Prevention (CDC) report given at the 2008 HIV Prevention Leadership Summit (http://www.cdc.gov/hiv/topics/aa/resources/slidesets/hpls_cleveland.htm), in 2006, blacks accounted for nearly half (49 percent) of new HIV/AIDS diagnoses in the United States in the 33 states with long-term, confidential name-based HIV reporting. See Cleveland, J. (June 2008. *Heightened National Response to the HIV/AIDS Crisis Among African Americans.* Paper presented at the HIV Prevention Leadership Summit, Detroit, MI.

According to an April 2008 CDC report (http://www.cdc.gov/hiv/hispanics/resources/factsheets/hispanic.htm), in 2006, Hispanics/Latinos accounted for 18 percent of the 35,314 new HIV/AIDS diagnoses in the 33 states with long-term, confidential name-based HIV reporting. See Centers for Disease Control and Prevention (October 2008). *HIV/AIDS Among Hispanics/Latinos.* Retrieved September 25, 2008, from http://www.cdc.gov/hiv/hispanics/resources/factsheets/hispanic.htm.

According to a 2005 CDC report (revised August 2008; http://www.cdc.gov/hiv/resources/factsheets/aian.htm), even though the numbers of HIV and AIDS diagnoses for American Indians and Alaska Natives represent less than 1 percent of the total number of HIV/AIDS cases reported to CDC's HIV/AIDS Reporting System, when population size is taken into account, American Indians and Alaska Natives in 2005 ranked third in rates of HIV/AIDS diagnosis, after African Americans and Hispanics. See Centers for Disease Control and Prevention (August 2008). *HIV/AIDS Among American Indians and Alaska Natives.* Retrieved September 25, 2008, from http://www.cdc.gov/hiv/resources/factsheets/aian.htm.

16. One of the findings of a 2006 report done by the Association of Community Organizations for Reform Now (ACORN; http://acorn.org/fileadmin/HMDA/2006/Rate_Shock_Report.pdf) is that America's low-income and minority communities receive a disproportionate amount of subprime loans. See also ACORN (August 15, 2006). *The Impending Rate Shock: A Study of Home Mortgages in 130 American Cities.* Washington, D.C.: ACORN Fair Housing.

17. According to the *Cradle to Prison Pipeline* report by the Children's Defense Fund (http://www.childrensdefense.org/site/DocServer/CPP_report_2007_summary.pdf?docID=6001), released in 2007, African American juveniles are about four times as likely as their white peers to be incarcerated. African American youths are almost five times as likely and Latino youths about twice as likely to be incarcerated as white youths for drug offenses. In 2007, 580,000 African American males were serving sentences in state or federal prison, while fewer than 40,000 African American males earned a bachelor's degree. At mid-year 2006, 837,000 African American men were incarcerated—many of them fathers. Although they represent just 39 percent of the U.S. juvenile population, minority youth represent 60 percent of committed juveniles. One in three African American men, 20 to 29 years old, is under correctional supervision or control (Children's Defense Fund 2007).

18. The wealth and income of Cuban Americans, Indian Americans, and similar groups shift the changing face of who is considered to be socially black in the United States. For example, see http://www.census.gov/prod/2007pubs/acs-03.pdf. The 2004 American Community Survey reports that Cubans had the highest homeownership rate among Hispanics and had a median income of $38,256, compared to $35,929 for all Hispanic households. Citation: R. Suro, Kocchar, R., Passel, J., Escobar, G., Tafoya, S., Fry, R., et al. (2004). *The American Community—Hispanics: 2004* (ACS-03). Washington, D.C.: US Census Bureau. http://www.census.gov/prod/2007pubs/acs-05.pdf.

The 2004 American Community Survey reports that Asian Indians had a median income of $68,771, which was the highest of all Asian groups. In fact, it was about $10,000 higher. (The homeownership number for Asian Indians is not very high compared to all Asians. It is 51.7 percent. As a group, Asians have a high homeownership rate—57.6 percent—but the highest homeownership rates seem to be with the Vietnamese, Chinese, and Filipinos. Citation: R. Suro, Kocchar, R., Passel, J., Escobar, G., Tafoya, S., Fry, R., et al. (2004). *The American Community—Asians: 2004* (ACS-05). Washington, D.C.: US Census Bureau.

19. This also excludes the number (although perhaps it is shrinking with the passage of time) of all-white suburban enclaves. For example, one research assistant who worked on this project recounts that she attended high school in such an enclave, where she was one of three African American students in a school with more than a thousand students. There were also three Latina girls, all of whom were housed together because they were in a special academic program. The town itself had similar demographics—the total nonwhite population was 1 percent (the majority of whom are Asians who, given the affluence of the community, many would consider honorary whites). The only brown faces in this suburban enclave were those of their nannies, landscapers, bus drivers, athletes from rival schools, and the six academically gifted students imported from inner cities.

20. See Feigenbaum, Henig, and Hamnett (1998).

21. John McCain's (and the Republican Party's) 2008 campaign illustrates the push to privatize everything from education to Social Security. However, the fall 2008 global credit crisis potentially dealt a serious blow to these beliefs, and apparently to the McCain campaign itself.

22. (Williams 1995, p. 25).

23. For analyses on racial isolation in neighborhoods that take social class into account, see Massey and Denton (1993). For a more recent overview, see Iceland, Weinberg, and Steinmetz (2002) and Wilkes and Iceland (2004). For effects of racial isolation in schooling, see Kozol (1991).

24. "Native American Kids: American Indian Children's Well-Being Indicators for the Nation and Two States." Angela A. A. Willeto. *Social Indicators Research*, August 2007, Vol. 83, Issue 1, pp. 149–176.

25. In 2006, 4.2 million white children were living below the federal poverty level in the United States. See S. Fass, and Cauthen, N. K. (November

2007). *Who Are America's Poor Children? The Official Story*. New York: Columbia University, Mailman School of Public Health National Center for Children in Poverty (http://www.nccp.org/publications/pub_787 .html).

26. While there are greater *numbers* of white children living in poverty than any other U.S. racial/ethnic group, the poverty *rate* for children of other racial/ethnic groups is disproportionately higher than that of whites. In 2006, while 10 percent of all white children lived in poverty, 27 percent of Latino children, 33 percent of African American children, and 40 percent of Native American children lived in poor families (http://www .nccp.org/publications/pub_787.html).

27. The focus on the race and gender politics of the Vietnam War era often overshadows the generational politics of the times. Widespread student unrest on college campuses against the Vietnam War affected the political outlook of an entire generation of college students. The experiences of middle-class college kids are often depicted as the politics of the generation itself, yet working-class kids of varying racial and ethnic backgrounds who did not take part in campus unrest also were politicized within this period.

28. The events of 1968, for example, illustrated this political uncertainty, if not the crisis facing American social institutions. This was a period of so much change that no one knew where it was going.

29. Here I present but one way of describing the generations that came of age and into U.S. politics in the post–Civil Rights era. The question of how to define these generations has sparked considerable debate. For varying definitions of how the hip hop generation and the generation that seems to be following it define themselves and their political identity, see Kitwana (2002) and Bynoe (2004).

30. For a sense of the politics of this generation, especially as they overlap with the Obama presidential campaign and the potential for progressive politics, see Connery (2008) and Goff (2008).

31. For a discussion of this period of African American student activism, see Collins (in press).

32. This image, titled "The Unknown Rebel," can be viewed at http://www .asianamericans.com/TiananmenSquare.htm.

33. Guinier and Torres show how the political left and right each endorses

a discourse on race that fosters an ideology of color blindness that ultimately hinders people's ability to organize politically around issues of race (Guinier and Torres 2002). David Theo Goldberg traces the inherent danger of the modern state's neoliberal allegiance to color blindness under the law. Goldberg asserts that in this context, racial inequalities are viewed as outcomes of private, individual choices, not products of a racially unjust system. Thus race gets rendered invisible under the law, while racial inequality remains a very real lived experience for millions of people (specifically, see chapter 8 and Goldberg 2002). Eduardo Bonilla-Silva writes about how color blindness affects racial behavior (Bonilla-Silva 2001; Bonilla-Silva 2003). In *Black Sexual Politics*, I examine the evolution from America's earlier forms of racism to contemporary, color-blind racism, highlighting how the new racism takes on gender-, class-, and sex-specific forms (Collins 2004).

34. This either/or thinking might explain some of the deadlock characterizing early-twenty-first-century U.S. public policy concerning racial issues. The Democratic Party routinely points to discriminatory institutional policies as the root of racial inequality, whereas the Republican Party blames personal irresponsibility and lack of individual initiative.

35. In crafting this framework, I draw upon disparate traditions of research about power. For the structural domain of power, I draw upon analyses of institutional power advanced by Marx and Weber, especially their treatment of capitalism, state power, and bureaucracies. This literature is vast; for an introduction, see Collins (1994, pp. 47–118). For the disciplinary domain of power, the work of French social theorist Michel Foucault has been invaluable, especially his classic work *Discipline and Punish* (Foucault 1979). For the cultural domain of power, I rely on discussions of ideology and hegemony as sites where the manipulation of ideas constitutes a source of power (see, for example, Gramsci 1971). Foucault has also catalyzed work on knowledge as a system of power (Foucault 1980). In addition, I expand this focus on knowledge as domination to include oppositional knowledge and prospects for empowerment that is found in the work of feminist and postcolonial theorists. This literature is vast; see, for example, Scott (1990), Scott (1985), Barsamian and Said (2003), and Smith (1990). Finally, for the interpersonal domain of power and its conception of empowerment, I draw from the work of American pragma-

tists, especially John Dewey; see, for example, Dewey (1954) and Dewey (2004). These four domains are not as clear-cut as I present them here, nor are all equally significant at the same time. The domains-of-power framework is a heuristic device, a technique to be used to guide questions and avenues of investigation (in this case about contemporary color-blind racism). This is *not* a theoretical model to be tested empirically, for example, with efforts to parse out whether the structural domain has more predictive power than the interpersonal domain, or how one might measure the interactive effects of the disciplinary and cultural domains.

36. In other places in my work, I refer to this domain as the *ideological domain* or the *hegemonic domain*. While the cultural domain, especially with the growth of mass media, does appear to be hegemonic, the term *hegemony* suggests that ideas are so powerful that one cannot overcome them. I see hegemony as a potential form of ideological control, but contemporary social relations might be better described as seemingly hegemonic. In chapter 3, I take up this issue of practicing resistance in the cultural domain of power.

37. For an earlier version of this model, see chapter 12 of *Black Feminist Thought,* revised edition (Collins 2000).

38. For discussions of this theme, see Sharpley-Whiting (2007). For discussions of Third World feminism among young women of color, see Hernandez and Rehman (2002). I take up these issues at length in chapter 4.

39. (Nelson 1994, p. 62).

40. Dismantling affirmative action by recasting it as "reverse racism" illustrates this point. The *Bakke* Supreme Court decision, California Proposition 209, Washington Initiative 200, and the Michigan Civil Rights Initiative (Proposal 2) all seem to use the Civil Rights Act to argue that "preferential treatment" is unconstitutional. For a link that summarizes important court rulings related to affirmative action, see http://www.pbs.org/wgbh/pages/frontline/shows/sats/race/summary.html.

41. (Massey and Denton 1993, pp. 2–3).

42. (Moss and Tilly 1996). For an extended discussion of the structural domain of color-blind racism, see Brown et al. (2003).

43. (Steele 1997).

44. The Bureau of Justice Statistics reports that, in 2002, African Americans

made up 40 percent of the jail inmate population; Hispanics, 19 percent; and whites, 36 percent. Bureau of Justice Statistics. (2004). *Profile of Jail Inmates, 2002* (Report No. NCJ-201932). Retrieved September 27, 2008, from http://www.ojp.usdoj.gov/bjs/pub/press/pji02pr.htm.

45. For a social-science analysis of this trend, see Waçquant (2001).

46. A prison society is a carceral society—*carceral* means relating to incarceration. This notion of the carceral society is fully explored in the work of Michel Foucault (Foucault 1979). For a discussion of contemporary carceral society, see Davis (1997).

47. In schools, the penalties for not behaving are severe. Black students are more likely than any other students to be in special education programs for children with mental retardation or emotional disturbance. The suspension rate among African American students in public school is three times that for white students. African American children are 50 percent more likely than white children to drop out of school. When African American children do graduate from high school, they have a greater chance of being unemployed and a lower chance of going directly to full-time college than white high school graduates (Children's Defense Fund 2007).

48. For example, I wonder whether the intense interest in the late twentieth century in so-called identity categories, especially questions such as "What is black?" "Who is really black?" and the question raised about Barack Obama during his 2008 presidential campaign, "Is he black enough?" were not part of these larger issues of coming to terms with the persistence of racial inequality in a context where color blindness was assumed to be the norm.

49. Experiences such as being disproportionately seated in restaurants next to the kitchen door or the restrooms, or being followed in stores by salespeople with insincere offers of "Do you need any help?" can be dismissed as examples of bad luck or bad service. These types of incidents could happen to anybody, I agree. What I stress here is the *pattern* of these events—the fact that they routinely occur to some individuals and groups more than others, patterns that shape the contours of the group—in this case, (social) blacks.

50. These words are taken from Martin Luther King's "I Have a Dream" speech, delivered in 1963 at the March on Washington. This one line,

"I have a dream that my four little children will one day live in a nation where they will not be judged by the color of their skin but by the content of their character," remains the most memorable line from the speech. Yet extracting this line without reading the entire speech enables a recasting of King's work. The speech talks of contemporary injustices and was delivered at the March on Washington for Freedom and *Jobs*. Reciting one line that emphasizes an unfulfilled dream erases the actual social context that gives meaning to the dream. To read the entire speech, see Carson and Shepard (2002, 81–87). This one sentence has been King's signature line, yet his many other speeches offer a more complex history of his more radical politics.

51. The case of Bob Jones University's position regarding the admission of African American students illustrates the complexities of race and its operation in the public and private spheres. For details, see the CNN article "Bob Jones University ends ban on interracial dating," broadcast on March 4, 2000 (http://archives.cnn.com/2000/US/03/04/bob.jones/).

52. For a discussion of these debates, see Collins (1998).

53. These latter terms originated in Spike Lee's 1988 film *School Daze* and refer to the two teams' differing appearances. Here is an excerpt from the brief exchange: "IMUS: 'That's some rough girls from Rutgers. Man, they got tattoos and—'McGUIRK: 'Some hard-core hos, Tom.' IMUS: 'That's some nappy-headed hos there. I'm gonna tell you that now, man, that's some—woo. And the girls from Tennessee, they all look cute, you know, so, like—kinda like—I don't know.' McGUIRK: 'A Spike Lee thing.' IMUS: 'Yeah.' McGUIRK: 'The Jigaboos and the Wannabes that movie that he had.'" For some of the transcript, as well as other remarks Imus has made in the past, see "Imus Called Women's Basketball Team 'Nappy-Headed Hos.'" (2007). Retrieved September 27, 2008, from http://media matters.org/items/200704040011.

54. Richards made several public apologies for his remarks, explaining that he was trying to defuse heckling by being even more outrageous, but that it had backfired. Kyle Doss, one of the members of the group that Richards had addressed, gave his version to CNN of the events that transpired prior to the cell phone video. He said that they had arrived in the middle of the performance and that "I guess we were being a little loud, because there was twenty of us ordering drinks. And Richards said,

'Look at the stupid Mexicans and blacks being loud up there.'" Richards then continued with his routine. Doss added, "And, then, after a while, I told him, my friend doesn't think you're funny," which triggered Richards' outburst. *Michael Richards.* (n.d.). Retrieved September 25, 2008, from http://en.wikipedia.org/wiki/Michael_richards. *The Situation Room.* (November 22, 2006). Retrieved October 9, 2008, from http://transcripts. cnn.com/TRANSCRIPTS/0611/22/sitroom.03.html.

55. Other examples from popular culture illustrate this point. For example, Bill O'Reilly took a call from a listener who stated that, according to "a friend who had knowledge of her," Michelle Obama "'is a very angry—' her word was 'militant' woman." O'Reilly later stated, "I don't want to go on a lynching party against Michelle Obama unless there's evidence, hard facts, that say this is how the woman really feels. If that's how she really feels— that America is a bad country or a flawed nation, whatever—then that's legit. We'll track it down." Bill O'Reilly: "I Don't Want to Go on a Lynching Party Against Michelle Obama Unless There's Evidence" (February 20, 2008). Retrieved September 25, 2008, from http://www.huffington post.com/2008/02/20/bill-oreilly-i-dont-w_n_87616.html.

56. (Bonilla-Silva 2003).

57. For an analysis that uses *The Cosby Show* to illustrate the emergence of color-blind ideology, see Jhally and Lewis (1992).

58. The myth of color blindness allows whites to imagine that they do not support racism because they don't hate African Americans and may even love and admire African American individuals. *The Cosby Show* in the 1980s ushered in a period of socially black respectability by depicting the normal life of the Huxtables, who were married professionals, rich, home-owning, and...well...black! A similar early-twenty-first-century version of these relations inflected through hip hop culture has markedly different content but serves the same purpose. Just as many middle-class whites could identify with the Cosbys, many middle-class young white adults can identify with rap and hip hop culture. Despite the numbers of genuinely supportive whites in both groups, one must ask, exactly what is the point of identification? The Cosbys were a fictional family created during a time of racial integration that helped assuage white fears of black people (they became honorary whites who were safely black through black-inflected markers of jazz and wall art). In a similar fashion,

white American youth driving fancy cars in suburbia with rap boom-
ing from mega-speakers may identify with black urban youth, but exactly
what is being imagined? For an extended argument of these issues, see
Greg Tate's *Everything but the Burden* (Tate 2003).

59. These social scripts resemble the roles of traditional social science. The
terms are similar but not the same. The term *role* suggests that one is
given a gender role or a race role that one simply acts out. In contrast,
the term *social script* gives greater space for how one plays the script or
whether one keeps to the script at all. One accepts roles and plays with
social scripts. For an introduction to the dramaturgical ideas expressed
here, see Irving Goffman's classic work, *The Presentation of Self in Everyday Life* (Goffman 1959). See also my discussion of filters and frameworks
in chapter 3. *Filters* and *frameworks* are more nuanced terms describing
elements of social scripts.

60. Lisa Jones, the biracial child of a white mother and an African American
father, describes how her mother became more politically active about
race when she saw the type of discrimination facing her children (Jones
1994).

3. WOULD YOU KNOW IT IF YOU SAW IT?

1. The *Washington Post* covered both of these events. For a story on the
Obama school decision, see "Obama Girls Will Go to Sidwell Friends:
Elite Primary School Is 'Best Fit' for Next First Family," *Washington Post,*
November 22, 2008, Style, pp. C1 and C8. For the follow-up story on
Anacostia High School, see "Rhee Seeks New Way to Avert Violence:
Anacostia High Fight Injured 5," *Washington Post*, November 21, 2008,
Metro, pp. B1 and B5.

2. The kind of binary thinking of the exclusion/inclusion framework can
be used to uphold either the policies of assimilation or multiculturalism discussed in chapter 1. For assimilation, the terms of inclusion require erasing differences. For multiculturalism, the terms of inclusion
require reworking assimilation's norms to have multiple standards. The
construct of *mestizaje* is not so easily positioned. How would *mestizaje* be
positioned within this exclusion/inclusion binary?

3. (Tatum 2007; Boger and Orfield 2005).

4. I am arguing here neither for nor against racial integration. Rather, I suggest a pragmatic approach to imagining resistance across a variety of school settings. People working with poor facilities and underprepared students can do much. For example, parents, teachers, and administrators in Southern schools under racial segregation practiced resistance to racism by setting high standards for African American children and providing them with as many opportunities to achieve those standards as was possible within the confines of segregated school systems. Yet this very type of school has been identified as the problem to be abolished. For a discussion of these issues, see Morris and Morris (2002).

5. As this example suggests, color-blind racism is not a stand-alone system —it often is bundled with similar gender-neutral policies and individualistic policies for poor students. I am thinking here of the reluctance to institute social policies that acknowledge social class differences in the U.S. context. There is much more willingness to help individual kids from poor backgrounds than to help poor people as a population. This applies from everything to social welfare policies to educational policy.

6. It also can be applied to other forms of social inequality (for example, sexism, class exploitation, heterosexism, and ethnic conflict), as well as intersections among these various systems of power.

7. I rely heavily on examples that concern African American students and public education, not because I think that African Americans' experiences are superior to those of other groups, but for three reasons: (1) in addition to indigenous peoples, African Americans have been at the center of issues of race and educational equity for several hundred years; (2) I have spent the vast majority of my career teaching African American students and researching African American issues and am therefore most familiar with this population and its issues; and (3) I have spent the bulk of my educational experiences, as a student, as a teacher, and as a scholar, in public institutions.

8. Dead Prez. "They Schools." Dead Prez is a two-man underground hip hop group known for its politicized, pan-Africanist lyrics and confrontational style. Composed of rappers stic.man and M-1, Dead Prez debuted in 2000 with their first album, *Let's Get Free* (Loud Records), from which "They Schools" comes. Scholars have shown an increasing interest in the effects of street culture on inner-city kids. For an analysis of the effects of street culture on schooling, see Dance (2002).

9. For a discussion of global youth, race, and social problems, see Green (2001).

10. Some readers may note the parallel to Virginia Woolf's famous essay about women writers, "A Room of One's Own."

11. In her novel *What Looks Like Crazy on an Ordinary Day*, Pearl Cleage recounts a similar use of space (Cleage 1997). Also, the process that Maya used illustrates sociologist C. Wright Mills's advice that we develop a sociological imagination by using our personal troubles to think through larger social issues (Mills 2000).

12. (Freire 1970).

13. Lecture-based classrooms and those organized around adversarial debate have been recently joined, in higher education much more so than in K–12 education, by the "different voices" model of people engaged in polite, harmonious conversation. This approach appears to be an improvement, yet in actuality it often fosters an equally unsatisfying classroom climate. This weak version of multiculturalism implies that all voices are equal, that there is a polite way to discuss differences.

14. I discuss this theme of empathy in greater depth in my earlier work. See Collins (1989).

15. (Walker 1983, p. 5).

16. (Fordham 1996).

17. For example, see Jablon, Robert. "School Walkouts Continue in California to Protest Immigration Law," *San Francisco Chronicle*, March 27, 2006. http://www.sfgate.com/cgi-bin/article.cfi?f=/n/a2006/03/27/state/no 84303S10.DTL/.

18. Power relations are often organized through variations of gender, race, and class that play out via these mechanisms of surveillance. Thus, socially black men should not stare at white women because race grants white women protection from black men's stares.

19. These ideas reflect the work of Michel Foucault (Foucault 1979).

20. (Carter 2005).

21. For an introduction to African American women's intellectual and political traditions, see the discussion of visionary pragmatism in the Afterword. Also see Collins (1998).

22. I'm thinking here of the dangers that face individuals who use testimonial traditions in Latin American societies. See, for example, Nobel Peace Prize winner Rigoberta Menchu's autobiography of political activism in Guatemala (Menchu et al. 1984).

23. An interesting aside—blogs deploy a similar testimonial practice, but they use Internet technology where anonymity provides privacy, even in a highly public space of mediated communities.

24. This is also a major premise of black feminist thought: the value of self-definition and self-determination. For a discussion of these themes, see Collins (2000).

25. In chapter 4, I develop this argument by examining the placement of African American youth in contemporary mass media in an increasingly interdependent black culture and sex-work industries.

26. I discuss these trends in greater length in chapter 4.

27. One important way to practice resistance in the cultural domain is what I'm doing in this book—namely, unmasking the fallacies of color blindness itself. To recap some of the main ideas that I have developed here about the myth of color blindness: When you see color, or when you claim you're seeing color, you are creating race and racism; and some people would say that you're being a racist. It's forbidden to see color, to talk about color, and to talk about color in negative or stereotypical ways in the public sphere. As a result, our speech has to be carefully measured in public institutions when we talk about race. This climate puts schools in a real bind—they should be teaching students to live in an imagined color-blind society and do so without talking about the painful, difficult current racial issues.

28. For example, Tricia Rose examines the social conditions within New York City that led to the creation of hip hop and argues that because African American youth had been written off by city schools and neighborhoods, they took to the streets, creating a vibrant hip hop culture of breaking, DJ-ing, graffiti art, and rap (Rose 1994). Yvonne Bynoe takes a similar position and encourages African American youth to go beyond the trappings of rap music itself and to begin to use the elements of hip hop to build new institutions (Bynoe 2004).

29. I develop these ideas more fully in chapter 4. As I suggested in my analysis of African American youth and popular culture, developing media literacy for poor and working-class youth in particular requires, at minimum, a careful comparison of one's own lived experiences with social injustice and media representations of those experiences. This critical process goes beyond simple coding of accuracy and/or a moral value of

"positive" or "negative" images. Rather, critical education for media literacy requires an analysis of how global media operate and how one is placed within these social conditions.

30. When it comes to race, using filters in everyday life resembles the process of racial profiling. Recall the story in chapter 2 of my white male colleague who had difficulty seeing me. In small-group, university-based settings (such as faculty meetings and social functions), he had no problems talking with me. Yet whenever I passed him in public spaces that were outside the college (or even on college grounds, but not in the formal school settings in which I worked with him), he looked right through me. I remained unseen by my white male colleague unless I was in a specific social context that gave him cues as to whether to see me at all. He seemingly could not see me because he used the filter of how he should treat African American women in public spaces as a shortcut for deciding whom he should see and how he should respond when he does see them.

31. (Goffman 1974).

32. The following section illustrates a few pedagogical techniques for developing media literacy. For additional ideas, see the Web sites of organizations that are dedicated to media literacy, such as the Media Literacy Online Project (http://interact.uoregon.edu/medialit/mlr/home/). For a site with concrete approaches and tools to media literacy, see the Center for Media Literacy (http://www.medialit.org/).

33. Here, I am using the actual racial categories used by the South African government. For a general description of these categories, see Fredrickson (2001).

34. Readers who attended the lectures may recall that I demonstrated a similar exercise using contemporary images of African American women. I projected a PowerPoint slide with four different images of women but with no text. I asked the audience to provide a title and some text that would explain what they saw. In the next slide, I added another image and asked how their titles and text might need revision with this additional image. I also shared information about how African American women are sexualized within mass media as shown by a simple Google search for the term *black girls*. I could not develop the several steps in this process of matching images to scripts to dominant frameworks on a given topic, but the exercise was suggestive.

35. For example, see the Center for Media Literacy (http://www.medialit
.org/).

36. This exercise was inspired by Sylvia Ashton-Warner's 1963 book *Teacher*,
in which she describes teaching Maori kids to read through the process
of helping them write their own books. Teachers felt that colonial education was so culturally biased that Maori kids needed to see themselves.

37. *Tsotsi*, directed by Gavin Hood and distributed by Miramax Films
(2005).

38. See, for example, the discussion of advanced capitalism and the media
in chapter 4.

39. (Martin and Robinson 2007; Metcalf 2007).

40. Many grassroots organizations make extensive use of media for political
organizing. I found this Washington, D.C., group to be particularly interesting. Inspired by the intellectual energies of the 2002 inaugural Words
Beats & Life (WBL) Hip-Hop Conference at the University of Maryland in College Park, the *WBL Journal* initially came to life as a venue
through which the contributions of hip hop culture could be explored
within higher education. The first issue of the *Journal* was the result of
a call for submissions that secured contributions from notable scholar
Mark Anthony Neal and internationally known spoken-word artist jes-
sica Care moore.

41. Compare this with the discussion of Nelly's entrepreneurial model, Pimp
Juice—metaphor and product—in chapter 4.

42. (Carson and Shepard 2002, p. 85).

43. This quote is from "A Talk to Teachers," in Baldwin (1985).

44. On the other hand, there is a counterargument that African American
teachers should teach in white districts because racial segregation leaves
privileged white kids adrift as well. Many of these kids have traveled and
have seen global elites of color, and if anything, they're being prepared
to live in the color-blind society. In some ways it might be better for a kid
to be in an all-white environment and have to come to terms with his or
her own limitations by analyzing the social cues of this setting than to be
helped along and coddled from one multicultural situation to the next.

45. I'm thinking of the paradox-of-choice model, which suggests that too
much choice can be just as debilitating as having too little of it. This
idea foreshadows the consumerism discussion in chapter 4.

4. SOMEBODY'S WATCHING YOU

1. MSNBC conducted this interview with Nelly as an up-and-coming hip hop entrepreneur (http://www.msnbc.msn.com/id/6011814; accessed September 27, 2008).

2. Philosopher Michel Foucault argues this very point in *Discipline & Punish: The Birth of the Prison.* According to Foucault, modern-day discipline and punishment is not only about the use of coercive force against lawbreakers, it is also about establishing a system of surveillance to make all citizens feel as though they are being watched and in turn monitor their own behavior. This concept, which he terms *panopticism*, has infiltrated society to the point that it is built into our modern-day perception of normalcy (Foucault 1979).

3. The American public is often depicted in a similar fashion—namely, as passive consumers of a government that increasingly uses the manipulation of mass media as a site of governing. See Max Horkheimer and Theodor W. Adorno's "The Culture Industry: Enlightenment as Mass Deception," in *Dialectic of Enlightenment* (Horkheimer and Adorno 1972)

4. I would argue that the media plays an important role in educating African American youth about their place in society. In chapters 2 and 3, I introduced the domains-of-power framework—the structural, the disciplinary, and the interpersonal domains. In this chapter, I emphasize the cultural domain; namely, how the media manufactures the pimp as the image of African American manhood and the "ho" as the image of African American womanhood. I suggest that these images help justify intersecting inequalities of class, race, gender, and sexuality.

5. In the words of Grace Palladino, "[T]eenagers are now riding the crest of a demographic wave that promises big business for years to come. . . . No matter what we profess to believe about teenagers . . . we tend to value them most as consumers" (Palladino 1996, xi). Teens are a great consumer market, and different segments of the teen market desire "black" cultural products for varying reasons. For example, white teens may be interested in black culture because it allows them to oppose their parents. In contrast, African American teens see consuming black culture as a way to reinforce their connection to African American culture.

6. This argument is not specific to issues of race or to socially black populations. In her classic work *The Second Sex*, Simone de Beauvoir argued
that women were not born but rather were made by their respective societies (de Beauvoir 1989).

7. The *beurre* youth of France illustrate the fluid form that social blackness can assume. This youth population typically consists of second-
generation Arab youth of north African decent. While these youth
are most certainly of "African descent," in Western treatments of the
African continent, the region south of the Sahara is typically depicted
as the "true" space of African descent, while populations of northern
Africa tend to get cast as less "authentically African" than their southern neighbors. Adding another layer of complexity, such youth are often
Muslim, a religious/ethnic category that renders this population superior on the African continent yet secondary within France itself. For an
analysis of the status of French youth in this socially black category, see
Begag (2007).

8. In some cases, groups with a Caucasian phenotype can be rendered
socially black via their political and economic status, for example, the
Kurdish population in Turkey. See Secor (2004).

9. (Tate 2003).

10. Another approach to conceptualizing this notion of social blackness is
to examine its obverse, namely, the category of whiteness and the Latin
American saying, "Money whitens." This small phrase captures the cor-
relation between race and poverty—the poorer you are, the more likely
you are to be treated as the black people of your given society. Conversely,
the richer you are, the more likely you are to be treated as an "honorary
white person." For discussions of the treatment of race in Latin American settings, see Winant (2001) and Fredrickson (2001). For an analysis
of color-blind racism in Brazil, see Twine (1998).

11. Note that the word *denigrates* means to cheapen, or blacken.

12. For discussions of how racial ideology has shaped contemporary policy,
see Lubiano (1992), Quadagno (1994), and Zucchino (1997).

13. See the discussion of social blackness in chapter 2.

14. Different segments of the American public have differential relationships to social blackness, some of which may be beneficial. For example,
social blackness may have some provocative links both to lived African

American culture as well as a commodified black culture. Part of the challenge with the ghettoization of black culture is that many young, middle-class African Americans buy into it because they perceive a commodified black culture as the route to authentic blackness. So they talk the talk, dress the dress, blast the music, get pulled over by the police, and give their parents anxiety because, even when they have so-called professional role models, many still aspire to have a pimp (or even "ho") persona. The idea of social blackness as a fluid category enables this population to imagine a black identity in much the same way that white teenagers might imagine a different form of social blackness for themselves.

15. (Wilson 1996).

16. These patterns can be explained by shifts in global advanced capitalism: The practices associated with advanced capitalism generate two areas of emphasis. One concerns how relations of production have been reshaped in a global context. New business practices, both in industrial and industrializing economies (for example, outsourcing, free trade zones, and mechanization; the increasing ability of multinational corporations to influence domestic labor policies and the concomitant effects on global labor markets and practices; and major domestic and transnational migrations), constitute distinctive features of globalization. This focus on production, on the effects of advanced capitalism on job markets, is one important dimension of globalization. Yet when it comes to youth, this overemphasis on production can obscure an equally fundamental effect of advanced capitalism. Thus, another area of emphasis concerns a renewed interest in relations of consumption. George Ritzer argues that societies are increasingly organized via the means of consumption, whereby the shift from production to consumption has catalyzed a parallel shift from the exploitation of workers to that of consumers. To ensure profitability, consumers could no longer be relied upon to decide on their own whether to consume, what to consume, in what proportions, and how much to spend (Ritzer 2005, p. 51).

17. Here I describe how African American men are dehumanized and treated as commodities, but these policies reach a heterogeneous population. Increasingly, poor and working-class African American women, Latinos and Latinas, poor whites, and immigrant populations are drawn

into the punishment industry. For a discussion of race and the punishment industry, see Davis (1997).

18. (Davis 1997).

19. This is an indication of Foucault's notion of the carceral society (Foucault 1979).

20. For a general discussion of black cultural commodification, see Stuart Hall's work on black popular culture (Morley and Chen 1996). See especially "What Is This 'Black' in Black Popular Culture?" (Hall 1992). Houston Baker's seminal work on blues is also useful here: "Blues, Ideology, and Afro-American Literature: A Vernacular Theory" (Baker 1993). For a discussion of the history of blackface minstrelsy, see Lott (1993). For an analysis of contemporary commodified black culture, see Neal (2002).

21. (Palladino 1996, p. 152).

22. (Palladino 1996, p. 124).

23. For an extensive discussion of this situation, see Kelley (1994).

24. I choose not to capitalize the word *black* in the phrases *black culture industry* and *commodified black culture* because these terms reference the marketing of a corporate-based version of African American and African heritage cultures. I also want to distinguish my use from that of Cashmore (Cashmore 1997), for whom "black" culture as an entity is a derivative product of white racism. As such, Cashmore sees no value in black culture. In contrast, I see a history of indigenous aesthetic and political forms of African American culture that, while they may be appropriated and commodified by corporate interests, in effect still speak to the lived experiences of African Americans. For works that approach contemporary black popular culture as a place where both trends are evident, see Rose (1994) and Perry (2004).

25. I develop a comprehensive analysis of these themes in *Black Sexual Politics* (Collins 2004); see especially chapters 1, 4, and 5.

26. I use the terms *representations, stereotypes,* and *controlling images* to refer to the depiction of people of African descent within Western scholarship and popular culture. Each term has a different history. Representations need not be stereotypical, and stereotypes need not function as controlling images. Of the three, controlling images are most closely tied to power relations of race, class, gender, and sexuality. For a discussion of controlling images, see Collins (2000, pp. 69–96).

27. In *Black Noise,* Tricia Rose discusses the dual nature of these sites of black popular culture that can function as spaces in which power is enacted *and* resisted (Rose 1994, p. 148).

28. My definition of the sex-work industry is expansive and is in line with emerging areas of research that approach sex work as a rapidly growing, global industry (Kempadoo and Doezema 1998). While he focuses especially on the sex-trafficking industry, Robert K. Schaeffer (2003) makes an argument linking the growing sex industry and globalization (including tourism). See Schaeffer (2003).

29. In essence, physical sexuality that is part of the human body can be commodified and sold, as can the actual bodies of people who provide sexual services. While the Western media may present pimps and prostitutes as the most visible and hegemonic images of commercial sex-work, the industry itself is much broader than these particular sex-work occupations.

30. Here I focus on race, gender, and age, although the industry also reflects inequalities of ethnicity, nation, and sexualities other than heterosexuality. For an analysis of these intersections, see Alexander (1997; 2005).

31. I realize that some may see my couching sex work in the context of individual choice as victim-blaming. Within the current neoliberal context, acknowledging individual choice seems to take away the structural forces of class, race, nation, and gender that are endemic to sex work. For a discussion of this point of view, *New York Times* columnist Nicholas Kristof has written extensively about sex work as modern-day slavery. For a recent example, see http://www.nytimes.com/2008/09/25/opinion/25kristof.html. Yet unionized sex workers argue that they engage in sex work as a matter of personal choice, and that they should be provided the rights and benefits that other categories of workers receive (Kempadoo and Doezema 1998). My intent here is to reject moral positions on sex work itself and to encourage readers to view sex work through both the individual-choice and structural-force approaches that are applied to political and economic arguments overall.

32. Cynthia Enloe's classic book *Bananas, Beaches & Bases: Making Feminist Sense of International Politics* discusses sex tourism, as well as prostitution and militarism (Enloe 2001). A 2006 ethnographic study by Alexandra K. Murphy and Sudhir Alladi Venkatesh, "Vice Careers: The Changing Contours of Sex Work in New York City," shows the movement of sex work from the street to indoor venues and identifies changes

in policies that catalyzed this move (http://www.sociology.columbia.edu/
pdf-files/murphyvenkarticle.pdf). Through ethnographic methods, Elizabeth Bernstein (2007) also documents the shifting organization of sex
work from the street to indoor venues.

33. I extrapolated my argument about a hierarchy of pimps from the growing body of research on the hierarchy of prostitutes, primarily female sex
workers. Popular culture can lead the way in shedding light on this issue via varying depictions of pimps that can be seen as class-stratified.
For example, the 2005 film *Hustle & Flow* (which won the Academy
Award for Best Original Song for Three 6 Mafia's "It's Hard out Here for
a Pimp") told the story of a street-level pimp who was trying to leave "the
life" behind and break into the music business. Cultural products such as
these point to a certain image of the pimp across class categories, but it
also can be reconfigured to shed light on class differences that influence
what it takes to be considered a successful pimp.

34. For a related application of the domains-of-power framework to education as an industry, see chapter 3.

35. The literature on the global sex work industry illuminates how to recast
ideas about sexuality. Feminist scholarship led the way in refocusing attention on the body itself as a site of objectification, commodification,
and exploitation. Rejecting biological notions of the body, this scholarship investigated how power relations of gender and sexuality operate by
writing cultural scripts onto women's bodies (Bordo 1993; Butler 1990).

36. Answering this question requires a gender analysis that includes both
women and men, but for the moment, I want to focus on women because
women's experiences give clear insight into the industry. For poor and
working-class women from socially black groups, good jobs are elusive
in both industrialized and developing countries. Under these circumstances, some women do not sell their bodily *labor* to produce a commodity, as is the case with some sex workers. Sex workers often exercise
considerable control over their conditions of employment, a fact that is
lost within moralistic arguments that see women primarily as victims
within pimp/prostitute interpersonal relations. At the same time, some
groups *are* victimized, primarily because they lack control over these jobs.
For a discussion of these issues, see Alexander (1997) and Kempadoo and
Doezema (1998). Here I focus on youth as a mark of disadvantage and

gender as a further disadvantage within youth (the sexual trafficking of girls). For a discussion of global sex work, see Wonders and Michalowski (2001).

37. See *Hip Hop America* by Nelson George (George 1998). George's book provides an early analysis of the political economy of hip hop. For a more nuanced elaboration of these ideas, see *That's the Joint! The Hip-Hop Studies Reader* (Forman and Neal 2004), particularly part VII, "I Used to Love H.E.R.: Hip Hop in/and the Culture Industries," which includes six essays on consumption, commodification, and capitalism.

38. Moreover, this commodified black sexuality remains linked to historical expressions of color-conscious racism that identified a hypersexuality as part of the essence of blackness and then profited from that identification. For further discussion on constructions of black hypersexuality that serve to legitimate racial domination, see my discussion of the controlling image of Jezebel, as well as my discussion of the sexualized predatory image of black men which historically served, in name, to protect white women and, in actuality, to justify the system of terrorism (such as lynching); these constructions of black hypersexuality continue to justify systems of domination today (Collins 2004, pp. 100–105).

39. The term *conspicuous consumption* describes behavior where people acquire material possessions so that they can show off before their friends and neighbors. A good deal of the ethos of hip hop, beginning in the 1990s, focuses on the conspicuous consumption of rap stars. By itself, conspicuous consumption can be benign. It becomes problematic when people assume excessive debt to sustain lifestyles of excessive consumption. The term certainly fits today, but it originates in Thorstein Veblen's *The Theory of the Leisure Class*, in which he introduces this term to describe similar conditions a century ago (Veblen 1998).

40. I am not thinking exclusively of a Civil Rights generation of youth as the "previous generation" of talented black youth, but I would also include early rappers who touted their lyrical abilities (that is, gifted abilities) as their cultural product. For discussions of generational differences in culture and politics written by members of the hip hop generation, see Kitwana (2002), Bynoe (2004), Connery (2008), and Goff (2008).

41. For an analysis of the jezebel, see Collins (2004, pp. 119–148). In essence, representations of African American women as mules, mammies, ma-

triarchs, and jezebels have morphed into a proliferation of sexual scripts within hip hop culture. Much has been written on the content of black women's representations within contemporary popular culture. Some argue that black girls confront sexual scripts such as divas, gold diggers, freaks, dykes, and gangsta bitches, all of which pivot on issues of sexuality, materialism, and submission to male authority (Stephens and Phillips 2003). For a discussion that extends this focus on representations to the involvement of young black women in various forms of sex work (for example, video vixens, pole dancers, and so on), see Sharpley-Whiting (2007).

42. (Kempadoo and Doezema 1998).

43. (Sharpley-Whiting 2007).

44. Many scholars have documented the inadequacy of welfare benefits and the need for women to find other means to supplement income. For example, in *Making Ends Meet: How Single Mothers Survive Welfare and Low-Wage Work* (Edin and Lein 1997), the authors' interviews with 379 low-income single mothers illustrate the myriad of ways in which women receiving welfare benefits found it necessary to devise creative strategies for caregiving and supplemental income support to make ends meet.

45. (Sack 2001). For a comprehensive analysis of the ideas outlined here, see Sharpe's (2005) study of African American women, sex, and crack cocaine.

46. For example, practices in the Mississippi Delta and across the rural South illustrate this situation. Between 1990 and 2000, Southern states with large African American populations experienced a dramatic increase in HIV infections among African American women. In Mississippi, 28.5 percent of those reporting new HIV infections in 2000 were Black American women, up from 13 percent in 1990. In Alabama, the number rose to 31 percent from 13 percent, whereas in North Carolina, it rose to 27 percent from 18 percent (Sack 2001). Most of the women contracted HIV through heterosexual contact, and most found out that they were HIV-positive when they became pregnant. The women took risks that may at first seem nonsensical.

47. Angela Davis and Hazel Carby argue that after the disappointment of emancipation, sexuality was one of the few areas of life where African American women in the 1920s felt like they had any control (Davis

1998; Carby 1986). In contrast to this work, Sharpe (2005) argues that the drug industry provides survival, but with far less of a sense of sexual freedom.

48. (Collins 2004, pp. 224–32).

49. (Luttrell 2003).

50. The black male body in prison resembles the sexualized, socially black male body in hip hop—this is certainly the case for African American and Latino men alike. The exploitation of socially black male bodies in hip hop and its connection to the prisoner's body is not insignificant; both sets of commodified bodies serve as consumers and exploited laborers for particular industries within advanced capitalism. However, a clear distinction can be made here between the exploitation of male and female bodies in hip hop—while the sexualized male body almost always belongs to the rapper, the sexualized female body is most often working in the background. Here, numbers matter—the typical formula is one sexualized black male body that has a voice and identity among a group of silenced, anonymous, and often fragmented sexualized black female bodies. I am indebted to Valerie Chepp for this insight.

51. For further discussion on the origin of sagging pants in prison culture, see http://www.nytimes.com/2007/08/30/fashion/30baggy.html and http://www.snopes.com/risque/homosex/sagging.asp.

52. For a discussion of African American men as ethnic entrepreneurs, see Basu and Werbner (2001). For a critique of black hip hop entrepreneurs as hustlers, see Smith (2003) and Neal (2004), among others.

53. http://www.forbes.com/2008/08/15/music-media-hiphop-biz-media-cz _zog_0818cashkings.html.

54. I am indebted to Valerie Chepp for this insight.

55. http://www.vibe.com/news/news_headlines/2005/07/nelly_pjtight _theme_song/.

56. For example, I spent my childhood as a working-class, African American girl in a country that classified people using categories of class, race, and gender and saw those categories as important. My place as a young African American girl was very different than it would have been had I been born into wealth, or had I been classified as white, or had I been male, and it would have been still more different had all of the above happened. A critical education that enabled me to see how the structures of

society, its disciplinary practices, its cultural ideas, and my own behavior and those of people in my everyday life were all affected by my classification enabled me to see my place. Becoming critical of my place meant that I did not have to accept it passively.

57. Ironically, creative people are often stigmatized for thinking the unpopular and doing the unthinkable. But in the act of practicing resistance, criticism and creativity nurture one another

58. I conceptualized racism as a system of power that has four domains. They are (1) a structural domain of power that shows how racial practices are organized through social institutions such as banks, insurance companies, police departments, the real estate industry, schools, stores, restaurants, hospitals, and governmental agencies; (2) an ideological domain of power that both manufactures the ideas that justify racial hierarchy and catalyzes the anti-racist knowledge that challenges it; (3) a disciplinary domain of power where people use the rules and regulations of everyday life to uphold and contest racial hierarchy; and (4) an interpersonal domain of power that shapes race relations among individuals in everyday life. This framework is useful in positioning an actual social group; for example, the way poor and working-class African American youth are treated. But it also serves as a useful way of mapping how social blackness itself operates from one society to the next.

59. In a nutshell, socially black youth, broadly defined, bear the brunt of advanced capitalism (global consumption) and global racism (as organized through relations of social blackness) as intersecting systems of power and the places to which they are being assigned may provide benefit to some, but those benefits rely on the continued disadvantage of many.

60. Before we become too critical of African American teenagers, one need only look at the 2006–08 mortgage crisis to get an idea of how these values pervade American culture overall.

61. For example, the blues reflected the pain of the Mississippi Delta, gospel the ethical and political strivings of a spiritual population, jazz the syncretic nature of African American life that spoke to the rights of African Americans to be here, and rhythm and blues the hope of the Civil Rights generation. See Porter (2001) and Neal (2002).

62. For example, the owners of Pimp Juice aim to bring it to new consumer markets. Here, the images of young, black, and sexy African Americans

(consuming Pimp Juice) expand the consumer market for the beverage. In essence, Pimp Juice is part of a global marketing campaign to expand into new youth markets, using imagined ideas of a sexualized, commodified black culture (the intense version represented by pimp juice, the metaphor) for profit. Here we see the marketing of images of commodified sexuality and social blackness to stimulate new consumer markets. In other words, the success of the Pimp Juice beverage relies upon selling a commodified, sexualized blackness in the global marketplace. One example of this was the Pimp Juice launch party in the Netherlands. One can see the fusion of the product, the image of Nelly, and Nelly the individual attending the launch party holding a can of Pimp Juice. One can only imagine that the song must have been playing in the background as well.

63. (Bynoe 2004, p. 152). I am indebted to Michelle Burstion for this analysis.

64. For information on the connection between Sumner Redstone and George W. Bush, see http://www.dailykos.com/story/2007/9/21/215027/970.

65. A good example here is Bill O'Reilly pressuring Pepsi to drop Ludacris from his contract with them (http://www.ew.com/ew/article/0,,345308,00.html).

66. I am indebted to Michelle Burstion for making this connection.

67. (Alexander 1997; Emeagwali 1995).

68. Access is important, but here, I focus on how youth use the access that is available. Many studies identify the digital divide as an important factor in limiting access to new mass-media technologies. See, for example, Martin and Robinson (2007). Martin and Robinson test the hypothesis that the diffusion of the Internet is becoming more polarized by family income in the United States and that the odds of access increased most rapidly for individuals at the highest family income levels and most slowly for individuals with the lowest income levels. These differential rates of diffusion, combined with an overall slowing of the diffusion of Internet use since 2001, suggest that it may be 2009 before a majority of the lowest-income Americans use the Internet. The slow diffusion among low-income groups is not apparent in comparable assessments of Internet diffusion in European countries. For a brief article that illus-

trates some key statistics on the digital divide among youth according to race and income, see Metcalf (2007).

69. http://notherapedocumentary.org.

70. Coined in 1990 by Aishah, the term *AfroLez femcentric* defines the culturally conscious role of black women who identify as Afrocentric, lesbian, and feminist. For three years, she coproduced two monthly public television programs for a PBS affiliate in Philadelphia. Her internationally acclaimed short videos "Silence . . . Broken" and "In My Father's House," which were produced in 1993 and 1996, explore the issues of race, gender, homophobia, rape, and misogyny. Since its official release in 2006, *No!* has been screened and distributed to racially and ethnically diverse audiences at film festivals, community centers, colleges and universities, high schools, correctional facilities, rape crisis centers, battered women's shelters, and conferences throughout the United States and in Italy, Spain, Hungary, Croatia, Rwanda, Kenya, Nepal, South Africa, Jordan, Burkina Faso, Peru, and Mexico. Further information can be found at http://notherapedocumentary.org.

AFTERWORD: THE WAY FORWARD

1. (Walker 1979, p. 165).

2. For biographical information on Hurston and a sample of her writings, see Walker (1979).

3. For an example of this, see the discussion of social blackness in chapter 4, "Somebody's Watching You."

4. Here, I make a distinction between principles and ideology, theology, or dogma. Principles are core ideas that may be realized in one's lifetime but that will always be tested in each new social formation. For example, taking action against color-conscious racism fostered the noble ethos of color blindness. Yet the very principle of color blindness was tested through the emergence of color-blind racism, a seeming oxymoron. Unless one can imagine a world where all vestiges of a five-hundred-year-old system of global racism are eradicated, there will always be the need to take action against racism.

5. (Carson and Shepard 2002, pp. 84–85).

References

PREFACE

Carson, Clayborne, and Kris Shepard, eds. *A Call to Conscience: The Landmark Speeches of Dr. Martin Luther King, Jr.* New York: Warner Books, 2002.

I. WHAT DOES THE FLAG MEAN TO YOU?

Addams, Jane. *Democracy and Social Ethics.* Urbana: University of Illinois Press, 2002.

Berry, Mary F. *Black Resistance, White Law: A History of Constitutional Racism in America.* New York: Penguin Press, 1994.

Boger, John C., and Gary Orfield, eds. *School Resegregation: Must the South Turn Back?* Chapel Hill: University of North Carolina Press, 2005.

Brodkin, Karen. *How Jews Became White Folks and What That Says About Race in America.* New Brunswick, N.J.: Rutgers University Press, 2000.

Bynoe, Yvonne. *Stand and Deliver: Political Activism, Leadership, and Hip Hop Culture.* Brooklyn: Soft Skull Press, 2004.

Canclini, Néstor García. *Hybrid Cultures: Strategies for Entering and Leaving Modernity.* Minneapolis: University of Minnesota Press, 1995.

Collins, Patricia Hill. *Black Feminist Thought: Knowledge, Consciousness, and the Politics of Empowerment*. 2d ed. New York: Routledge, 2000.

Connery, Michael. *Youth to Power: How Today's Young Voters Are Building Tomorrow's Progressive Majority*. Brooklyn: Ig Publishing, 2008.

Cooper, Anna J. *A Voice from the South; By a Black Woman of the South*. New York: Oxford University Press, 1990 (orig. ed. 1892).

Dewey, John. *Democracy and Education*. Mineola, N.Y.: Dover Publications, 2004.

————. *The Public and Its Problems*. Athens: Ohio University Press, 1954.

Du Bois, W. E. B. *The Souls of Black Folk*. New York: Dodd, Mead, & Company, 1979.

Edin, Kathryn, and Laura Lein. *Making Ends Meet: How Single Mothers Survive Welfare and Low-Wage Work*. New York: Russell Sage Foundation, 1997.

Feigenbaum, H., J. Henig, and C. Hamnett. *Shrinking the State: The Political Underpinnings of Privatization*. New York: Cambridge University Press, 1998.

Freire, Paulo. *The Pedagogy of the Oppressed*. New York: Herder and Herder, 1970.

Glazer, Nathan, and Daniel Patrick Moynihan. *Beyond the Melting Pot: The Negroes, Puerto Ricans, Jews, Italians, and Irish of New York*. Cambridge, Mass.: MIT Press, 1968.

Glenn, Evelyn N. *Unequal Freedom: How Race and Gender Shaped American Citizenship and Labor*. Cambridge, Mass.: Harvard University Press, 2002.

Goff, Keli. *Party Crashing: How the Hip-Hop Generation Declared Political Independence*. New York: Basic Books, 2008.

Goldberg, David Theo. *Multiculturalism: A Critical Reader*. Cambridge, Mass.: Blackwell, 1995.

————. *Racist Culture: Philosophy and the Politics of Meaning*. Cambridge, Mass.: Blackwell, 1993.

Gordon, Linda. *Pitied But Not Entitled: Single Mothers and the History of Welfare*. Cambridge, Mass.: Harvard University Press, 1994.

Guglielmo, Jennifer, and Salvatore Salderno, eds. *Are Italians White? How Race Is Made in America*. New York: Routledge, 2003.

Guinier, Lani, and Gerald Torres. *The Miner's Canary: Enlisting Race, Resis-

ting Power, Transforming Democracy. Cambridge. Mass.: Harvard University Press, 2002.

Haynes, Jo. "World Music and the Search for Difference." *Ethnicities* 5 (3) September 2005: pp. 365–85.

Ignatiev, Noel. *How the Irish Became White*. New York: Routledge, 2005.

Katz, Michael B. *The Undeserving Poor: From the War on Poverty to the War on Welfare*. New York: Pantheon, 1989.

Kitwana, Bakari. *The Hip Hop Generation: Young Blacks and the Crisis in African-American Culture*. New York: Basic Books, 2002.

Leipold, Anita. *Syncretism in Religion: A Reader*. New York: Routledge, 2004.

Lubiano, Wahneema. "Black Ladies, Welfare Queens, and State Minstrels: Ideological War by Narrative Means." In *Race-Ing Justice, En-Gendering Power*. Toni Morrison, ed. New York: Pantheon Books, 1992: pp. 323–63.

Marable, Manning. "Beyond Identity Politics: Towards a Liberation Theory for Multicultural Democracy." *Race and Class*, 1993, 35(1): pp. 113–30.

———. *The Great Wells of Democracy: The Meaning of Race in American Life*. New York: BasicCivitas, 2002.

Miller, Marilyn Grace. *The Rise and Fall of the Cosmic Race: The Cult of Mestizaje in Latin America*. Austin: University of Austin Press, 2004.

Mills, C. W. *The Power Elite*. New York: Oxford University Press, 2000a.

———. *The Sociological Imagination*. New York: Oxford University Press, 2000b.

Neubeck, Kenneth J., and Noel A. Cazenave. *Welfare Racism: Playing the Race Card Against America's Poor*. New York: Routledge, 2001.

Perry, Theresa. *The Real Ebonics Debate*. Boston: Beacon Press, 1998.

Quadagno, Jill. *The Color of Welfare: How Racism Undermined the War on Poverty*. New York: Oxford University Press, 1994.

Ritzer, George. *The McDonaldization of Society*. Thousand Oaks, Calif.: Pine Forge Press, 2004.

Scott, James C. *Domination and the Arts of Resistance: The Hidden Transcripts*. New Haven, Conn.: Yale University Press, 1990.

———. *Weapons of the Weak: Everyday Forms of Peasant Resistance*. New Haven, Conn.: Yale University Press, 1985.

Seidman, Steven. *Contested Knowledge: Social Theory Today*. 3d ed. Malden, Mass.: Blackwell Publishing, 2004.

Smith, Dorothy E. *The Conceptual Practices of Power: A Feminist Sociology of Knowledge*. Boston: Northeastern University Press, 1990.

Takaki, Ronald T. *A Different Mirror: A History of Multicultural America*. Boston: Little, Brown, 1993.

Tatum, Beverly D. *Can We Talk About Race? And Other Conversations in an Era of School Resegregation*. Boston: Beacon Press, 2007.

Ward, Geoffrey C. and Ken Burns. *Jazz: A History of America's Music*. New York: Knopf, 2002.

West, Cornel. *Democracy Matters: Winning the Fight Against Imperialism*. New York: Penguin, 2004.

Westbrook, Robert B. "Pragmatism and Democracy: Reconstructing the Logic of John Dewey's Faith." In *The Revival of Pragmatism: New Essays on Social Thought, Law, and Culture*. Morris Dickstein, ed. Durham, N.C.: Duke University Press, 1998, pp. 128–40.

Williams, Patricia J. *The Rooster's Egg*. Cambridge, Mass.: Harvard University Press, 1995.

Woodson, Carter G. *The Miseducation of the Negro*. Washington, D.C.: Associated Publishers, 1969 (orig. ed. 1933).

Young, Robert J. C. *Colonial Desire: Hybridity in Theory, Culture, and Race*. New York: Routledge, 1995.

Zucchino, David. *The Myth of the Welfare Queen*. New York: Scribner, 1997.

2. SOCIAL BLACKNESS, HONORARY WHITENESS, AND ALL POINTS IN BETWEEN

Barsamian, David, and Edward W. Said. *Culture and Resistance: Conversations with Edward W. Said*. Cambridge, Mass.: South End Press, 2003.

Bell, Derrick. "Brown v. Board of Education and the Interest Convergence Dilemma." *Harvard Law Review*, January 1980, 93(518): pp. 518–30.

———. *Silent Covenants: Brown v. Board of Education and the Unfulfilled Hopes for Racial Reform*. New York: Oxford University Press, 2004.

Bonilla-Silva, Eduardo. *Racism Without Racists: Color-blind Racism and the Persistence of Racial Inequality in the United States*. Lantham, Md.: Rowman & Littlefield, 2003.

———. *White Supremacy and Racism in the Post–Civil Rights Era*. Boulder, Colo.: Lynne Rienner Publishers, 2001.

Brown, Michael K., Martin Carnoy, Elliott Currie, Troy Duster, David E.

Oppenheimer, Marjorie M. Shultz, and David Wellman. *Whitewashing Race: The Myth of a Color-Blind Society*. Berkeley: University of California Press, 2003.

Bynoe, Yvonne. *Stand and Deliver: Political Activism, Leadership, and Hip Hop Culture*. Brooklyn: Soft Skull Press, 2004.

Carson, Clayborne, and Kris Shepard, eds. *A Call to Conscience: The Landmark Speeches of Dr. Martin Luther King, Jr*. New York: Warner Books, 2002.

Children's Defense Fund. *America's Cradle to Prison Pipeline Summary Report*. Washington, D.C., 2007

Cole, Elizabeth, and Safiya Oman. "Race, Class, and the Dilemmas of Upward Class Mobility for African Americans." *Journal of Social Issues*, December 2003, 59(4):785.

Collins, Patricia Hill. *Black Feminist Thought: Knowledge, Consciousness, and the Politics of Empowerment*. 2d ed. New York: Routledge, 2000.

——. *Black Sexual Politics: African Americans, Gender, and the New Racism*. New York: Routledge, 2004.

——. *Fighting Words: Black Women and the Search for Justice*. Minneapolis: University of Minnesota Press, 1998.

——. "Freedom Now! 1968 as a Turning Point in Black Student Activism." In *1968 in Retrospect: History, Theory, Politics*. Gurminder K. Bhambra and Ipek Demir, eds. London: Conference Proceedings, in press.

Collins, Randall. *Four Sociological Traditions*. New York: Oxford University Press, 1994.

Connery, Michael. *Youth to Power: How Today's Young Voters Are Building Tomorrow's Progressive Majority*. Brooklyn: Ig Publishing, 2008.

Daniels, Jessie. *White Lies: Race, Class, Gender and Sexuality in White Supremacist Discourse*. New York: Routledge, 1997.

Davis, Angela Y. "Race and Criminalization: Black Americans and the Punishment Industry." In *The House That Race Built: Black Americans, U.S. Terrain*. Wahneema Lubiano, ed. New York: Pantheon, 1997, pp. 264–79.

Dewey, John. *Democracy and Education*. Mineola, N.Y.: Dover Publications, 2004.

——. *The Public and Its Problems*. Athens, Ohio: Ohio University Press, 1954.

Do Nascimenta, Abdias, and Elisa L. Nascimento. "Dance of Deception: A Reading of Race Relations in Brazil." In *Beyond Racism: Race and Inequality in Brazil, South Africa, and the United States.* Charles V. Hamilton, Lynn Huntley, Neville Alexander, Antonio S.A. Guimaraes, and Wilmot James, eds. Boulder, Colo: Lynne Rienner Publishers, 2001, pp. 105–56.

Feagin, Joe R., and Melvin P. Sikes. *Living with Racism: The Black Middle-Class Experience.* Boston: Beacon Press, 1994.

Feigenbaum, H., J. Henig, and C. Hamnett. *Shrinking the State: The Political Underpinnings of Privatization.* New York: Cambridge University Press, 1998.

Ferber, Abby L. *White Man Falling: Race, Gender, and White Supremacy.* Lanham, Md.: Rowman and Littlefield, 1998.

Foucault, Michel. *Discipline and Punish: The Birth of the Prison.* New York: Vintage, 1979.

———. *Power/Knowledge: Selected Interviews and Other Writings, 1972–1977.* Colin Gordon, ed. New York: Pantheon, 1980.

Fredrickson, George M. "Race and Racism in Historical Perspective: Comparing the United States, South Africa, and Brazil." In *Beyond Racism: Race and Inequality in Brazil, South Africa, and the United States.* Charles V. Hamilton, Lynn Huntley, Neville Alexander, Antonio S.A. Guimaraes, and Wilmot James, eds. Boulder, Colo.: Lynne Rienner Publishers, 2001, pp. 1–26.

Goff, Keli. *Party Crashing: How the Hip-Hop Generation Declared Political Independence.* New York: Basic Books, 2008.

Goffman, Erving. *The Presentation of Self in Everyday Life.* Garden City, N.J.: Doubleday, 1959.

Goldberg, David T. *The Racial State.* Malden, Mass.: Blackwell Publishing, 2002.

Gramsci, Antonio. *Selections from the Prison Notebooks.* London: Lawrence and Wishart, 1971.

Guinier, Lani, and Gerald Torres. *The Miner's Canary: Enlisting Race, Resisting Power, Transforming Democracy.* Cambridge. Mass.: Harvard University Press, 2002.

Hernandez, Daisy, and Bushra Rehman, eds. *Colonize This! Young Women of Color on Today's Feminism.* New York: Seal Press, 2002.

Iceland, John, Daniel H. Weinberg, and Erika Steinmetz. *Racial and Ethnic*

Residential Segregation in the United States: 1980–2000. Washington, D.C.: U.S. Government Printing Office, 2002.

Jhally, Sut, and Justin Lewis. *Enlightened Racism.* Boulder, Colo.: Westview Press, 1992.

Jones, Lisa. *Bulletproof Diva: Tales of Race, Sex, and Hair.* New York: Doubleday, 1994.

Kitwana, Bakari. *The Hip Hop Generation: Young Blacks and the Crisis in African-American Culture.* New York: Basic Books, 2002.

Kozol, Jonathan. *Savage Inequalities: Children in America's Schools.* New York: HarperCollins, 1991.

Lacey, Karen. *Blue Chip Black: Race, Class, and Status in the New Black Middle Class.* Berkeley: University of California Press, 2007.

Massey, Douglas S., and Nancy A. Denton. *American Apartheid: Segregation and the Making of the Underclass.* Cambridge, Mass.: Harvard University Press, 1993.

Moss, Philip, and Chris Tilly. "'Soft' Skills and Race." *Work and Occupations,* 1996, 23:252–76.

Nelson, Jill. *Volunteer Slavery: My Authentic Negro Experience.* New York: Penguin, 1994.

Park, Robert E. *Race and Culture.* Glencoe, Ill.: The Free Press, 1950.

Patillo-McCoy, Mary. *Black Picket Fences: Privilege and Peril Among the Black Middle Class.* Chicago: University of Chicago Press, 1999.

Scott, James C. *Domination and the Arts of Resistance: The Hidden Transcripts.* New Haven, Conn.: Yale University Press, 1990.

———. *Weapons of the Weak: Everyday Forms of Peasant Resistance.* New Haven, Conn.: Yale University Press, 1985.

Shapiro, Thomas. *The Hidden Costs of Being African American.* New York: Oxford University Press, 2004.

Sharpley-Whiting, T. D. *Pimps Up, Ho's Down: Hip Hop's Hold on Young Black Women.* New York: New York University Press, 2007.

Smith, Dorothy E. *The Conceptual Practices of Power: A Feminist Sociology of Knowledge.* Boston: Northeastern University Press, 1990.

Steele, Shelby. "A Threat in the Air: How Stereotypes Affect Intellectual Identity and Performance." *American Psychologist,* 1990, 52:613–29.

Tate, Greg, ed. *Everything but the Burden: What White People Are Taking from Black Culture.* New York: Broadway Books, 2003.

Twine, France W. *Racism in a Racial Democracy: The Maintenance of White*

Supremacy in Brazil. New Brunswick, N.J.: Rutgers University Press, 1998.

Waçquant, Loic. "Deadly Symbiosis: When Ghetto and Prison Meet and Mesh." *Punishment and Society,* January 2001, 3(1):95–134.

Wilkes, R., and John Iceland. "Hypersegregation in the Twenty-first Century: An Update and Analysis." *Demography,* February 2001, 41(1): 23–36.

Williams, Patricia J. *The Rooster's Egg.* Cambridge, Mass.: Harvard University Press, 1995.

3. WOULD YOU KNOW IT IF YOU SAW IT?

Baldwin, James. *The Price of the Ticket: Collected Nonfiction 1948–1985.* New York: St. Martin's Press, 1985.

Boger, John C., and Gary Orfield, eds. *School Resegregation: Must the South Turn Back?* Chapel Hill: University of North Carolina Press, 2005.

Bynoe, Yvonne. *Stand and Deliver: Political Activism, Leadership, and Hip Hop Culture.* Brooklyn: Soft Skull Press, 2004.

Carson, Clayborne, and Kris Shepard, eds. *A Call to Conscience: The Landmark Speeches of Dr. Martin Luther King, Jr.* New York: Warner Books, 2002.

Carter, Prudence L. *Keepin' It Real: School Success Beyond Black and White.* New York: Oxford University Press, 2005.

Childress, Alice. *Like One of the Family: Conversations from a Domestic's Life.* Boston: Beacon Press, 1986.

Cleage, Pearl. *What Looks Like Crazy on an Ordinary Day.* New York: Avon Books, 1997.

Collins, Patricia Hill. *Black Feminist Thought: Knowledge, Consciousness, and the Politics of Empowerment.* 2d ed. New York: Routledge, 2000.

———. *Fighting Words: Black Women and the Search for Justice.* Minneapolis: University of Minnesota Press, 1998.

———. "Toward a New Vision: Race, Class and Gender As Categories of Analysis and Connection." *Workshop on Integrating Race and Gender into the College Curriculum,* Center for Research on Women. Memphis State University, 1989.

Dance, L. Janelle. *Tough Fronts: The Impact of Street Culture on Schooling.* New York: Routledge, 2002.

Fordham, Signithia. *Blacked Out: Dilemmas of Race, Identity, and Success at Capital High*. Chicago: University of Chicago Press, 1996.

Foucault, Michel. *Discipline and Punish: The Birth of the Prison*. New York: Vintage, 1979.

Fredrickson, George M. "Race and Racism in Historical Perspective: Comparing the United States, South Africa, and Brazil." In *Beyond Racism: Race and Inequality in Brazil, South Africa, and the United States*. Charles V. Hamilton, Lynn Huntley, Neville Alexander, Antonio S.A. Guimaraes, and Wilmot James, eds. Boulder, Colo.: Lynne Rienner Publishers, 2001, pp. 1–26.

Freire, Paulo. *The Pedagogy of the Oppressed*. New York: Herder and Herder, 1970.

Goffman, Erving. *Frame Analysis: An Essay on the Organization of Experience*. New York: Harper & Row, 1974.

Green, Charles. *Manufacturing Powerless in the Black Diaspora: Inner City Youth and the New Global Frontier*. Lanham, Md.: Rowman & Littlefield, 2001.

Martin, Steven, and John P. Robinson. "The Income Digital Divide: Trends and Predictions for Levels of Internet Use." *Social Problems*, February 2007, 54(1):1–22.

Menchu, Rigoberta, Elisabeth Burgos-Debray, and Ann Wright. *I, Rigoberta Menchu: An Indian Woman in Guatemala*. London: Verso, 1984.

Metcalf, DaVinci. "Reducing the Digital Divide." *American Libraries*, February 2007, 38(2).

Mills, C. W. *The Sociological Imagination*. New York: Oxford University Press, 2000.

Morris, Vivian Gunn, and Curtis L. Morris. *The Price They Paid: Desegregation in an African American Community*. New York: Teachers College Press, 2002.

Rollins, Judith. *Between Women: Domestics and Their Employers*. Philadelphia: Temple University Press, 1985.

Rose, Tricia. *Black Noise: Rap Music and Black Culture in Contemporary America*. Hanover, N.H.: Wesleyan University Press, 1994.

Tatum, Beverly D. *Can We Talk about Race? And Other Conversations in an Era of School Resegregation*. Boston: Beacon Press, 2007.

Walker, Alice. *In Search of Our Mother's Gardens*. New York: Harcourt Brace Jovanovich, 1983.

4. SOMEBODY'S WATCHING YOU

Alexander, M.J. "Erotic Autonomy as a Politics of Decolonization: An Anatomy of Feminist and State Practice in the Bahamas Tourist Industry." In *Feminist Genealogies, Colonial Legacies, Democratic Futures*. M.J. Alexander and Chandra T. Mohanty, eds. New York: Routledge, 1997, pp. 63–100.

———. "Imperial Desire/Sexual Utopias: White Gay Capital and Transnational Tourism." In *Pedagogies of Crossing: Meditations on Feminism, Sexual Politics, Memory, and the Sacred*. M. J. Alexander, ed. Durham, N.C.: Duke University Press, 2005, pp. 66–88.

Baker, Houston A. *Black Studies, Rap, and the Academy*. Chicago: University of Chicago Press, 1993.

Basu, Dipannita, and Pnina Werbner. "Bootstrap Capitalism and the Culture Industries: A Critique of Invidious Comparisons in the Study of Ethnic Entrepreneurship." *Ethnic and Racial Studies*, March 2001, 24(2):236–62.

De Beauvoir, Simone. *The Second Sex*. New York: Vintage Books, 1989 (orig. ed. 1949).

Begag, Azouz. *Ethnicity and Equality: France in the Balance*. Lincoln: University of Nebraska Press, 2007.

Bernstein, Elizabeth. *Temporarily Yours: Intimacy, Authenticity, and the Commerce of Sex*. Chicago: University of Chicago Press, 2007.

Bordo, Susan. *Unbearable Weight: Feminism, Western Culture, and the Body*. Berkeley: University of California Press, 1993.

Butler, Judith. *Gender Trouble: Feminism and the Subversion of Identity*. New York: Routledge, 1990.

Bynoe, Yvonne. *Stand and Deliver: Political Activism, Leadership, and Hip Hop Culture*. Brooklyn: Soft Skull Press, 2004.

Carby, Hazel. "It Just Be's Dat Way Sometime: The Sexual Politics of Women's Blues." *Radical America*, June/July 1986, 20(4): 9–22.

Cashmore, Ellis. *The Black Culture Industry*. New York: Routledge, 1997.

Collins, Patricia Hill. *Black Feminist Thought: Knowledge, Consciousness, and the Politics of Empowerment*. 2d ed. New York: Routledge, 2000.

———. *Black Sexual Politics: African Americans, Gender, and the New Racism*. New York: Routledge, 2000.

Davis, Angela Y. *Blues Legacies and Black Feminism: Gertrude "Ma" Rainey, Bessie Smith, and Billie Holiday*. New York: Vintage, 1998.

————. "Race and Criminalization: Black Americans and the Punishment Industry." In *The House That Race Built: Black Americans, U.S. Terrain.* Wahneema Lubiano, ed. New York: Pantheon, 1997, pp. 264–79.

Edin, Kathryn, and Laura Lein. *Making Ends Meet: How Single Mothers Survive Welfare and Low-Wage Work.* New York: Russell Sage Foundation, 1997.

Emeagwali, Gloria T., ed. *Women Pay the Price: Structural Adjustment in Africa and the Caribbean.* Trenton, N.J.: Africa World Press, 1995.

Enloe, Cynthia. *Bananas, Beaches, and Bases: Making Feminist Sense of International Politics.* Berkeley: University of California Press, 2001.

Forman, Murray, and Mark A. Neal, eds. *That's the Joint! The Hip-Hop Studies Reader.* New York: Routledge, 2004.

Foucault, Michel. *Discipline and Punish: The Birth of the Prison.* New York: Schocken, 1979.

Fredrickson, George M. "Race and Racism in Historical Perspective: Comparing the United States, South Africa, and Brazil." In *Beyond Racism: Race and Inequality in Brazil, South Africa, and the United States.* Charles V. Hamilton, Lynn Huntley, Neville Alexander, Antonio S.A. Guimaraes, and Wilmot James, eds. Boulder, Colo.: Lynne Rienner Publishers, 2001, pp. 1–26.

George, Nelson. *Hip Hop America.* New York: Penguin, 1998.

Gross, Daniel. "Dirty Work: What Are the Jobs Americans Won't Do?" Posted Friday, Jan. 12, 2007, on Slate.com (http://www.slate.com/id/2157483/).

Hall, Stuart. "What Is This 'Black' in Black Popular Culture?" In *Black Popular Culture.* Gina Dent, ed. Seattle: Bay Press, 1992, pp. 21–33.

Horkheimer, Max, and Theodor W. Adorno. "The Culture Industry: Enlightenment as Mass Deception." In *Dialectic of Enlightenment.* New York: Seabury, 1972 (orig. ed. 1944), pp. 120–176.

Kelley, Robin D. G. *Race Rebels: Culture, Politics, and the Black Working Class.* New York: Free Press, 1994.

Kempadoo, Kamala, and J. Doezema. *Global Sex Workers: Rights, Resistance, and Redefinition.* New York: Routledge, 1998.

Koppel, Niko. "Are Your Jeans Sagging? Go Directly to Jail." *New York Times.* Aug. 30, 2007. "Style" section, p. 1.

Kristof, Nicholas. "A Heroine from the Brothels." *New York Times.* September 24, 2008. "Opinion" section, p. 29.

Lott, Eric. *Love and Theft: Blackface Minstrelsy and the American Working Class*. New York: Oxford University Press, 1993.

Lubiano, Wahneema. "Black Ladies, Welfare Queens, and State Minstrels: Ideological War by Narrative Means." In *Race-Ing Justice, En-Gendering Power*. Toni Morrison, ed. New York: Pantheon Books, 1992, pp. 323–63.

Luttrell, Wendy. *Pregnant Bodies, Fertile Minds: Gender, Race, and the Schooling of Pregnant Teens*. New York: Routledge, 2003.

Martin, Steven, and John P. Robinson. "The Income Digital Divide: Trends and Predictions for Levels of Internet Use." *Social Problems*, February 2007, 54(1):1–22.

Metcalf, DaVinci. "Reducing the Digital Divide." *American Libraries*, February 2007, 38(2), p. 29.

Morley, David, and Kuan-Hsing Chen. *Stuart Hall: Critical Dialogues in Cultural Studies*. New York: Routledge, 1996.

Murphy, Alexandra, and Sudhir Venkatesh. "Vice Careers: The Changing Contours of Sex Work in New York City." *Qualitative Sociology*, Summer 2006, 29(2):129–54.

Neal, Mark A. *Soul Babies: Black Popular Culture and the Post-Soul Aesthetic*. New York: Routledge, 2002.

———. "Up From Hustling: Power, Plantations, and the Hip-Hop Mogul." *Socialism and Democracy*, 2004, 18(2):157.

Palladino, Grace. *Teenagers: An American History*. New York: Basic Books, 1996.

Perry, Imani. *Prophets of the Hood: Politics and Poetics in Hip Hop*. Durham: Duke University Press, 2004.

Porter, Thomas. "The Social Roots of African American Music: 1959–1970." In *African American Jazz and Rap: Social and Philosophical Examinations of Black Expressive Behavior*. James L. Conyers, Jr., ed. Jefferson, NC: McFarland & Company, Inc., 2001, pp. 83–89.

Quadagno, Jill. *The Color of Welfare: How Racism Undermined the War on Poverty*. New York: Oxford University Press, 1994.

Ritzer, George. *Enchanting a Disenchanted World*. Thousand Oaks, Calif.: Pine Forge Press, 2005.

Rose, Tricia. *Black Noise: Rap Music and Black Culture in Contemporary America*. Hanover, N.H.: Wesleyan University Press, 1994.

Sack, Kevin. July 3, 2001. "AIDS Epidemic Takes Toll on Black Women." Accessed December 2, 2001. Available at http://www.nytimes.com/2001/07/03/health/03AIDS.html?pagewanted=print.

Schaeffer, Robert K. *Understanding Globalization: The Social Consequences of Political, Economic, and Environmental Change.* Lanham, Md.: Rowman & Littlefield Publishers, Inc., 2003.

Secor, Anna. 2004. "'There Is an Istanbul That Belongs to Me': Citizenship, Space, and Identity in the City." *Annals of the Association of American Geographers.* June 2004, 94(2): 352–368.

Sharpe, Tanya Telfair. *Behind the Eight Ball: Sex for Crack Cocaine Exchange and Poor Black Women.* New York: Haworth Press, 2005.

Sharpley-Whiting, T.D. *Pimps Up, Ho's Down: Hip Hop's Hold on Young Black Women.* New York: New York University Press, 2007.

Smith, Christopher H. "'I Don't Like to Dream About Getting Paid': Representations of Social Mobility and the Emergence of the Hip-Hop Mogul." *Social Text,* Winter 2003, 21(4):69–97.

Stephens, Dionne P., and Layli D. Phillips. "Freaks, Gold Diggers, Divas, and Dykes: The Sociohistorical Development of Adolescent African American Women's Sexual Scripts." *Sexuality and Culture,* Winter 2003:3–49.

Tate, Greg, ed. *Everything but the Burden: What White People Are Taking from Black Culture.* New York: Broadway Books, 2003.

Twine, France W. *Racism in a Racial Democracy: The Maintenance of White Supremacy in Brazil.* New Brunswick, N.J.: Rutgers University Press, 1998.

Veblen, Thorstein. *The Theory of the Leisure Class: An Economic Study of Institutions.* New York: Oxford University Press, 2008 (orig. ed. 1899).

Wilson, William J. *When Work Disappears: The World of the New Urban Poor.* New York: Knopf, 1996.

Winant, Howard. *The World Is a Ghetto: Race and Democracy Since World War II.* New York: Basic Books, 2001.

Wonders, Nancy A., and Raymond Michalowski. "Bodies, Borders, and Sex Tourism in a Globalized World: A Tale of Two Cities—Amsterdam and Havana." *Social Problems,* 2001, 48(4):545–71.

Zucchino, David. *The Myth of the Welfare Queen.* New York: Scribner, 1997.

AFTERWORD: THE WAY FORWARD

Carson, Clayborne, and Kris Shepard, eds. *A Call to Conscience: The Landmark Speeches of Dr. Martin Luther King, Jr.* New York: Warner Books, 2002.

Walker, Alice, ed. *I Love Myself When I Am Laughing: A Zora Neale Hurston Reader.* Old Westbury, N.Y.: Feminist Press, 1979.